Victoria Wood
Unseen on TV

Victoria Wood was a writer, actor, director, singer, composer and stand-up comedian. She first appeared on national television in 1974 in the talent show *New Faces* and her debut stage play *Talent* was televised in 1979. In the 1980s her sketch show *Wood and Walters* was followed by *Victoria Wood As Seen on TV* and *An Audience with Victoria Wood*. She became the preeminent stand-up comedian of the age, selling out the Royal Albert Hall forty times while, in the nineties, creating the TV film *Pat and Margaret* and the sitcom *dinnerladies*. In 2005 she turned her much-loved soap parody *Acorn Antiques* into a West End musical, then wrote and starred in the wartime drama *Housewife, 49*. In 2014 she filmed her stage musical *That Day We Sang* for television. Given an OBE in 1997, she was made a CBE in 2008. Among countless other awards, her work won eight BAFTAs. Since her death in 2016 at only 62, her work has continued to pulse through the British bloodstream.

Jasper Rees is an arts journalist and author who has written for the *Daily Telegraph*, *Sunday Times* and *theartsdesk.com*, which he co-founded. Previous books include *I Found My Horn* and *Bred of Heaven*, both of which were abridged for Radio 4's *Book of the Week*, and a biography of Florence Foster Jenkins. His most recent book was *Let's Do It: The Authorised Biography of Victoria Wood*, which was written with the full cooperation of her family, friends and colleagues including Julie Walters, Celia Imrie, Duncan Preston, Dawn French, Anne Reid and Michael Ball.

Victoria Wood
Unseen on TV

Edited and introduced by
Jasper Rees

First published in Great Britain in 2021 by Trapeze
This paperback edition published in 2022 by Trapeze
an imprint of The Orion Publishing Group Ltd
Carmelite House, 50 Victoria Embankment
London EC4Y 0DZ

An Hachette UK Company

1 3 5 7 9 10 8 6 4 2

ISBN (Mass Market Paperback) 978 1 3987 0747 4
ISBN (eBook) 978 1 3987 0748 1

Typeset by Input Data Services Ltd, Somerset
Printed in Great Britain by Clays Ltd, Elcograf S.p.A.

www.orionbooks.co.uk

'Comedy. Psychological insights or the same old tired one-liners? I'll be swapping gags with Ben Elton, Jim Bowen and Charlie Williams as we test the very latest in contraceptives. But if you like your comedy female-style, take a look at this!'

Unused script from *Victoria Wood's All Day Breakfast* (1992)

CONTENTS

I

CONTINUITY ANNOUNCEMENT

Victoria Wood had more to say and do. Loving to work, she would certainly have carried on creating through her sixties, well into her seventies, and perhaps beyond. This helps to explain the widespread sense of loss when she died in 2016. While working on *Let's Do It: The Authorised Biography of Victoria Wood*, and after its publication, I found that the same lament was voiced again and again by fans old and new: what a struggle it was to accept that 'We would never again come across a new joke from that irreplaceable source, to go with the thousands she had already given us.'

Happily, I knew this to be not quite true. After the contents of Victoria's office were archived and made available for research, I started to encounter material that had never seen the light of day. In particular, in a box containing scripts from *Victoria Wood As Seen on TV*, I opened one folder labelled 'multiple provisional scripts' and, leafing through a thick pile of A4, came across a sheet with five and a bit typed lines under the title 'CONTINUITY':

Susie: Well, we certainly seem to have lots of goodies for you in our new season. For lovers of TV magic, and there can't be many, there's a new series of 'I crack the jokes round here', comedy magic from all over the world. And the series opens with the Magic of – someone I've never heard of. Looks quite a bumptious little prat from the photograph.

Under it Victoria has scrawled '20 secs'. This was written for the *As Seen on TV* continuity announcer, played with such craft and beady charm by Susie Blake. I could hear her reading it so clearly that I imagined I actually had – yet I couldn't have because it was never broadcast. As if by magic, the folder promptly yielded up a sketch called 'Magic Show', in which a florid conjuror struggles with an uncooperative lady volunteer. One had been written to cue in the other and both had apparently been sacrificed together. There was more, including several sketches set in department stores, or at a terrible dry-cleaner's. A long monologue for a woman running an extremely local radio station from her home had clearly been earmarked for Victoria to play herself. There was a sketch called 'Private Lives' in which two characters straight out of a play by Noël Coward turn out to be something else altogether. In 'Tupperware Party', written for Julie Walters, a nervous housewife hawks sex aids. These were all from the first series. In the end, from the show's thirteen episodes, there were in the region of sixty sketches written in the inimitable voice of Victoria Wood. Further delving yielded another cache of unseen material for Victoria's three Christmas shows from 1992, 2000 and 2009.

The reason for all this overwriting goes back to *Wood and Walters*. A pilot of Victoria's first sketch show was broadcast early in 1981. A year on came a series which proved bruising for a set of interlocking factors. Just before it went into production, her trusted producer Peter Eckersley died. His successor scheduled recordings for the afternoon, which meant a sketch show fronted by two young women was performed in a studio packed with unsmiling pensioners. It was only as her gags wilted before this bewildered audience that she realised she couldn't ditch anything: she didn't have a surplus. And yet even with *Wood and Walters* the archive contains offcuts which, for specific reasons, did not make it into the show. One sketch, an astute parody of 1940s radio comedy with its baffling catchphrases, was written fifteen years before *The Fast Show* gave us Arthur Atkinson's wartime show 'How Queer!'[1]

---

1 When Arthur Atkinson was included in *The Sketch Show Story*, a history of sketch comedy presented by VW in 2001, she didn't mention that she'd got there first.

From then on, Victoria Wood wrote too much. The early months of 1984, when she sat alone at home in a quiet village on Morecambe Bay and came up with the first series of *As Seen on TV*, must count as the most intense and brilliant period of comic productivity to issue from a single pen in this country since Coward or even Wilde in their pomp. As Victoria wrote, she stockpiled sketches and songs to make sure she would never go short again.

The question can be legitimately asked: if sketches didn't make the cut, can they be as good as the ones that did? On one level that's for the reader to decide. But it's important to stress that many were discarded for reasons that had nothing to do with their quality. When her producer Geoff Posner oversaw the edit, he tended to favour sketches that featured Victoria and Julie Walters over those written for other members of the company. There was also the question of balance. Victoria wrote copiously about bad theatre, naff television and – connected to her own experience – compulsive eating. Some sketches covering similar terrain were in competition with each other and, sometimes before they were filmed or even rehearsed, a swift decision had to be made to favour one or the other.

The idea that Victoria cannot have valued these sketches because she didn't let them be seen on TV does not hold water. If she really regarded something as a failure, she would chuck it in the bin. There is no trace in the archive of the several plays and film scripts she attempted to write in the 1980s. Everything else she kept and, in some cases, published. *Up to You, Porky*, her first sketch collection from 1985, compiled sketches from *Wood and Walters* and the first series of *As Seen on TV* plus monologues from her stand-up show *Lucky Bag*. Among them Victoria smuggled in four sketches that were not seen on TV.[2] Its successor *Barmy*, published two years later, consisted of sketches from the second series, the complete *Acorn Antiques* and sketches that were yet to be broadcast in the *As Seen on TV Special*. There were also nine unseen sketches.[3] Evidently, they had been filmed because the

---

2 'Cleaning', 'Madwoman' and a sketch each featuring 'Kitty' and 'Margery and Joan'.
3 'Nora', 'Men Talking', 'Salesman', 'Reports Local', 'Wine Bar', 'We're Half Asleep', 'Lady Police Serial' and two 'Margery and Joan' sketches.

casts were listed. While it didn't make the cut, Victoria was happy to allow this work to be consumed in written form. Indeed, when she submitted the typescripts of *Barmy* to Geoffrey Strachan, her publisher at Methuen (see p. 209), she made no distinction between seen and unseen sketches.[4] 'Vic simply delivered them all with the contents she wanted, in the sequence she wanted and with the presentation she wanted,' he told me. 'If you have writer–performers of genius who know how to present their work in book form, you cherish and salute a professional to her fingertips, publish and rejoice!'

They sold well, and had an important role to play in keeping her sketches alive when video-recording was still in its infancy. Yet Victoria pretended to be modest about these publications. 'I didn't really know what I was going to talk about tonight,' she said in a speech to launch *Barmy*. 'The publisher's no help – they just want you to say "Buy My Book Tell Your Friends Buy My Book Tell Your Friends" till it's time to sit down. Then he said, "You could tell them how you came to write it," and I said, "Well, I didn't, it's just a load of old sketches, I didn't even type it."'

This collection pulls together a load of new old sketches covering three decades. Wherever the scripts in the archive indicate who Victoria wanted to be in them, or who actually was before they fetched up on the cutting-room floor, that information is included. But wherever it isn't, you the reader are encouraged to do your own casting, and directing and designing too.

But there is much more in the Victoria Wood archive than sketches. Several character monologues that were once enjoyed by live audiences are nowadays less than widely recalled. Victoria's shows were crafted to fill an evening, and when it came to memorialising them in an album or a video, not everything could fit in. Two stage monologues were included in *Up to You, Porky*,[5] and three more in *Chunky*.[6] But

---

4 Methuen published nine titles by VW: two editions of *The Lucky Bag Songbook*; *Up to You, Porky*; *Barmy*; a volume of her play scripts *Talent* and *Good Fun*; *Mens Sana in Thingummy Doodah*; *Pat and Margaret*; *Chunky*; and *dinnerladies: First Helpings*.
5 'Brontëburgers' and 'This House Believes'.
6 'Fattitude', 'Toupée Time' and 'Madeline'.

scholarly fans are aware that for her live show between 1983 and 1985, she came on in the second half in the character of a slatternly northern comic called Paula Du Val. The lyrics of the song Paula sings were included in Victoria's very first publication, *The Lucky Bag Songbook*, but there was no space for her monologue on the *Lucky Bag* album released in 1984. Tapes of the whole show survive, recorded at the King's Head Theatre in Islington and at other venues – so Paula Du Val now rides again, as do other vibrant characters from Victoria's live shows up to 1990.[7]

As for her songs, at a conservative count Victoria composed somewhere in the region of two hundred of them and probably no more than a fifth are widely known to even her most ardent fans. Yet to begin with, performing at the piano is what got her noticed. This collection revisits some of her finest lyrics from the 1970s and beyond. Even without a melody, her gift for rhyme and rhythm can convey a sense of a song's energy on the page. Some of these songs were written when Victoria was still a drama student at Birmingham University. In the same era she began to find her voice as a writer of monologues and sketches and, in the case of a script she submitted to BBC Birmingham, a whole half-hour drama. All are part of her story and are unveiled here.

So is 'Sex'. The sketch Victoria wrote for herself and Julie Walters to perform in the summer of 1978 is the foundation stone of her career in comedy. As she would often say, it was where she discovered how to make an audience laugh. But those audiences were minuscule. *In at the Death*, the revue of which 'Sex' was a part, was seen every night for three weeks by the ninety or so people who crammed into the tiny Bush Theatre above a pub in west London. It was briefly revived a few years later.[8] It has never been published.

Meanwhile, when the occasion was right, Victoria would sometimes stand up and tell her own story in the form of a well-made

---

7 For her tours in 1993–94, 1996–97 and 2001–02, VW invented fewer stage characters, instead relying on Kimberley's friend, a succession of fitness instructors, and Stacey Leanne Paige to get her on after the interval and/or the encore.

8 As part of a charity revue at the Theatre Royal Stratford East in March 1982.

speech. Not quite the same as stand-up, this was a skill she developed at her book launches and then when accepting honorary degrees. There were laughs to be had in looking back over her life. But when there were students in the audience, she also knew that her unique odyssey as the First Lady of British entertainment meant that she had something important to tell them – not just about herself, but about us all. She still does.

A note on sources and presentation. The sketches, lyrics and speeches, as they exist in the archive, don't all come in the same form. There are manuscripts and prompt cards in Victoria's hand. Studio scripts are more formal documents for use by cast and crew, but even here she would often make cuts and edits. Once she moved to computer almost everything is, naturally, in the merry font known as Comic Sans. Wherever she wrote or typed, Victoria was not pernickety about punctuation – she was a serial employer of the dash – but rather than stay scholastically faithful to holy writ, this edition discreetly dots the odd i, crosses a t or two, and here and there respectfully adds an inverted comma. But often, particularly when written by hand, Victoria's less punctuated prose conveys a sense of a monologue's rhythm. In such cases it would have felt quite wrong to pepper her work with commas and semi-colons.

The scripts use the following abbreviations: CU for close-up, Ext for exterior, Int for interior, OOV for out of vision, VO for voiceover. Footnotes refer to Victoria Wood and others who are regularly mentioned by their initials: GD (Geoffrey Durham), JW (Julie Walters), CI (Celia Imrie), DP (Duncan Preston), GP (Geoff Posner). The same goes for shows: *GF* (*Good Fun*), *W&W* (*Wood and Walters*), *LB* (*Lucky Bag*), *ASOTV* (*As Seen on TV*), *AVW* (*An Audience with Victoria Wood*), *ADB* (*All Day Breakfast*), *DL* (*dinnerladies*), ATT (*All the Trimmings*), *H49* (*Housewife, 49*) and *MLX* (*Mid Life Christmas*).

The footnotes, which offer further context and commentary, are there to be enjoyed or ignored. For the benefit of some younger fans of Victoria's work, they briefly explain who on earth she is talking about when, for example, a stage character of hers asks, 'Mother Teresa,

Mary O'Hara, Rosalind Runcie: what do they have in common?'[9]

To capture the development of Victoria's voice and the journey of her career, I have edited the material to run more or less chronologically. She begins with a jolly poem and, nearly fifty years on, ends with one. But first, here's another new continuity announcement . . .

Susie: Well, now's the time to catch up with any re-pointing or exterior paintwork you may have been putting off, while those of us with no excuse to leave the house catch up with yet another episode of *Acorn Antiques*.

---

9 Although I have worked on the assumption that Mother Teresa needs no footnote.

2

STARTING OUT

SCHOOL

As a teenager Victoria wrote for *Cygnus*, the annual magazine of Bury Grammar School for Girls. The edition that came out in the summer of 1966 contains a mock-heroic ode. This was the first published piece of work by Victoria Wood. Even in the upper fourth, she reveals an early feel for meter and rhyme, and for the poetry to be found in domestic items. A year later, in the term she turned fourteen, an unsigned and unpunctuated paragraph titled 'Pardon?' foresaw an entire career. Once in the sixth form Victoria started writing shows with songs, including *Pearl: A Melodrama*. The script hasn't survived but the mock advert she inserted into the script has. It riffs on the idea of TV dramas being funded by soap powders. On the top right of the typescript it says 'lyrics by V. WOOD!' This was her first spoof of what she'd seen on TV.

AN ODE

Most venerable object,
We hail thee with acclaim.
Of articles most famous
We praise thy holy name.

Throughout the whole of England,
As one we all agree,
One fact we all unite on,
We can't do without thee.

The time has come to name thee,
This object without sin.
At last I will pronounce it: –
The Famous Safety-Pin!

PARDON?

I was born with a warped sense of humour and when I was carried home from being born it was Coronation Day and so I was called Victoria but you are not supposed to know who wrote this anyway it is about time I unleashed my pent-up emotions in a bitter comment on the state of our society but it's not quite me so I think I shall write a heart-warming story with laughter behind the tears and tears behind the laughter which means hysterics to you Philistines but let it pass if anyone is having any trouble with his toenails or dustbins please write to oh I mustn't say it must I the following passage has been censored by a brigade of white mice who think it unsuitable so I shall have to think of something else anyway I liked that joke about not calling you ladies as I know you too well it's alright chaps I've passed the little pencil line and can continue normal service back to the rats it's no use I shall have to write a poem about November the fifth happy days with the dustbin lids no I didn't get that off anybody else goodnight all mind how you go here's a jolly game try and put the punctuation in . . .[10]

THE CUPID'S KISS CORNPLASTER SONG[11]

Are your toenails troubled . . . ?
Are you going lame?
Did you think there was no remedy . . . ?
Are your ankles weary . . . ?
Are your feet in pain . . . ?
If you thought there was no answer
You will have to think again.

With a Cupid's Kiss Cornplaster
You can run much faster
You can live a life of bliss . . .
With a CUPID'S KISS!
With a Cupid's Kiss Cornplaster
You'll have feet like alabaster
Be a Mrs not a Miss . . .
With a CUPID'S KISS!

10 Under 'Pardon?' in her copy of *Cygnus* VW pencilled 'Vicky Wood'.
11 VW mentioned the song in her speech to launch *The Lucky Bag Songbook* (see pp. 81–2).

UNIVERSITY

Victoria began to study drama at Birmingham University in 1971. There were not many female roles to go round and invariably she missed out. In 1973, she was especially miffed not to be cast in *Loot*. As a sop she was invited to sing hymns before and after the show, and during the interval. Instead, she paraded her own compositions. Among them was 'Going Home Again', an exuberant attack on middle-class students pretending to have proletarian roots.

News of her performance resulted in her first ever gig. On the evening of Wednesday 27 June 1973, Victoria performed a dozen of her own songs in a venue at a hall of residence. 'My next song,' she says on a scratchy mono recording of the concert, 'is called "Sad Salad Sunday" because it's about those three things.'[12] A witty teenage take on the stultifying lives of adults, it was to have the longest lifespan of all her early songs.

Then in her final year, as part of a course in television, Victoria wrote a song to accompany an experimental film shot by fellow student Catherine Ashmore. 'King Kong' told of a statue commissioned by the city council in Birmingham which was later rejected and ended up in the forecourt of a car dealership.

Songs were to remain her primary creative output, but as her thoughts turned towards television, she submitted an untitled script set in a girls' school to the BBC's drama department in Birmingham. It was rejected, and she refashioned it for her TV course. While it's possible to see why it wasn't right for television, it nonetheless shows Victoria finding her voice and exploring the themes of female friendship that would be the focus of *Talent* and *Nearly a Happy Ending* and, in a different way, *Pat and Margaret*. For the first time she contrasts two young women, one confident, the other awkward. It was written

---

12 The recording was by Sahlan Diver, who organised and performed in the concert and played a saxophone obbligato during the second chorus of the song. His tape spent forty-five years in various attics and miraculously survived to be digitised in 2019.

around the time Victoria had her first dalliance with an older man, and she used the script to explore her ambivalent feelings.

Its rejection did not dissuade Victoria from continuing to write. As friends of hers performed in practical examinations, she would supply them with scripts. In the summer of 1973 she wrote a monologue for Alison Sabourin, who was sitting her finals, in which Victoria drew on the experience of breaking up with her boyfriend. A year later she wrote a sketch for first-year student Chrissie Poulter. Once more it explored with even more striking directness the power dynamics in female friendships. Though she did not overtly write herself into this snapshot of two flatmates, Victoria found it easy to imagine herself into the mindset of both the alpha aggressor and the beta victim. Titled 'Sketch One', it was the first Victoria Wood sketch to be performed to an audience.

She wrote the second when, after finishing as a student, she stayed on in Birmingham and remained embedded in the lives of friends in the years below. In the summer of 1975 Robert Howie asked her to write something for himself and Chrissie Poulter to perform. She wrote it rapidly and they went on just before the interval. Thus the programme listed a first half consisting of work by John Ford, Percy Bysshe Shelley, TS Eliot, Edward Albee, Edward Bond and Victoria Wood.

GOING HOME AGAIN[13]

Put back your accent where you found it
And climb into the train
You've got to pass
As middle class
You're going home again.

Conversation should be tactful
Or you'll cause your mother pain

---

13 The melody is jaunty, sung to a sprightly piano accompaniment. VW slowed down in the final couplet.

Keep off the Jews
You know their views
You're going home again.

In the lies about your father
I think that you have rather
Strayed from the path
He's not a crippled miner, he's a winer and diner
More at home in a sauna than an old zinc bath.

Hope your friends don't discover
The truth about your mother
She's never been near a loom
She's not dying of bronchitis
She's just got conjunctivitis
Magnolia emulsion in the new spare room.

They're bound to meet you at the station
All resistance is in vain
You'll have to wait
They're always late
You're going home again.

If only they were trendy
With morals that were bendy
It wouldn't be such a bore.
You could sit around on cushions
Have political discussions
About the possibility of a Third World War.

If you sprinkle marijuana
On your custard and banana
They won't even look up
They're too busy watching auntie

Do Jimmy Durante[14]
With a very silly voice and a plastic cup.

You'll leave the college for the suburbs
And stare into the rain
Although you curse
It could be worse
You're going home again
Although you curse it would be worse
You're going home again.

MONOLOGUE FOR ALISON SABOURIN[15]

I must look awful. I never thought you'd be back so early. Have you a hanky I've run out of tissues not like me. Not like me at all must be old age ha. Thank you. It's a nice big one. I didn't know you had a middle name.

Anyway – I liked her. I did like her. But she wasn't like me or my friends. She used to swear a lot. Not just bloody or any of those – And she used to wear those dresses from charity shops – all flowered down to her ankles – and platform shoes. I didn't know Roger liked platform shoes – he used to say they were like barges. She suited hers though . . .

Well I suppose it was when her window got stuck. Well my friends and I used to go to the launderette on Saturday mornings – Roger would drive us wait for us at the flat then drive us back. He didn't like the launderette. But she wouldn't come with us. She didn't like it either. Well after he'd mended her window he said what a nice room it was – all pictures. Roger did ART at school you see. So I bought one

---

14 Popular American vaudevillian (1893–1980). He retired in 1972, the year before the song's composition.

15 Handwritten script. The sketch was never performed. 'I was looking for something to do for my final performance assessment,' says Alison, 'and Vic said, "Would you like me to write you something?" And she did. In the end I did something with two other people and felt much happier. I absolutely should have done it.' VW would continue to draw on the raw pain of being dumped in scripts she wrote in her fifties.

at Boots. I don't know anything about them but I thought it must be good or they wouldn't have it. It was abstract. A sunset over a lake with a black tree at the front. Well when I showed it him he said he wanted her to see it. So he took it upstairs. I could hear them laughing.

He saw her a few times after that. He said she was lonely. And then on our anniversary – we'd been going out for a year – we were having a meal in my room. I'd made it – it was beef curry and rice. We had candles. And wine. And I'd bought a new dress. It was red gathered under the bust with a low neck and puffed sleeves. Full length. And I'd had my hair done – it was long then. It went up like this and a ringlet in front of each ear. And my white shoes.

Well from where he was sitting he could see into the garden. And she was there. It was summer so it was still light – and she was in the middle of the lawn with her legs crossed. She had those denim jeans on cut off at the top and a blue T-shirt. She was brown as well. I suppose it was because she was a student. They have more time in the day than we do.

Roger kept looking at her. She just sat there with all her hair over her face not combed or anything.

And because it was our anniversary I got a bit upset and started to cry – smudged all my new make-up. But he didn't say anything – just kept looking out of the window.

Then he stood up and sort of smiled . . . Then he went out. I drew the curtains then . . .

This room's a mess isn't it. I ought to go to the launderette really . . .

SAD SALAD SUNDAY[16]

Children be nice to your father
He is still alive at thirty-five

---

16 The looping melody is wistful and, unusually, VW slowed down for the chorus. She delivered the last line in the voice of a well-spoken middle-aged man. She was proud enough of the composition to include it in *The Camera and the Song*, a commission from BBC Two to write a suite of songs on an overarching theme. VW recorded them early in 1975, although it was not broadcast until May 1976. It was repeated at the end of 1977.

While your eyes get brighter
His trousers get tighter
His wife's hair is as hard as her voice
And his freedom of choice is blown out through the window
That cost him so much to put in.
While the light that streams through them is making him sad
His daughter is rolling her eyes saying DAD!
The salad's ready for the ninetieth time.

Chorus:
Sad salad Sunday,
Sad greens and blues
Everybody's feeling they've nothing left to lose
Sad salad Sunday,
Sad blues and greens
Everybody's feeling things might have been.

Children be nice to your mother
She is nearly alive at thirty-five
As she hitches her skirt and says look at the dirt
In the sunlight that streams through the windows
That cost her so much to put in.
And she hopes it doesn't matter that she's really rather fatter than
  she was the year before the year before the year before the year
  before that
She wasn't fat
And she feels there is something she should have had
And she doesn't know what but it makes her sad
And she doesn't know but she knows she hasn't got it whatever it is.

Repeat chorus.

Children be nice to your father
Or he won't survive on the eight oh five he takes to work on Monday
  trying to lose that Sunday feeling
The men in the office will say

'What kind of weekend have you had?'
He'll say, 'Not so bad, old boy, not so bad.'

KING KONG[17]

A sunny shopping Saturday I chanced to pass
The most beautiful gorilla ever seen in fibreglass
And as I stood beneath the sky
A sky of jungle blue
I said, 'King Kong I'll write a song and sing it just for you.'

Chorus:
Ding dong King Kong
Loved you from the minute I saw you
You caught my eye, I don't know why
I thought everybody would adore you.
Dong dong was wrong
Which caused me so much pain
But whatever I do wherever I go
I will get you back again.

Lady from the council decided he wasn't right
'I've seen him twice and he's not quite nice
He frightened the kiddies who think he'll bite'
An unexpected saviour
And expert in car dealing
Came in the end to save our friend
Which showed he wasn't lacking in the finer feelings.

Repeat chorus.

---

17 Typically of VW's songs at the time, she flitted between a slow verse and an up-tempo chorus. The final chorus is repeated at even higher speed.

Man from the garage has decided the gimmick is dead
Where will he go we don't know
Where he can lay his big black . . . head
Too bad, how sad
They don't want him at the zoo
Who'll give a pillow to a fibreglass gorilla
Maybe it could be you.

Repeat chorus.

UNTITLED TELEVISION SCRIPT

1: Int. School room. Day.

A small room full of plastic chairs, a desk and chair for the form mistress. No blackboards or anything schooly. There are two doors, one leads on to the corridor, one into a locker room. Christine comes in from the corridor, drops her satchel near the door, takes a hymn book and bible from the windowsill, pushes a chair into a corner with her foot and sits on it with her hands jammed deep into her blazer pockets. The bible and hymn book need re-covering. Her uniform doesn't fit properly, her socks are grey and woolly, her shoes need cleaning.[18]

She sits. Barney comes in from the locker room. Her uniform is clean and smart; she wears a shirt and tie as well as a little jumper and looks as if a quirk of fashion had made her the 'school uniform look' in this year. Her hymn book and bible are covered in flowered paper. She smiles when she sees Christine, and goes and sits near her.

Barney: It's a good morning, isn't it?

Christine: What?

Barney: It's a good morning.

Christine: Hm.

Barney (*going to window and waving*): There's Charlie. (*She mouths violently through the window.*) Have you got your clean overalls

---

18 This was VW's look as a sixth-former.

on, Charlie? (*Pause.*) Your overalls. (*Pause.*) Doesn't matter. (*Comes back to Christine.*) Deaf as a post. (*Pause.*)

Christine: Who's Charlie?

Barney: He's my friend. One of the boiler-men. He put the heel back on my shoe that day I chased Heather Thing out of the common room.

Christine: Heather Douglas?

Barney: Yes.

Christine: But she's a sixth-former. She's allowed to be there.

Barney: Not with a face like that she isn't.

Christine: Didn't she mind?

Barney: She thought it was quite an honour, considering no one's spoken to her for about six years. Oh, I did personally congratulate her on the occasion of her falling over the Bishop's tin leg in the Carol Concert, but apart from that she's rotted quietly away in that rather disgusting locker room, hearing no sound save the slow steady drip of her hair onto her meek and lowly shoulders. Not bad that, for a Monday morning. Do you always come in this early? Yes you do don't you, at least you're always here when I come. I came in early though to finish that essay on the Seven Deadly Sins. 'The Seven Deadly Sins' starring Heather Douglas as at least three of them.

Christine: She laddered her stockings.

Barney: When I threw her out? You mean you've looked at her legs? You must be mad. She wouldn't wear stockings anyway. She shouldn't wear legs either come to that. Have you done the essay?

Christine: No.

Barney: Oh, I wish you had. It could have been a really beautiful moment as she picked up the essays and saw they were all there. Never mind, I'll put them in her locker and take away the bottom seven, that's me, Stevenson, Taylor, Turtem, you, Wilkinson and Wood.[19] Then she'll think she's lost them,

---

19 VW did this once when she had not completed her homework.

because people like Maureen and Wendy always give them in.

Christine: Will you really do that?

Barney: Of course. Did you have a good weekend?

Christine: Just the same as the week really. Different clothes and no school dinners, that's all.

Barney: Sounds a bit miserable. What did you do?

Christine: Nothing.

Barney: You must have done something. (*She tries to think of suggestions but can't think of anything Christine might have been doing.*) (*Pause.*)

Christine: What did you do?

Barney: Played tennis on Friday night with that boy with the knees. Then went to torment that old woman, if I keep on long enough either she'll die and leave me her money or I'll get the Good Deeds Shield. Saturday morning crawled out to orchestra, staggered through a few symphonies, crawled back, took my sister out for a drink, bought some new shoes, played dominoes with Buster, then Dad brought a man back for me . . . Sunday morning climbed trees with Buster, ripped my jeans, sewed them up, watched 'The Golden Shot',[20] 'Stars on Sunday', 'Doctor at Large',[21] put Buster to bed, went out for a drink with my Dad, got pissed a bit, came home, fell over, said my prayers and went to bed.

Christine: It sounds nice. (*Pause.*) Is Buster your brother?

Barney: Yes, he's five.

Enter Maureen and Wendy who wear sensible poplin macs and carry handbags and shopping bags with their books in. Judith and Gill wear slightly less sensible coats and carry their books in Boots carrier bags. They take their coats and go in and out of the locker room during this bit.

Barney: What did you do this weekend, Maureen? Oh, it was your party wasn't it on Saturday night.

Wendy: Yes it was and we didn't see you there, did we?

---

20 ATV game show, broadcast from 1967 to 1975.

21 LWT comedy based on the books by Richard Gordon. Shown in 1971.

Barney: You know I'd been looking forward to it all week then come Saturday afternoon, after orchestra, there I am trying to borrow my sister's black dress when THUMP, there I am out cold on her carpet.

Maureen: You fainted?

Barney: I did. (*She nudges Christine's arm and Christine smiles, flattered to be in her confidence.*) When I came to six minutes later, there they all are running about getting hysterics with wet sponges, and so I spent my Saturday night in bed. (*She coughs once for Christine's benefit.*)

Wendy: I hope you're alright now.

Barney: Oh, I think so. Was it a good party?

Maureen: Very enjoyable. This Wendy got a bit tiddly didn't you, Wendy?

Wendy: Only a bit, Maureen.

Maureen: Well, we shall know what to blame if you don't get B+ for your Scripture essay this week.

Wendy: Oh be fair, Maureen. (*Barney is looking out of the windows, Christine is hunched into the corner.*)

Judith: When do you think you'll let him?

Gill: After my exams, I suppose.

Mrs Burton comes in.

Barney: Hello.

Mrs Burton: Good morning, Barney. Are we all here?

Maureen: Pat's gone to the dentist, Paula's got a feverish cold, and Linda's gone to her great aunt's funeral in Yorkshire.

Mrs Burton: Ah yes. Thank you, Maureen. Shall we go in? Put that satchel in the locker room, Christine, for the fiftieth time.

Christine goes in the locker room, comes out after Judith has left. Barney goes out first, then Maureen and Wendy, Gill and Judith in pairs. Mrs Burton finishes the register.

Come on, Christine, cheer up for heaven's sake. What's the matter?

Christine: Nothing.

Mrs Burton: Well stand up straight for heaven's sake. And that blazer
could do with a clean, couldn't it? Oh, and Miss Herbert wants
to see you after prayers – about a missing essay. Not really
good enough is it, Christine?

They go out to the prayers.

Music – shot of Christine and Miss Herbert, Christine's head is down.

Music – mistress stops her as she walks along corridor, tells her to pull her socks up. She pulls them up.

Music – last lesson of day – Barney is holding forth – mistress and girls are laughing, Christine sits in corner. Bell goes, mistress leaves, Christine goes out first.

2: Ext. By the canal.

Christine walks home by the canal, sees man leaning against canal bridge, she walks past him and looks over at the same side. He moves up to her.

Man: Nice day, isn't it?

Christine: Yeah.

Man: On your way home are you?

Christine: Well, yes. But I'm not in a hurry.

3: Int. Next day. School room.

The same form room before prayers. Barney is standing at the window smoking a cigarette – Christine comes in from the outside door, drops her satchel on the floor near the door and goes to stand next to Barney.

Barney (*as Christine enters the room*): Hello, darling.

Christine (*smiling*): Hello.

Barney: You don't look like a miserable sod this morning.

Christine: Do I usually?

Barney: Yes. (*Small pause.*) I mean I don't mind, it just confounds the
theory that these are the best days of your life. I suppose they
could be. You'd have to have a bloody miserable life when you
left though.

Christine: I thought you like school.

Barney: I'm talking about you. I'm a ray of sunshine.

Christine: Is that difficult?

Barney: Mornings like this it can be. (*Pause.*) Why don't you?

Christine: What?

Barney: Look like a miserable sod.

Christine: Just in a good mood.

Barney: Why?

Christine: I'm just thinking about what somebody said to me.

Barney: When?

Christine: Last night.

Barney: What did he say?

Long pause while Christine scrunches up her toes.

Christine: He said I had nice eyes.

Short pause.

Barney: Well you have. (*Pause.*) I didn't know you had a boyfriend.

Christine: Oh yes. He doesn't often say things, that's all.

Pause.

Barney: Go on.

Christine: What?

Barney: Tell me about him. (*Short pause.*) What's his name?

Christine: George.

Pause.

Barney: And?

Christine: I don't know his other name.

Barney: No I mean tell me about him. I mean I'm not surprised that you've got one, it's just you've never said anything about him. I'd like to hear about him.

Christine: Have you got one?

Barney: Sort of. There's that actor I never see and that man from my father's department, I can't get rid of. No one exciting. Is he exciting, George?

Christine: Well. (*She shuts her eyes, opens them.*) He's twenty-one. (*Short pause.*) And he works for a newspaper.

Barney: Which one?

Christine: The *Guardian*. (*Pause.*) He's six foot two and he wears a
denim suit (*pause*) not jeans and a Levi jacket – a suit.

Barney: Where do you meet him?

Christine: Where did I meet him?

Barney: No. Where do you go when you go out together? Or do you
go to your house?

Christine: I go to his flat. (*Pause.*) I make his tea and he wears an
apron and pretends to be Fanny Cradock[22] and puts garlic in
the baked beans. It's nice.

Barney (*smiles*): It sounds great. (*Pause.*) What happens after the
beans?

Christine: We go into his living room. It's a big room with one wall all
curtains and a big television and a desk where he writes. And
a blue phone.

Barney: Pale blue?

Christine: Navy. (*Pause.*) Then he puts the television on and turns the
sound down till it comes on to the adverts.

*Christine isn't looking at Barney. Gill and Judith and Maureen and
Wendy come in from outside. Barney gestures to Gill and Judith and they
come and sit with Barney, Maureen and Wendy in the locker room.*

. . . because he likes them best because his friend Paul's on one
for beer and then after a bit he turns it off and tells me to come
and sit next to him on the sofa.

Barney: A big sofa.

Christine: Wide. Dark blue velvet.

Gill: Are the lights on?

Christine: Only the one by the sofa. A blue light.

Judith: What does he say?

Barney: What does he do?

Christine: I sit on his knee (*pause*) and he hugs me (*pause*) and I look
at his shirt.

Barney: Well what does he do?

Judith: Has he asked you to?

---

22 Celebrated television cook (1909–1994). Later in life VW would ritually watch a
particular clip of her every Christmas.

Gill: Or doesn't he want to?

Christine: He always wants to.

Gill: Do you let him?

Maureen and Wendy have come in – they see the set-up and stand apart but watching.

Christine: Yes.

Gill: What's it like? Was the first time awful?

Christine: It hurt a bit but I like it all the time now.

Judith: Do you do it a lot?

Christine: Nearly every night. That's why I can't do these essays.

Pause.

Barney: Hadn't you better tick her off, girls?

Gill: What?

Barney: The list.

Gill: Oh yes. You've got it, Judith, haven't you?

Judith: In my handbag, hang on. (*She takes from the handbag by her chair a printed list of names – all the girls in the sixth form.*) Now. Upper VI B. Christine Trent. (*She marks a tick against the name.*)

Gill: How many is that now, Judith?

Judith: Well that's – four out of ten in Upper VI L, three out of ten in Upper VI W, and now three out of nine in ours.

Christine: Is that you and me and Gill?

They don't answer.

Gill: I suppose you're still not going to tell us, Barney?

Barney: I've told you, darling. I'm waiting for Buster to grow up. I've always had a fancy for incest.

Gill and Judith: Oh Barney.

Gill and Judith go into the locker room to disrobe. Maureen and Wendy have sat down some time (perhaps on essays).

Barney: Well you're well in now.

Christine: Am I?

Barney: Member of the fraternity, pal. To you is afforded the dubious honour of sitting in the Whore's Corner in the common room, discussing orgasms, relative sizes of organ . . . things like that.

Christine looks at Barney to see if they are friends.

4: Int. The Assembly Hall.

The Assembly Hall – the girls sit in a row – Maureen, Wendy, Gill, Judith, Christine, Barney. Maureen is reading the bible, which is on a lectern. Judith and Gill are not listening. Gill is looking at a photograph of her boyfriend who is in the army. Wendy is listening to Maureen. Barney is nodding in agreement with the bible reading to make Christine laugh. Christine laughs silently.

5: Int. School Room.

After prayers. Mrs Burton in form room, others coming in.

Mrs Burton: Just a minute, girls, before you go to your first lesson. As I was late this morning we didn't have time to vote about whether you should bring your boyfriends to the sixth-form party. Now Upper VI L votes against. Upper VI W voted for, so it's up to us really. (*Pause. The six girls are seated.*) Maureen?

Maureen: I vote against.

Mrs Burton writes it down.

Mrs Burton: Wendy?

Wendy: So do I.

Mrs Burton: Judith?

Judith: Ooh yes.

Mrs Burton: You vote for?

Judith (*laughing*): Yes.

Mrs Burton: Barney?

Pause.

Barney: I abstain.

Pause.

Mrs Burton: Oh. (*Short pause.*) That leaves the casting vote to you, Christine.

Pause. Christine thinks hard. Gill and Judith stare at her. Barney looks at her. Maureen and Wendy are unaware of the implications.

Christine: I vote for.

Mrs Burton: Beg your pardon?

Christine (*clears throat*): For. I vote for.

Mrs Burton: Right. Thank you. I'll tell the Headmistress. (*Girls get up to go out.*) Move that satchel, Christine.

6: Int. School corridor.

Christine in front of the homework lockers – small square lockers in blocks with the names of mistresses on each door on little plastic strips.

Christine: Perhaps they wouldn't laugh at him if he came. (*Pause.*) He's not like what I said though. (*Pause.*) I could say I had two. Barney's got two, and one's quite old. (*Pause.*) I could get him a suit. (*Pause.*) I could say I was ill. I could say he was ill. Or on a job. (*Pause.*) They'd laugh if I brought him. He'd be embarrassed. He'd be embarrassing. He's horrible.

She begins to cry but tries to stop as Barney comes round the corner with a dead rat. She stops near Christine.

Barney: Hey, I'm sorry about that essay.

Christine: It doesn't matter.

Barney: Do you like my rat? (*She puts it in a locker.*) That's what happens if you eat custard creams while you're marking one of Barney Murdoch's essays.

Christine smiles with the side of her mouth nearest to Barney. Barney goes away.

Christine: If he was like I said he was I could have brought him. They would have been jealous. (*Pause.*) They might like him.

She walks down the corridor. Barney comes back round the corner, takes the rat out of the locker. Christine turns round.

Barney: I changed my mind.

7: Int. The Evening Before. A small dark room.

A bed with not enough bedding, a table, chair, big empty wardrobe door won't shut. Christine sits on the bed with her satchel held to her. The man stands looking out of the window. Pause.

Man: The kettle won't be much longer. (*Pause.*) I'll just go down
     and . . .

*He goes out. Christine pulls her socks up, licks her finger and takes a mark
off one of her shoes. She looks in her satchel, takes out half an old bar of
chocolate, puts too much in her mouth, hears him coming back, takes it
out and puts it back in her satchel. The man comes in with two tea cups.
He puts them on the table. He puts sugar in both and starts to drink his,
leaving the other on the table. Christine puts her satchel on the bed. Takes
the cup on the table and stands next to him looking out of the window.
Pause.*

     What's your name?

Christine: Barney.

Man: Is that a proper name then?

Christine: Yes.

Man: Never heard it before.

Pause.

Christine: Do you like it?

Man: Sounds more like a boy's name. (*Pause.*) Have you got a boy-
     friend?

Christine: Not this week.

Man: What do you mean?

Christine: I mean, I had one last week, but I haven't this week.

Man: Chucked him, did you?

Christine: Yeah. He was stupid.

Pause.

Man: I bet you have a lot, don't you?

Christine: Boyfriends?

Man: Yes. I bet you tell them where to get off.

Christine: Well—

Man: Or do you let them? (*Christine looks down.*) You've got a nice
     bust. (*Pause.*)

Christine: Have I?

Man: Yes, it's nice.

He puts his arm round her. Pause. Christine thinks.

Christine: Yes, I do let them.

8: Int. Same. Afterwards.

Man sits on bed. Christine near door just going.
Man: I'll meet you by that bridge then, tomorrow.
Christine: Yes. Goodbye.
She goes.
Man: Goodbye, Barney.

9: Ext. A bus stop.

Christine stands with other girls.
Girls: You don't usually come this way, do you?
Christine: No.

10: Ext. The canal bridge.

The man stands smoking. He finishes his cigarette, grinds it out on the bridge wall, throws it into the water and walks in the direction of his room.

11: Int. School room. The morning after the party.

Barney, Gill, Judith, Maureen, Wendy all sitting together before prayers. (Two other girls sit apart, Paula and Pat – not absolutely necessary.)
Barney: I'm surprised he got here at all with a jacket like that. (*They all laugh.*) Did you notice one of our illustrious members was conspicuous by her absence? (*Small pause.*)
Gill: Christine Trent.
Judith: She said she was coming, she . . .
Gill: She said she was going to bring that journalist. I wanted to see him.
Barney: Well she didn't come. And we didn't see him.
Maureen: I bet he wasn't a journalist.

Gill: Probably a paper boy.

Wendy: Well I can't see a journalist going out with someone like that,
can you? She's so scruffy.

Judith: He's probably as scruffy as she is.

Barney: Surely, girls, you are erring rather on the charitable side in
this affair. We are informed by Miss Christine Trent that she
is ravished nightly by a member of the Press, and yet he won't
even accompany her to so humble a function as the sixth form
party. What are we to assume? (*Short pause.*) Did he exist at all?

Maureen: I bet she made it all up.

Wendy: To get attention.

Judith: Who'd want to sleep with her anyway?

Barney: Her accounts to me of their intercourse seemed sadly lacking
in the knowledge of basic anatomy.

Wendy: She did it to get attention.

Gill: We'll have to cross her off the list, Ju.

Judith: Hey, yeah.

*Christine comes in. While the others are looking at each other, Barney
gives Christine an extra special friendly smile while nudging Judith.*

Barney: Morning, darling.

SKETCH ONE[23]

Jennifer lying on a table reading. She throws down her book, sighs, drums her heels, throws it on the floor.

J: Fuck. (*Pause.*)

    Balls. (*Pause.*)

    Shit. (*Pause.*)

(*Shouts*) WILLY!

Pause – then doorbell rings. She's back feeling better. She opens the door and gets back on the table.

    Apologise.

S: Sorry?

J: Apologise for getting me off the table. I could have left you out there, with the bins and the Pakistanis. I would ask you to get down on your knees but it might make you start praying, so a verbal apology will suffice.

S: I don't know what made me forget my key; I must have left it in my locker. (*Flustered – doesn't know what to say.*) Whatever are you doing on the table? I only polished it yesterday.

J: Just checking the shine. It's the modern equivalent of running your finger over the ornaments. No – I'm letting my sense of the absurd run away with me. I'm hoping the dizzy heights of the table top will instil some excitement into my jaded existence.

S: I got the tomatoes.

J: So I can get off the table? Whoopee. (*She does so.*) You look pink. Somebody been fondling your acne?

---

23 There is no trace of other sketches so the title is an anomaly. In the manuscript VW gives a name to one of the characters but only an initial to the other. The repartee between two friends – one always quipping, the other perennially on the back foot – would be developed in *GF* (1980). The sketch is 'close to the bone', says Chrissie Poulter, for whom the role of S was written. 'Though I now wonder how much was me and how much was her. I always thought the easily-fooled one was me . . . the church stuff, good causes etc. were me pre-university and I've never worn make-up. But there are aspects of her in both characters, as when she cut off all my hair or got me to buy outrageous luminous knee-length moon boots.'

S: No.

J: There's definitely something different about you. Lost your faith?

S: No.

J (*slumps back on table*): Bore. (*Pause.*) What are you doing tonight? Brownies? Convicts Welfare?

S: Well, actually—

J (*not listening*): I'm starving. It's your day.

S: Correct me if I'm wrong. I seem to remember it was my day yesterday, so unless we have been blessed with two Tuesdays this week . . .

J: Shut up God-rot and make the bloody tea.

S (*coyly*): Well, I don't know whether I've got time, even you can't go wrong with salad. Barn dancing went on later than usual, so I'm a bit late already.

J: Late for what?

S: I'm – going out.

J: Going out? You've not been out since you sampled the delights of the Health Service with housemaid's knee.

S: Tennis elbow.

J: Prostitute's pelvis – the point remains the same – you never go out. (*S combing her hair – polishing her shoes etc.*) Wherever are you going? Church bazaar – an extra hand with the bran tub, the institute of further education – the Household Arts – ways and means with bandage and ballcock.

Pause.

S: No I'm not.

J: Not what?

S: Going to the bazaar. That's Sunday.

J: Oh Jesus. (*S applies make-up ineptly.*) Come here for God's sake, you look like a mothy old panda.

S (*not hearing*): Sorry?

J (*taking eye make-up off her*): Who are you going out with?

S: Roger.

Pause. Both think, one complacent, the other thoughtful. J takes up blue stick, smears it on eyelids with horrible effect.

J: What are you going to wear?

S: Well I thought I'd ask you actually. You always look nicely turned
out. (*J mimes vomiting.*) What do you think?

J: The one your mother sent is nice.

S: That blue one?

J: Yes.

S: You said it made me look like part of a three-piece suite.

J: I was only joking. Go and put it on.

S: I haven't got any tights – can you lend me some?

J: Sorry I ruined my last pair today. You know what those tables are
like. Tell you what – wear those knee-socks and your flat shoes.
That's very fashionable.

S: Is it?

J (*enthusiastically*): Yes. Go on.

S exits to change.

J: How did this little romance come about then? (*Applies eye make-up,
combs hair etc.*)

S (*off*): Well – we were in the canteen, I'd just come out of New
Testament. I was exhausted.

J: I can imagine.

S (*off*): And I was hovering over the puddings, as it were, trying to
choose between rhubarb crumble and prunes.

J: Lovely.

S (*off*): And he came up from the other side and said would I let him
in?

J: And did you?

S (*off*): Well I didn't like to say no, though Deirdre Armstrong looked
furious. Course, he'd only come up for some cigarettes so it
didn't really count. He does smoke a lot, silly boy. I wonder if
I could get him to stop.

J (*softly*): Nothing like a good pig's influence. Better take your glasses
off.[24]

S: I can't see a blind thing without them.

J: (I know.) Makes you look better though.

---

24 There is no stage direction but 'Better take your glasses off' is clearly spoken at normal
volume. In J's next speech VW's brackets indicate that 'I know' should be muttered too.

S: Alright. (*She blunders uncertainly into the room.*)

J: You look really nice.

S: Do I? I feel a bit silly.

J: Come here, I'll just put some lipstick on you. (*She does so.*) Great.
The finishing touch. Wait a minute though – you say he
smokes a lot – maybe it'd look better if you were smoking too
when he came.

S: I don't know. I haven't had one since Christmas Day.

J lights one for her.

J: You can't get cancer on two a year. You don't want to look as if
you're sitting in judgement.

S: No. (*Starts coughing and J puts cigarette in her mouth – she begins to
choke.*)

Bell rings.

J: I'll get it. You just sit there and look pretty. Smile!

*S sits smiling, choking and holding herself self-consciously. J advances
sexily towards the door.*

J and S: Hello!

Blackout.

DO YOU WANT TO KNOW
WHAT I'VE GOT IN MY POCKET?

*A launderette. C enters, puts her clothes in a machine, puts the money in
and sits down, starts reading a magazine. B enters carrying a small parcel
in opaque plastic bag. He sits very close to C and watches her washing
going round.*[25]

B: They'll be nice and clean, won't they?

C: Hope so.

Pause.

---

25 C is Chrissie, as in Chrissie Poulter, B is Bob, as in Robert Howie, who says, 'David
Hirst – who directed and didn't cast Victoria in *Loot* – ran an option on Violence in the
Theatre. I asked Victoria to write something for us, and "Do You Want . . ." is what she
produced. Very quickly, I remember.'

B: Do they take a long time?

C: About twenty minutes.

B: And they come out all dry?

C: No, I wish they did . . . no, you have to put them in the dryer – see over there.

B: We don't have them.

C: Sorry?

B: In our laundry.

C: Oh.

Pause.

B: Will it get the stains out?

C (*doubtful now*): Should do.

B: We have a lot of trouble with stains in our laundry.

She reads, he looks at her washing.

      What are them little blue things?

C (*knowing what he means*): Jeans.

B: No, them little blue things.

C: Knickers.

B (*laughing*): They're nice, aren't they?

C: Marks and Spencer.

B: Have you got any more of them?

C: Oh lots – keep looking and you'll get a panoramic view of my entire underwear – my particular favourites are those striped ones nestling near that tea towel.

B: I bet you look pretty in . . .

C: In the tea towel? Knockout. I have matching tea cosy and oven gloves. (*Carries on reading.*)

B: When I'm a bit better they said they'll move me from the laundry to the dinner room. Then I'll have big dinners and get fat (*laughs*).

C turns the page, he reads it.

B: Lil-Lets, I know what they're for. 'Feel safe all day.' My auntie used them, but she still couldn't go swimming 'cause she couldn't swim (*laughs*). She won't come back now. They took her away – in an ambulance. At least it had beds in but it didn't make a noise, no bells. I had to go away with a lady after that. I liked

her, but she was always talking. She said she wasn't cross with
me but I think she was.

C: Do you live in a house?

B: Mm, a big house. I used to live with my auntie but they had to
take her away. I didn't mind . . . She wouldn't talk to me. She
wouldn't get up off the floor even when I said I was sorry . . .
Do you want to know what I've got in my pocket?

C: Look, I'm reading a magazine, OK?

B: It's only little . . .

C (*standing up to check the machine, smiling*): Really?

B (*standing between her and the door*): It's a little knife. I have to be
careful in case I cut myself. Will you help me wash my parcel?
I don't know how to make the washing machine work. (*Takes
out something wrapped in bloodstained paper.*)

C: What . . . ?

B: Don't be cross with me – I couldn't get that ring off her finger, she
had big fingers, it's a lovely ring . . . So . . .

*B starts to unwrap the paper. C hits him in an effort to reach the door,
he falls hitting his head on the bench. She drags him into a corner out of
sight and starts to put her clothes in her bag. Woman enters and nearly
trips over her.*

W: Ooh sorry . . . just looking for my husband – you haven't seen
him, brown hair, duffel coat?

C: No.

W: Men. He said he'd come straight here after he'd been to the butcher's. Sorry, am I in your way? (*Lets C through the door and sits
down to wait.*)

3

SHOW BUSINESS

In Victoria's early years as a professional entertainer she was seen exclusively as a songwriter. It began auspiciously: in the autumn of 1974, in her first appearance on national television, she won her heat of *New Faces* with a song called 'Fashion'. No tape of the show has surfaced, but she kept the lyric sheet and there are recordings. One is on a BBC variety show broadcast in the Midlands called *Mother Muffin's Music Stand*, on which she also performed 'Nice Girl'. Then, for her next appearance on *New Faces*, she composed 'Lorraine'. All three songs reveal her preoccupation, as she started out in show business, with young women being expected to conform – and the rebellion that simmers inside them.

After *New Faces*, Victoria tried to forge a career as a cabaret singer. She struggled because she had not yet created a rapport with audiences, leaving her songs – some of them slow and gloomy – to do all the heavy lifting. She fared better when in 1975 she was invited to share the bill with GRIMMS, the male collective consisting of Roger McGough, John Gorman and Andy Roberts, in a show called *Wordplay* which opened in Edinburgh and transferred to the Hampstead Theatre Club. Roberts, a musician, urged her to steer away from comic whimsy and approved of her nuclear doomsday song 'We're Having a Party for the End of the World'.

She took him at his word when she composed a song about her struggles with body image. 'Nobody Loves You When You're Down and Fat', which she performed on tour with John Dowie in 1977, was an introspective dirge. She paid a far bouncier and more characteristic visit to the same territory in 'Never Spend a Fortnight on a Health Farm'. This was her first attack on the diet industry – she would later set *Mens Sana in Thingummy Doodah* (1989) in just such a hellhole.

By 1976 Victoria felt confident that she'd amassed enough songs for an album and recorded a demo of thirteen of her compositions at Zella Records in Birmingham. They included some from her student days, others from the previous two years of cabaret performing and sporadic TV, among them a couple of songs written that year for *That's Life!* The most personal was a lament composed to mark the end of a period in her life when she had had on–off liaisons with older men. It was one of the first songs she played to her future husband Geoffrey Durham, whom she met over the summer.

Over the same period Victoria had a commission to write a Christmas entertainment for children from Jude Kelly, who studied drama at Birmingham and had just taken over Solent People's Theatre. She took the Cinderella story as a template and wrote about a shy girl called Gail Wilkins who has an unloving parent and two older sisters, and dreams of love. *Sunny Intervals* was rejected, and the demo tape of the songs does not survive, but the script, and particularly the untitled lyric included here, suggest Victoria put much of herself into Gail.

A snapshot of Victoria's repertoire, and her state of mind, was captured in the earliest surviving audio interview, broadcast on BBC Radio Blackburn at the start of 1978. Her career had not taken off despite considerable television exposure, and at the age of twenty-five there was no sign of an upswing. Of the seven songs she recorded, the most optimistic shows her turning her gaze away from herself and harking back to Bury Grammar to write about characters.

FASHION[26]

Dorothy picked up a magazine
And sadly flicked through its pages
Wondering if she could afford a facelift
Out of her typist's wages
Reading the fashion columns
Wishing she could follow their advice
But she has to wear what her mother buys
And mother is boringly nice.

She sees herself in black satin
With no back and no sides and no top
The sort sexy ladies pop out of
Except Dorothy's got nothing to pop.
She sees herself in silver boots
With twelve-inch platform soles
Her mother sees her in lace-ups
And what mother says goes.

She'd really like to be daring
But it's hard when your mother knows best
If she wore a see-through blouse
Through it you'd see her . . . vest.
Dorothy bought some perfume
Exuding an aura of sin

26 The tempo is slow but picks up whenever Dorothy imagines herself dressing as a
vamp. 'Written for BBCTV', VW pencilled on the lyric sheet, so *New Faces* was actually its second outing.

Dorothy's father is a bit of a wag
Said it smelt like Rin Tin Tin.[27]

She sees herself in blue denim
In a torn and faded shirt
In a floating dress of dazzling white
Because her mother says it shows the dirt.
She sees herself in cotton
The thin kind that's easy to rip
She sees herself in black leather
With a very fetching whip.

Will you dream forever?
Will you stay in your sartorial rut?
Will you stay in your nylon trousers,
The kind that go under the foot?
From the safety of your lumpy jumpers
Will you marry into cavalry twill
As your nice dress fades into the sunset?
My guess is you probably will.

NICE GIRL[28]

Mummy's glad I'm not rough
And she loves me enough
To tell me twice.

---

27 German shepherd that became a canine star of silent films. After his death in 1932
his name was inherited by other screen dogs. He later cropped up as part of a sex gag in
'I've Had It Up to Here' (*GF*):

Full of self-congratulation
They expect a combination
Of Olga Korbut, Raquel Welch
And Rin Tin Tin.

28 The melody is cheerful and raunchy. On *Mother Muffin's Music Stand* VW was
backed by a traditional jazz band.

What she doesn't know
And I hope it doesn't show
Is that I hate being nice.
I want to go home tonight
And tread on the cat
To hear the sound as I whirl it around
I've always wanted to do that.

But I'll be sitting down
In my pink dressing gown
And my cocoa
While my father pats his bulge
And says you shouldn't indulge
But want a smoke? No?
I'll take his cigarettes
I'll take his matches too.
While casually inhaling I'll nail him to the railings
That'll give me something to do.

While I'm resigned to the life
As a very cute wife
Of a civil engineer
A plan I'll hatch
In my semi-detached
And just disappear
I might turn up as a stripper in a den of vice
I'll be introduced as Sadie, a rather evil lady
Won't that be nice?

LORRAINE[29]

There's a tin in the office cupboard
Labelled Lorraine

---

29 Slowish, with a chuntering piano accompaniment.

Because I've gone and got engaged again
I wonder what they'll give me
Money'd be ideal
Probably be something practical in stainless steel.

I hope to get thin for the wedding
Lose a couple of stones
Cos on the day I might fade away
And be just a veil and a pile of bones.

Bit doubtful about the reception
Hear the whispers as they drink the toast
She had to get married, he had to be carried,
I give it two years at the most.

Mothers getting together
Thinking that's never real fur
Hope if there's a baby
It won't look like her.
Fathers getting matey
Help yourself to wine
Each one's thinking
His wife's as boring as mine.

I don't think his mother likes me
I can tell by the look in her eyes
As she sips her port and lemon
Says I've got a little premon-
-ition you're in for a surprise.
I know what she's trying to tell me
I've heard about marital rites
It sounds like 'ell so it's just as well
It only happens on Saturday nights.

The worst thing about this is Richard
He's very nice but thick

Slaps people on the back
Says 'Call me Dick'
He's very conscientious
He's very seldom late
In fact if you go a bomb on greasy hair he's great.

He must have some more good points
Hang on a minute I'll check
I don't think I've seen a cleaner Cortina
He washes it more than his neck.

Still it's better than staying single
And it's better than being dead
And to tell you the truth
I don't know what I can do instead.

WE'RE HAVING A PARTY
FOR THE END OF THE WORLD[30]

We're having a party for the end of the world
And everyone's gonna be there
We're having a party for the friends of the world
We'll sing and dance and pretend we don't care
Who would have thought that the man in the park
With the placard of doom was right?
Well never mind, we'll stand a glass raised in our hand
And sing to the turning off of the last light
Sing to the turning off of the last light
We'll sing to the turning off of the last light
We'll sing do do do do . . .[31]

---

30 The melody and piano accompaniment match the anxiety and introspection of the lyrics.

31 The scat resolves into a snatch of the title tune from *Singin' in the Rain*.

It might not be good, this last party of ours
It might not occasion much laughter
Still we'll stand in the cold
And say at least we'll never grow old
And we won't have to worry about the morning after
Be quite informal, an informal affair
In fact you can come as you are
And together we'll stand
And say, strike up the band
And sing to the fading of the last star
And sing to the fading of the last star
We'll sing to the fading of the last star
We'll sing do do do do . . .

NOBODY LOVES YOU WHEN YOU'RE DOWN AND FAT[32]

As the clock moves to half past
Order another bun
You didn't like him really
You knew he couldn't come.
The tears soften your sandwich
And run into your cup
Still you'll tell a good story tomorrow
About being stood up.

Chorus:
People can be very cruel
There's no use denying
Inside every jolly fat girl
Is another one crying
So get thin or keep smiling

---

32 The melody strides along at medium tempo.

And that's that.
Nobody loves you when you're down and fat.

Order a toasted teacake
To help you to forget
You'll have to dry your tears now
You're making it all wet.
Brush the crumbs off your new jumper
And lumber into the street
Stop at the fish and chip shop
You deserve a treat.

Repeat chorus.

Your mother says you'll get a man soon
Comfort as she makes the tea
Does she know what she's talking about?
She was deserted in 1953.[33]
So ready with another chocolate
And ready with another joke
And all I hope is that one day one of them will make you choke.

Repeat chorus until last line:
Nobody loves you nobody loves you when you're nobody loves you
    when you're down and fat.

---

33 The year gives VW the rhyme, but 1953 was also the year of her birth and it popped
up throughout her work. There is a Miss Bognor Regis 1953 in her very earliest play,
written in a school exercise book when she was seventeen. In 'Keeping Fit', her stand-
up monologue about Morecambe, she refers to 'the Sunset Jigsaw Club formed in 1953'.
In 'Service Wash' (*ASOTV*) VW plays an old woman in a launderette: 'I'll never forget
the coronation, 1953 . . .'

NEVER SPEND A FORTNIGHT
ON A HEALTH FARM[34]

I remember when I used to be healthy
Everything infectious I could catch
And all I wore was blotchy food-stained cardigans
With blotchy legs to match.
The only exercise I had was yawning
And chocolate was the only food I ate,
I never ever got up in the morning
I was really really bleurgh but it was great.
And then I won this contest in the paper –
Two weeks on a health farm was the prize.
You're supposed to have a wonderful fortnight
Except it was like prison in disguise.
I didn't mind the exercise, the lemon juice or eggs
I couldn't bear the bouncing bottoms and the flabby legs.
Never spend a fortnight on a health farm
You'll end up with fourteen days of health.

Wouldn't be so bad without the others
But the people there they really get you down –
They eat their half a carrot and their orange
And their Mars bar that they've smuggled in from town.
I couldn't stand the gentlemen in underpants and ties
And the way they said 'Oh yoghurt!' like it was a big surprise.
Never spend a fortnight on a health farm
You'll end up with fourteen days of health.

---

34 High-speed with a rumpty-tumpty accompaniment, it has a similar energy to 'At the Chippy' (*ASOTV*). When performing it for BBC Radio Blackburn, VW introduced it as 'Healthy, Poor and Very Stupid'. It stayed in her repertoire and in 1981 she recorded it for *The Little and Large Party* on BBC Radio 2.

I wonder what it is about a tracksuit
That makes every single person look so funny.
Still I did lose thirty pounds in fourteen days there,
The trouble is that most of it was money.
And the jogging in the garden in the early morning mist
Drinking half a glass of grapefruit juice and wishing I was . . .
    drunk.[35]
Never spend a fortnight on a health farm
You'll end up with fourteen days of health
You'll end up with fourteen days of health.

NO MORE OLD MEN[36]

No more old men, no more affairs
On my brown pillow case no more grey hairs,
No more Black Magic, no more Milk Tray
If I want to get fat it'll have to be another way.

But they help out with minor debts,
So quick to pass the cigarettes,
And they're so pleased to find you nice –
So overwhelmed to do it twice.

They turn away, put on the suit,
A dented mattress, the smell of Brut.
Some look ashamed, make you feel tarty
The smell they leave is Hai Karate.[37]

---

35 Promising a salty rhyme and then withholding it was a favourite tactic of VW's.
36 Dirge.
37 A budget aftershave. It spawned a series of television commercials in which a stumpy
nerd wearing the lotion resorts to martial arts to fend off a beautiful woman played
by a barely dressed Valerie Leon, then best known for half a dozen *Carry On* films. It
cropped up again in the wife-swapping scenario VW imagined in her 1990 stand-up
show: 'She's getting her g-string out of the airing cupboard, he's frantically splashing his
private parts with Hai Karate.'

No more accept the convenient lift
Or help to choose her birthday gift,
No more the bed from six till eight
Pretend to come so he's not late.

What will I do? Where will I find
Someone so boring, someone so kind?
You tiptoe down my unlit stairs –
No more old men, no more affairs.

UNTITLED (HOW NOT TO BE SHY)[38]

My dad says that I'm just a shy girl
I don't know what life's all about
He says 'Gail, come out of your shell more'
But it seems safer in than out.
I never wish to be clever
'Cause I know wishes never come true
But there's got to be something I'm good at –
There must be a job I can do.

I know everyone laughs at me
Well why not?
I suppose being funny
Is all I've got.

I know that I'm not good-looking
It's a topic my sisters discuss
They decide that they're both rather stunning

---

38 The song comes at the end of the first scene of *Sunny Intervals*. Gail's older sisters
Marilyn and Deirdre have already introduced themselves in a duet ending with a joke
about exams that would become a favourite of VW's:
    We left with our scarves wrapped round our necks
    With CSE knitting and O level Sex.

And I'm like the back of a bus.
I did have a dormouse that loved me
They threw him away and I cried
They said that he smelt a bit funny
But it's only two years since he died.

Why does everyone laugh at me
All the time?
Why should not being pretty
Be treated like a crime?

My dad thinks I'm nice but I'm useless
My sisters are glad to agree
One day I know I'll meet someone
Someone who's going to need me.

And then nobody will laugh at me
There'll be no reason why
Until then I'd better learn
How not to be shy
Not to be shy
Not to be shy.

UNTITLED (LORD DISMISS US WITH THY BLESSING)[39]

Lord dismiss us with thy blessing,
Thanks for mercies past received
Agatha the large headmistress speaks to girls about to leave.
Dusty sunlight, stained-glass windows,
Scraping of green canvas chairs,
Agatha feels sentimental
Watching 6A's last school prayers.

---

39 After the reflective opening verse the pace picks up.

Elizabeth Owen fair and slender, senior prefect known as Liz
Loved by many and was once on *Junior Criss Cross Quiz*[40]
Role-plays in Latin, taught us Spanish, nobody was to guess
She'd fade into an English teacher, hairy legs and sleeveless dress.

Patty could play blues piano, never wants to do games or gym,
Reduces friends to helpless laughter, putting rude words in the
    hymn,
Called her physics master Henry, play the drums and wouldn't
    wear specs
Then as planned on her fifteenth birthday, gave up music, took up
    sex.

Brenda egged on by her mother, disregarded smirk and smear
Always came top and never used tampons, then became an engineer
Encountered no discrimination, no one tried to change her plan
Probably cos Brenda's colleagues all think Brenda is a man.[41]

Agatha surveys her favourites,
Tears drip proudly down her wart.
But I backed the girl in the filthy blazer –
The one who's burnt her school report.

---

40 Children's version of Granada quiz show based on noughts and crosses, ran from
1957 to 1967.
41 In 1983 VW would revisit the idea of a song about school contemporaries in 'Funny
How Things Turn Out': 'Remember Bobbie Field/Jennifer Hill/Brenda James?'

4

IN AT THE DEATH

In June 1978 Victoria was asked to write songs for a revue at the Bush Theatre in west London called *In at the Death* which responded to stories in the news. She found herself in – for her – the unusual position of composing for another performer. Though it was written for a male voice, Victoria would include 'Love Song' in her live show and publish it in *The Lucky Bag Songbook*. She herself performed the other songs she contributed. In the jaunty 'Dear Mum' a woman callously racks up excuses for not visiting her elderly parent, while 'Children' was inspired by a newspaper report of a woman who'd had an abortion and ended up in a mental hospital.[42] ('You could actually feel the audience pausing to think,' wrote Steve Grant in his review for *Plays and Players*.) Her jolliest song was 'Guy the Gorilla', inspired by the recent death of London Zoo's most famous resident. No recordings of these songs have surfaced.

While Victoria was becoming a familiar voice as a songwriter, audiences and critics knew nothing of her talent for comic dialogue. That changed when, at short notice, an extra sketch was needed. One lunchbreak Victoria hastily wrote 'Sex' for the three women in the cast. It was packed with jokes and was the hit of the show. In Julie

---

42 VW returned to the subject in *Talent*. 'I mean an abortion's not much to get steamed up about these days,' says a male character. 'Cath's sister had one; and she helped us paint our kitchen ceiling the week after.'

Walters, whom she met and bonded with at the start of rehearsals, Victoria had found her muse.

Her success in the show led to *Talent*, which opened at the Sheffield Crucible in November. It was too short to make up a full evening in the theatre so Victoria and her boyfriend Geoffrey Durham, in the guise of the Great Soprendo, supplied the second half. Victoria began her section with a song whose strategic function was to get the audience in the mood. There would be many better-known show openers, but 'I Only Hope to God It Goes Alright' was her first.

DEAR MUM

Sorry we weren't able to get down to you last week.
Daniel's still revising, General Studies next week, then Greek.
And till they mend the Maxi, we just daren't drive too far.
You're really very lucky not to have a car.

Sorry for the silence, your card was not ignored –
I put 'must write to Mother' on the kitchen noticeboard.
Mind you, my lousy writing, and my spelling's not too hot,
I'm sure you can't be bothered if I write to you or not.

But we'll definitely be there, or perhaps you could come to us,
But the train is so expensive, and it's five hours on the bus.
Things are frantic here as usual, not surprised I'm going grey,
You don't know how I envy you, not a thing to do all day.

I'm still busy with the barbecue, I don't know where to turn,
I'm baking eighteen dozen vol-au-vents in aid of Age Concern.
The dining room's been painted, avocado, sage and lime
And I've joined another Women's Group – Consciousness Through
   Mime.

But we'll definitely be there, end of April, early May.
Anyway start boasting, dotty daughter's on the way.
Bet your friends are jealous, family back so soon.
But we'll definitely be there, end of May or early June.

CHILDREN[43]

I lost my pills on Monday,
Got pregnant the week after,
Told Gerald on the Tuesday,
We were both in fits of laughter.
He said I was the last girl
To ever have a kid –
I'll have an abortion
If you lend me fifty quid.

We did discuss it slightly
But it's hard to talk to Gerald –
He said we'd never fit a baby
In the Triumph Herald.
They said I wouldn't feel a thing,
Just a little prick –
Gerald made a joke.
I felt sick.

It's not as if they're people,
I can always have one later,
I don't believe those old wives' tales
Screams from the incinerator.
I don't know why I dream about you, baby,
My conscience is clear
And I really was very busy
With my job that year.

Went off my food afterwards,
Lost my curves,
I keep having these nightmares –
They get on Gerald's nerves.

---

43 In the typescript of the lyrics there is an alternative title: 'You Won't Feel a Thing'.

It's nice here, very quiet,
I can spend all day in bed
Just talking to the baby that lives in my head.

GUY THE GORILLA

Jane and Sam keep busy,
Up by half nine,
Straight to the airing cupboard
To make disgusting wine,
Printing patterns with potatoes
On a bamboo roller blind,
Checking their biorhythms
To see if they're aligned.
And if they're not, and they're usually not,
No chance of sex that day,
They flick through *Cosmopolitan*
For another game to play,
Go and see Guy the Gorilla,
Very *Cosmo* thing to do,
So they borrow a black deprived three-year-old
And drag it to the zoo.

Chorus:
Guy the Gorilla, Guy the Gorilla,
Died of chocolate,
Not usually a killer,
In cottage flat and villa
They're crying on the piller
Cos of the death of Guy the Gorilla.

Tom's a bad actor,
Leather jacket and charm,
Done fourteen walk-ons in *Emmerdale Farm*,
And one shampoo advert,

Though in this case,
They borrowed his dandruff
And didn't use his face.

Repeat chorus.

Mel's a bit weedy,
Wears sandals and socks,
He's got spots on his back
And a sponge bag that locks,
He's into Pet Clark and Dennis Lotis,[44]
Screwed his girlfriend,
She didn't notice.
To bring out the best in him
She said 'Go and see Guy'
Mel took his woolly and thermos
And gave it a try.
As he stared at the animal,
It dawned on Mel
That Guy the Gorilla was boring as well.

Repeat chorus.

SEX

Julie in library behind the counter, slashing wrists with library ticket, sorting tickets and crying. Vic approaches counter with books, gives Julie her ticket. Julie stops suicide. Julie snots all over it, and can't get it into the computer.
J: It won't go in.
V: That's cos it's got snot all over it.
J: It's the computer.
V: I know, they can't deal with it, can they?
J: Pardon?

---

44 Popular singer in the 1950s.

V: Snot.

J tries again but it won't go in.

V: Oh it doesn't matter – I didn't want to read them anyway.

J bursts into tears.

What's the matter? Are you having a do? Time of the . . . ladies' trouble?

J: I wish I was. I'd be running about with a sanitary towel on my head, singing.

V: Are you late?

J nods.

Oooh pet, are you married?

J: No.

V: Engaged?

J: No.

V: Well has he been to tea with your mum and dad cos that's as good as?

J: No I've only met him the once.

V: Did you?

J: Yes.

V: Oooh dear, whatever made you do it right off like that? Was he right nice?

J: He was smashing. Name's Brett.

V: Lovely.

J: And he was right funny, you know a man came up to us in the pub and said, about me, 'I bet your tart bangs like a shithouse door,' and Brett said, 'Get lost or I'll cut your ears off.'

V: What happened?

J: Brett cut his ears off. You know he's really witty. We were at the bus stop and he got out his . . .

V: Doodah.

J: His thingy – he got it out, hung my handbag on it[45] and said,

---

45 VW also used the image of an erection doubling as a hook in *We'd Quite Like to Apologise* (1989). 'These are the men we're having dinner with tomorrow, Victoria,' says Joyanne, showing her a photograph. 'He on the left, Nobby – you'll like him – he's very witty. I bet you've never seen a medallion hung round that before.'

'Shut that door.'[46] I was dying laughing. I nearly swallowed my chewy. (*Tearful.*) Course, once he got what he wanted . . . I haven't seen him since – I think I might be in the . . .

V: Up the . . .

J: Doodah.

V: Thingy. Well, I pity you, I really do. Though personally why you want to go doing it at all . . .

J: Haven't you ever done it?

V: Oh, I'm not a prude. I've done it and I don't like it. August 1967 that was – I said to Elvis, my husband, there must be better things to do on a Bank Holiday than lying on your back getting pine needles up your roll on.

J: Like crazy golf.

V: I was put off when I saw his . . .

J: Donger.

V: Pinkie. I mean the basic equipment's so ridiculous – how's he expected to take you to the brink of ecstasy with something that looks like a school dinner without the custard?

J: Spotted.

V: Oojah.

J: Does your husband . . .

V: Elvis.

J: Does he not mind your not doing it?

V: Well, I tend to just make excuses or just make it difficult for him – separate sleeping bags, wearing a leotard, Carmen rollers in your pubic hair.

J (*crying*): You've never been pregnant then? Don't you want children?

V: I certainly do – I found a Mothercare token in the precinct and I'm not wasting it. We're having one done in a test tube.[47] From your husband's . . . You post it off.

---

46 This was the camp catchphrase of the comedian Larry Grayson, and the title of his ATV comedy chat show, which ran for five years from 1972. VW plays on it in *Talent* in a reference to a face-pack which pledges to 'shut that pore!'

47 At Oldham General Hospital on 25 July 1978 Louise Brown became the first human to be born via in vitro fertilisation. *In at the Death* had opened twelve days earlier. VW revisited the subject in 'Today in Hospital' (*ASOTV*):

J: How does it stay in the envelope?

V: That was a problem. We put it in a Tupperware in the end.

J: And they send the baby back?

V: No, you grow it in the test tube; when it gets a bit bigger it's going in a tropical fish tank we had off Aunty Kathleen.

J: Suppose you don't like it?

V: You can send it back as long as you've not had it out and played with it.

J (*bursting into tears*): I shan't want to play with mine.

V: Or perhaps you don't have to have it. Couldn't you afford an abortion?

J: I'm only on 23 pounds 50 and I'm still paying my fine for shop lifting.

V: What happened?

J: A duvet fell into my shopping bag. Very expensive abortions, aren't they?

V: Unless you do it yourself. Mind you, button hooks aren't cheap these days.

J: I could ask Mr Bailey, our caretaker. He's been through the WVS. No, ARP, that's it.[48] (*Calls.*) Mr Bailey, can you stop mopping a minute? Got a little sexual problem here.

Mr B:[49] Oooh, don't ask me. I haven't had so much as a sniff at a surgical stocking since the Coronation, and that's only cos it were too wet for pigeons.

V: You manage alright without it then?

Mr B: Oh aye. If I start getting a bit under the . . .

V: Y-fronts.

Conrad: We want a test-tube baby.

Corin: Why, are there problems . . . ?

Elaine: Yes, we've only got a maisonette, so a little tiny test-tube one would be . . .

Corin: No, they grow to a normal size – they're conceived in the test-tube.

Elaine: Well, we'll never both fit in.

48 The Women's Voluntary Service, subsequently to feature in *H49*, was formed in 1938 to prepare women for civil defence work, in the same year as Air Raid Precautions.

49 Philip Jackson, who later appeared as part of the Fettlers and Warp and Weft Adjusters Silver Band in 'Brassed Up' (*ATT*).

Mr B: Only for pigeons, I use a rusty nail file usually.

(*Stumped silence.*)

V: That woman might know – she looks very educated, doesn't she?

J: She does. She's probably done CSEs and typing. Shall we ask her? Excuse me?

A:[50] Ah, I was just coming to enquire actually – I don't seem to be able to find the books I want – vegetarian recipes for the one-parent family and competitive yoga.

J: I don't think we've got those – gymnastics for the hard of hearing?

V: We wondered if you could help us – little matter of pregnancy.

A: Well, I've just started on a new contraceptive.

V: Oh yes.

A: Lentils. (*Stumped silence.*) What exactly is the problem?

J: My period's late.

A: How late?

J: Five minutes.

A: When did intercourse take place?

J: Beg parden?[51]

A: Where are you in the menstrual cycle?

J: Taurus.

A: Did he – use anything?

Mr B (*clarifying*): A johnny.

J: You what?

Mr B: A manhole cover.

J: He didn't use anything. He didn't even take his trousers off.

A: Where were you?

J: Well, I was in the chippy. He was at the bus stop, and when I came back it was all over.

A: He didn't actually enter you?

J: Ooo. No, I'm a Catholic.

A: You can't be pregnant then.

J: Can I not?

V: You never actually did it.

---

50 Alison Fiske.

51 This is as VW spells it in the typescript.

J (*disappointed*): Did I not?

Mr B: I'll give you a go now if you like in the stockroom.

J: Oh will you? (*To A & V.*) Do you want to come and watch? And
    help us out a bit?

V: Yes, why not? I've missed the half past now. (*They go off.*)

Mr B: I'm probably a bit rusty, but it's roughly the same as the lizard,
    isn't it?

I ONLY HOPE TO GOD IT GOES ALRIGHT[52]

This is to tell you
That I'm very glad you're here
Cos without you, I would be bored tonight
I only hope to God it goes alright.
I cannot tell you what a funny show it is
I am not sure about it any more.
Prob'ly because I've heard it all before.
You'd better know before we start
I can't tell jokes
I forget the ends, even those that start 'knock knock'
Except the one about the mangled cock.
In case you're wondering I am not Pam Ayres[53]
She wears dresses and sits in chairs
(I like the chairs better)

---

52 No recording survives. The tempo is clearly upbeat.

53 Comic poet who delivers her verse in a distinctive Berkshire burr. Like VW she
got her break on a TV talent show – in her case *Opportunity Knocks* in 1975 – which
perhaps helped to merge their identities in the public mind. VW first mentions her in
Talent:

    Maureen: They don't take girls from offices to be on television.

    Julie: They do – what about Pam Ayres?

    Maureen: She probably knew someone.

    Julie: Slept her way to the top? Come in, Miss Ayres, get your corsets off and read us
    a poem about hedgehogs?

And I am not Jake Thackray,[54] he is taller
He plays guitar and his tits are smaller.
So here we are and I think I had better start
Cos if I don't
I cannot think who will.
Did you know Rochdale lost again one-nil?
I only hope you manage to enjoy yourselves
I am convinced it will be one brill night
I only hope to God it goes alright.

---

54 Observational singer-songwriter from Leeds (1938–2002). Like VW he featured in an
episode of *The Camera and the Song* and guested on *That's Life!*

5

WOOD AND WALTERS

'At the moment I'm recording a comedy (ho ho) series with pal Julie Walters,' Victoria wrote to her school friend Lesley Fitton in October 1981. 'It was a lot of work to write.' On the strength of a single pilot episode of *Wood and Walters* broadcast at the very start of the year, Victoria was commissioned to come up with material for a seven-part series. In the end there was enough to fill six episodes, so the seventh repeated the best of the songs and sketches. In fact, her archive does nevertheless contain some leftovers.

The exclusion of several items was connected with the show's conception – or misconception, as Victoria came to think of it. Although the title positioned the stars as a double act, it was not always a comfortable fit. Victoria attempted to write introductory patter for them both to deliver, but Julie was an actor to her marrow and much preferred dressing up and playing characters to coming on as herself. In one episode Victoria confronted the issue by having Julie make a late entrance in a silly outfit. In a couple of items, introduced with the words 'Hi chaps', Victoria got round Julie's shyness by opening the show on her own, but these were not used. In the second half of the series the episodes would just go straight into sketches. She wrote other material for two alter egos she referred to in the typescripts as 'Vic and Jules'. Some were fillers, others were add-ons intended for the end of the show. In many of these the stars deprecate themselves as unloved or unfunny. 'Starspotting', which has an elaborate set-up for the same sort of pay-off, may have been a self-reference too far.

Of the other sketches deemed surplus, 'The Rebel' featured neither Wood nor Walters, while 'Comedy Ration Book' is the most regrettable omission. A spoof of catchphrase-stuffed Forties radio comedy, it was out of step with a show that mainly took the mickey out of contemporary television. Plus the show contained another sketch making fun of wartime tropes.[55] Viewers would have spotted an unexplained glimpse over the closing credits of the highlights episode, with a tiny clip from it plus a shot of the cast togged up in posh period outfits and waving to the camera. But the words were never broadcast.

---

55 'This Week's Film', later published in *Up to You, Porky*.

HI CHAPS 1

Hi chaps. My friend and I have come to an agreement about introducing the show. I will crack a joke and she will show her bunions. If you can't get laughs get sympathy. We begin tonight's show with a documentary following the lives of three Manchester strippers – viewers should be warned the film contains outspoken language, nudity and scenes of an explicit sexual nature. What? I beg your pardon. It's been cut – we're having a sketch instead. Thank you.

VIC AND JULES 1

Vic: We've had another letter.

Jules: We haven't.

Vic: We have.

Jules: How many's that we've had now?

Vic: Two. It's one of those letters.

Jules: From a man? Making demands of a certain nature? You can tell me. I'm old enough.

Vic: This is true.

Jules (*suggestively*): Does he want something?

Vic: He does.

Jules: What does he want? My high-sided bikini pants in a Jiffy bag? A warm stocking?

Vic: That's not what he wants.

Jules: Does he want me on the ironing board in a corset and a balaclava?

Vic: He doesn't say so.

Jules: Does he want me nude covered in pork scratchings?

Vic: No. He wants to see something on the programme. It's quite a long word. Ends in 'O', I think.

Jules: I know what it is, don't read it out, no need to upset people.

This man needs help, no one's to blame . . .

Vic: Barry Manilow! He wants Barry Manilow!

Jules: Oh. Right. (*Pause.*) We're not having Barry Manilow, are we?

They wander off.

Vic: Are we heckers like.[56] He'd want paying. He'd want his bus fare from Bolton. He'd want the piano tuned – a proper orchestra. I'm not sitting here all day watching him trying to remember the last verse of 'Copacabana' . . .

STARSPOTTING

Jules: It's him, isn't it? I'm right, aren't I?

Vic: Eh?

Jules: He was in thingy, wasn't he?

Vic: You what?

Jules: He was in whatsit, on telly.

Vic: I don't know who you mean.

Jules: You do. Imagine him on a moped.

Vic: Oh yeah, I've got him now.

Jules: What the bloody hell is it called, that programme?

Vic: Oh come on, you should know, we can't shift you half past eight of a Friday.

Jules: He's not in that. He's in that bloody office thing.

Vic: And he comes in with that daft hat on . . .

Jules: And she caught for one and he wouldn't marry her?

Vic: That's right – cos she ran out in front of a bus and you said that's never Auntie Annie on the top deck and it wasn't . . .

Jules: And then the adverts came on and you said Barry Manilow

---

56 The original producer of *W&W*, as well as VW's three Granada dramas (*Talent, Nearly a Happy Ending, Happy Since I Met You*), was Peter Eckersley. Her nickname for him was Peter Eckerslike. She most probably wrote this sketch before his death in August 1981. She would express her bond with him by making herself the daughter of Willy Eckerslike in 'Brassed Up'.

plucks the hairs out the backs of his hands.

Vic: And Dave said pluck or not he'd like to see Barry Manilow in the abattoir at eight o'clock in the bloody morning and our Viv ran upstairs crying.

Jules: Then she came down in a housecoat and said she was pregnant by a Persian student.

Vic: Then Mam broke the toilet flushing a dead pigeon down it, and Cousin Harold had one of his funny dos and posted his underpants through next door's letterbox.

Jules: But we were still watching that programme *after* the police had left . . . I can't think what the hell it's called.

Vic: Well you should do, you directed it.

Jules: Well you wrote the bloody thing.

TIE-INS

Man (*VO*): Fans of *Wood and Walters* may be interested to know there is now a *Wood and Walters* inflatable woman on sale.

Vic/Jules (*VO*): It's fully clothed with a permanent headache. Ha ha!

HI CHAPS 2

Hi chaps – I'm afraid Jules is still in her dressing room, giving up smoking. She's rather worried by the new Government Health Warning 'Most Doctors Don't Smoke'. This is cos they're too drunk to light their cigarettes.[57] Tonight's programme will be followed by a discussion on BBC Two, led by Joan Bakewell,[58] who will be asking

---

57 VW liked this joke enough to keep it in her live show for several years. She often accused doctors of drunkenness. *LB*: 'He had a touch of the DTs – in fact I thought his desk had clicked on to final rinse and spin.' In 'Today in Hospital' an incapacitated drunk rises from his bed and pulls on a white coat to treat a patient.

58 VW had sung on shows fronted by Joan Bakewell three times: on *Woman's Week*

the question 'Have we started?'

THE CORNER SHOP

Ingratiating lady assistant behind the counter. Customer comes in.

Man: Four cans of lager, two bags of crisps and twenty cigarettes, please.

Lady: Having a nice night in in front of the telly?

Man: That's right.

He leaves. Lady customer comes in.

Customer: My magazines, please, bottle of lemonade and a packet of wine gums.

Lady: Having a nice cosy evening in, reading?

Customer: I thought I would.

She leaves. Another man comes in.

Man: Box of tissues, please.

Lady: Having a nice night in picking your nose?

HI CHAPS 3

Hi chaps. Welcome to part 17 in our series 'Acrylic Knitwear – does it suit the larger Comedienne?' I'm sorry we can't bring you our interview with Professor Temple, who committed suicide after spending thirty years teaching a dolphin to speak, and then found it didn't have anything interesting to say. Following the success of *Brideshead Revisited*,[59] Granada have recorded a new serial for children which they hope will have the same winning combination of Romance, Nostalgia and the

---

in 1975, *Pandora's Box* in 1977 and *On the Town* in 1980, when she was promoting the King's Head production of *GF*. There would be plenty more gags about Bakewell in the years to come, most memorably in *AVW* (1988) when as a plant in the celebrity audience she was required to ask, 'Do you think large bosoms are a handicap?'

59 Also made by Granada, the eleven-part series began broadcasting in October 1981 just as *W&W* was in production. For more on *Brideshead* see p. 280.

inbuilt Tragedy of the Aristocracy. It's about two very posh mice making a nest out of a *Radio Fun Annual* and choking to death on a picture of Arthur Askey.[60]

THE REBEL

An office. Weedy bloke is being interviewed by older man.

Man: Well, Frank, that's the boring part of the interview over – tell me something about your background. Do you come from a poor family?

Frank: We were pretty deprived. We couldn't have a piece of cake unless we'd had two slices of bread and butter first. My parents found me hard to control – I once stayed overnight at a friend's house and we talked until quarter to ten. I told lies – I'd tell my mother I'd cleaned my teeth under the cold tap, that kind of thing.

I got in with a wild crowd at school, they kept daring me to go to the toilet without washing my hands – I never actually went that far but once I wet a paper towel and stuck it to the mirror. I was a rebel – I wore shirts that weren't ironed. I had posters of Francis Chichester[61] all over my bedroom walls, hid under the bedclothes listening to the King's Singers.[62]

Man: Your father died, didn't he?

Frank: Yes, in a typical attention-seeking gesture – he was run over. Suddenly I was the man of the house, faced with all these terrifying decisions. Did I want luncheon meat on my sandwiches or beef paste . . . By the time I was fifteen I was virtually self-sufficient – I could make cocoa, I knew where the back door was – things a kid that age should know nothing about.

Man: And you were working for your exams?

---

60 Actor and comedian (1900–1982). He was a judge on *New Faces*, and at five foot two a famous name VW liked to make fun of.

61 The first person to sail single-handed around the world.

62 A cappella group formed in 1968 by six choral scholars, five of them from King's College, Cambridge.

Frank: Yes, I don't think people understand how hard it can be for a
        kid to study in a house like ours. The constant noise for one
        thing – my sister ironing, my mother putting pound notes
        into Christian Aid envelopes.

Man: What about girls?

Frank: I've always been pretty aware of the opposite sex. Even at
        ten I used to look through my sister's keyhole and watch her
        blanket-stitching a Brownie Duster. I think she knew but she
        never said anything.

Man: Do you have a girlfriend at the moment?

Frank: Girls are frightened of me – they realise I have no sense of per-
        sonal danger. I go out with wet hair, I don't always remember
        to put the quilted lining inside my gabardine . . .

Man: Well, Frank – I think you seem eminently suitable for the job.
        It's not easy, it can be frightening, you have to be constantly
        on the alert.

Pull back to show they are in a mobile library.

        People try and take out five books on a four-book ticket, they
        underline words, they tear adverts out of the periodicals . . .

VIC

Vic: Now, we've been having a lot of letters complaining that there
        aren't enough men in the show. Well, here's some.

Cut to lots of men standing about with their coats on.

        OK, boys? We hope to bring you more men later.

*The following sketch, whatever it is, should have lots of men stood at the
back with an explanatory caption.*

YOU WANT IT REALLY

A girl's flat. Vic/Jules in chair, butch man lounging on settee. Both have cups of tea.

Man: Come on, come and sit over here. I'm not going to bite you.

Girl: I'm OK over here, thanks.

Man: I mean, there's plenty of room for two on the sofa, isn't there?

Girl: I'm OK, really.

Man: Be more cosy sitting together, wouldn't it? I mean – we're adults – we know what we're doing – no one's going to get hurt. How about it?

Girl: No thanks.

Man: Come on, you want it really.

Girl: No, thank you.

Man: That's great, isn't it? I come all the way over here, you make me a cup of coffee [sic], ask me to sit down . . . your type make me sick. There's a word, you know, for girls like you, there's a word. Alright then, OK – if you didn't want – you know what – what did you ask me up here for, eh? Eh?

Girl: To tune the piano.

Man (*picking up case*): Oh yeah. Sorry. Through here is it?

VIC AND JULES 2[63]

Vic sitting outside door marked band room.

Vic: Ssh!

Jules: Who's in there?

Vic: Well you know on Michael Parkinson he has like Stéphane Grappelli and Yehudi Menuhin[64] and they play jazz together?

---

63 The last three lines of the sketch from 'Was it a dumb idea?' were included in the montage closing the *W&W* compilation episode.

64 Grappelli (1908–1997) was known as the grandfather of jazz violin. Menuhin (1916–1999) became synonymous with the classical violin in the UK and beyond.

Jules: Yeah?

Vic: Well I thought we could do that. Mingle two musical styles.

Jules: Who've you got in there then?

Vic: Winifred Atwell[65] and Edward Heath.[66]

Jules: What are they doing?

Vic: Not a lot. (*Looks through keyhole*.) Hang on. She's picking fluff
     off her cardi and he's doing the *Daily Mirror* Quizword. Was
     it a dumb idea?

Jules: Yes it was.

Vic (*holding hand out*): Smack. Thank you.

CLOSING CHAT

Vic, Jules in empty studio.

Jules: Nice working in television though isn't it?

Vic: Yeah.

Jules: What's the best thing about it?

Vic: Subsidised gravy.

Jules: I suppose once we've done a couple of programmes the security
       men will get to recognise us and just let us in.

Vic: Oh yeah.

Jules: No wonder I'm always late, stopping off at the car park every
       morning to show them my birthmark.[67] What's that?

Vic: It's for you. An offer of work. Updated remake of Jane Eyre they
     want you for.

---

65 Trinidadian ragtime pianist (birthdate uncertain: 1910 or 1914–1983), much played
in the Wood household in VW's childhood. One of the warm-up acts on *W&W* was
Mike Terry, a large and flamboyantly bejewelled pianist from Wakefield. 'I spent five
wonderful years with a lady,' he said to audience sniggers, 'for experience in piano playing. The greatest lady ever on a keyboard.' He then played a tribute to Winifred Atwell
and VW joined in one-handed at the top end.

66 Conservative Prime Minister from 1970 to 1974. A keen pianist and organist, he had
a Steinway grand installed at 10 Downing Street.

67 This gag was acted out at the start of one episode as VW and JW try to get into the
studio.

Jules: What part?

Vic: Just says 'woman in launderette'. (*They get up.*) Is your mum coming to pick you up?

Jules: Yeah.

Vic: Bit embarrassing at your age isn't it?

Jules: What?

Vic: Being pulled home in a shopping trolley.[68]

COMEDY RATION BOOK

A living room. Spotty adolescent listening to new-wave music on transistor, granny stands by disapprovingly.

Granny: I don't know how you can listen to that rubbish. It doesn't make sense. In my day, we had proper radio programmes.

Flashback. A BBC studio, on stage are three men in smart suits and two ladies in frocks, fur stoles and hats. They are grouped round the mike with scripts. It is 1940.

Announcer: This is the BBC Home Service. Welcome once again to 'Comedy Ration Book'.

Ecstatic applause from audience. Between every catchphrase there is a round of applause and huge laughter. Each catchphrase is preceded by sound effect, door opening, closing, buzzer, bell, etc.

Woman (*knock knock*): Come in!

Man (*cockney*): It's not enough, lady!

Woman (*little boy*): Can I burst your blister, mister?

Man (*posh*): They're not going to like it!

Woman (*cockney*): 'Ere! I've just ironed that!

---

68 The rest of the sketch was used at the end of the first episode of the series:
Looking at shot card on camera as they pass.

    Jules: They've got Marti Caine in tomorrow.

    Vic: She lives in Ullswater.

    Jules: No wonder she's so thin . . . They were a nice studio audience, weren't they?

    Vic: Very appreciative. Funny how they were all wearing canvas jackets laced up at the back.

Woman (*old*): We never did that in Delhi!

Man (*northern*): He's at it again!

Woman (*old cockney*): That's what I told the coalman!

Man (*Brummie*): It was alright when I posted it.

Two Women (*northern*): We wouldn't mind, but we've missed our bus.

Man (*Welsh*): You're not putting that here, boy!

Woman (*posh*): You do tell some whoppers!

All: He's under the cistern!!

Announcer (*over music and applause*): That was 'Comedy Ration Book' with . . .

Back to present.

Adolescent: 'Ere. You're sat on my headphones!

Round of applause and laughter as before. Both look puzzled.

VIC AND JULES 4

Vic centre right. Jules enters.

Jules: Hey, Vic!

Vic: What?

Jules: I've just had my doodles analysed.

Vic: We'll just stop the conversation there, shall we?

6

GETTING ON

The double bill with the Great Soprendo stayed intact until early 1983, whereupon Victoria struck out on her own and – unusually for the era – planned to lay on a whole evening of entertainment. To provide variety, she and Geoffrey Durham worked out that for the second half she would need to come on as a character, so she invented Paula Du Val, a potty-mouthed, ukulele-strumming northern comic – Victoria was not a fan of women doing blue material. She then needed to perform a smooth transition out of Paula's wig and costume while staying on stage, and came up with a canny solution – the creation of a posh, gawky actress doing an audition. Not untypically of Victoria's writing in the 1980s, the script has autobiographical flavourings. A similar figure would turn up the following year in 'To Be an Actress', the mini-documentary in *As Seen on TV*. The comic format of providing one half of the conversation with an unseen interlocutor was surely inspired by Joyce Grenfell.

The monologues appeared in *Lucky Bag*, and she would continue to perform them, and tinker with the text, until 1985. The release of *Lucky Bag* as an album was followed by Victoria's first publication. *The Lucky Bag Songbook* collected songs with the piano score and lyrics. In October 1984 the book was launched in Manchester, where Victoria gave the speech included here. It was the first time she stood up in front of an audience and told a more or less authentic version of her life story.

PAULA DU VAL

Alright put those hands together please for the one and only Miss
Paula Du Val!

Eh up. It's a bloody old life, int it, girls? If you didn't laff you'd puke,
wouldn't yer, eh? I'm Paula Du Val, comedienne and vocaliste. I'd just
like to say it's absolutely fabelous[69] to see you all here this evening I
think we're going to have a really fabelous time. Nice to be out though
girls, int it, nice to be out. I nearly didn't get here this evening, me.
I'm int lounge, right, putting on me panty girdle – don't that elastic
itch you, girls? I like a right good scratch when I take it off don't you?
Fabelous. Anyway, I'm int lounge and he comes crawling round, dunt
he, the old feller, wanting a bit. Wouldn't mind, he brought bloody
darts team with him! Good job I'm broad-minded – as me mother
said when she married a whippet. Ee that John Travolta's something
else, int he? Oo nice meat and two veg on him, eh ladies? Makes my
old feller look like Christ knows what. If I brought him here tonight
you'd say who's put a vest on that tripe? Eh it's a great gag that, love
it. (*Gets out ukulele.*) I played this the other night. Drove 'im mad, 'e
said, what you doing? Havin' a pluck. Why not, it were bath night.
He said well plucking pluck off and pluck it somewhere else! They're
writin' some fabelous stuff for me at the moment. Oo girls don't you
just hate it when they gob int ashtray? I say if you must do it do it in
your bloody turn-ups, do you know what I mean?

Exercise is the thing these days, girls, int it, exercise. Joggin'. Couldn't
go joggin'. Not with these. One jog I'd get concussion! I tell you one
good thing, one good thing, they're so far in front of me, right, they
could get home first make me a cuppa tea, what do you say? It's the
men that need the exercise though int it girls and they won't do it. If
my old feller has to poke his ear out with a matchstick ee's buggered.

---

69 This is VW's spelling in her handwritten draft. She pronounced it 'fabberlous'.

We're all part of one happy family really, ladies and gentlemen, even the men we wouldn't really change them for the world would we girls? Although I am here to entertain you here this evening and laughter is my business, I have had my share of troubles. A dropped womb and two lads in Parkhurst. Show business *is* a fabulous [sic] business and it's people like you that have helped me keep goin'. It's a very special night for me tonight, ladies and gentlemen, it's ten years to the day since I got done for shoplifting. I'd just like to thank my fabelous manager Frankie, who's seen me through a lot. I would also like to thank everyone at that fabelous agency Frankie's All Star Artistes Limited Prestwich.[70] Also my lovely lovely musical director Brian who can't be with us this evening owing to VAT problems and ear trouble. Nevertheless I would like to do a little number for you now, ladies and gentlemen, this one was written specially for me by two very close very dear friends of mine, Betty and Derek Dewsbury. They've written many many beautiful songs for me and this one is off of my new album, *Paula Du Val Sings Fabelous*, one ninety-nine available in all good petrol stations. I'd just like to say it's been absolutely fabelous sharing time with you this evening and if any of you should happen to be in Smethwick[71] next Monday Tuesday Wednesday then do feel free to pop along to the Dolce Vita[72] and say hi to Paula Du Val. So let's get into a little bit of music here and here's a song for human people everywhere. It just goes something like this . . .[73]

NASTY THINGS

There's nasty things where you look[74]
There's nasty things in every book

---

70 VW's birthplace.

71 Where JW grew up.

72 VW did her first audition for *New Faces* at the Dolce Vita nightclub in Birmingham.

73 'Nasty Things' was performed in the style of George Formby. The lyrics and music were published in *The Lucky Bag Songbook*.

74 Pronounced to rhyme with fluke.

You're down and out
You've got no rent
Your leg's been mashed in an accident
There's nasty things wherever you looook.

There's nasty things wherever you go
There's nasty folks around, and I know.
They offer you life's brimming cup
Then they make you puke it up
There's nasty things wherever you gooo.

Grease and grime
Sludge and slime
Evil doing and skuldugg'ry
Do we fight
To put them right?
Let's face it, do we bugg'ry.

There's nasty things all over in life
There's nasty things in being a wife
You make things nice
But does he care
Keeps maggots in your Tupperware
There's nasty things all over in liiife.

If life's a boat
Then mine don't float
My oars come out my rowlocks
You say, not at all
Life's a ball
Then my reply is – arseholes.

There's nasty things whatever you do
There's nasty things just waiting for you.
At the pearly gates
You make your bow

They say heaven's shut – it's Bingo now.
There's nasty things just waiting for you.

AUDITION[75]

I'm sorry, it was just called Paula Du Val. I thought it would be nice
for an audition you know sort of not to do Juliet or Lady Macbeth
or something like that.[76] Paula's a character I devised myself when I
was at drama school . . . Sorry? Oh, Wisbech.[77] No I didn't actually
write it. Two friends of mine wrote it for me. Oh, oh you won't have
heard of them – they're called Nick and Rob. They write for *Week
Ending*[78] and *Three of a Kind*[79] and things like that. Well they're hoping
to, they sort of haven't actually heard anything . . . I'll take the wig
off, shall I? Do you want to see my hair? I'm afraid it's rather a mess
through the wig. Normally it's more sort of punky than this. I . . .
I brought these in case you want me to do any improvs . . . Right,
well I've worked mainly in children's theatre and education theatre and
some fringe work. I started my career in Peebles[80] . . . Well we toured
all round there actually. It's a very nice play called *Ogo Pogo and the
Wibbly Wobblies*. One of the Ogo Pogo plays. It's a sequel to, er, *Ogo
Pogo and the Booly Oolies*. I had a very nice part – well I had two parts
actually. Played Winifred Wibbly Wobbly, which is a very important

75 The monologue has no title.
76 VW once recited Juliet's speech for a drama college audition. She didn't get in.
77 This is a clear improvement on VW's first and second choices: in the handwritten
draft she crossed out Bury St Edmunds and replaced it with Poole. Wisbech resurfaced
in her speech to launch *Barmy* when she recalls being invited to an awards do: 'I said
if that's the Grosvenor House Hotel Wisbech forget it.' 'Now,' says the pretentious
director John in *Acorn Antiques: The Musical!*, 'some of you may be intimidated by the
reputation I made at the Wisbech Festival.'
78 Long-running BBC Radio 4 satirical comedy.
79 BBC Two sketch show which had three series between 1981 and 1983. VW had
worked with two of its stars. Lenny Henry was in ITV's *The Summer Show* (1975).
Tracey Ullman, having played Julie in *Talent* at the Liverpool Everyman in 1980, had a
small role in *Happy Since I Met You* (1982).
80 Originally Kirkcaldy.

part plotwise. And, um, and I also played a raspberry. Yes, not not, not so rewarding. I toured with them for two years and then I joined Lorryload . . .[81] Oh sorry, they're an educational theatre group based in Canvey Island[82] . . . i-i-i-in a lorry. It's great fun actually because you did everything in the lorry. You sort of toured in the lorry and you lived in the lorry and you did shows from the lorry. One of the girls died. She was hanging a leotard out on the back axle. So that's closed down. And then I was out of work, which was nice because it gave me a chance to sit and think and redefine my goals, you know . . . Sorry, how long? Er, three years . . . Yes it is a long time. My mother has a cattery so she gave me lots to do . . . Right, radio and television? Yes well I've done quite a lot of radio. I've done a lot of radio commercials for my local radio station Radio Stamford Bridge. In fact I did rather, rather, rather a good one, um, it went, 'Can't stop to chat, Jean, I'm off to Whitworth and Biddy's Carpet Bonanza.' That's quite a good one . . . Television, yes well I've worked on *Nationwide*.[83] Rather a nice piece actually about Common Market milk, you know, did it taste any different? And I happened to be coming *out* of Marks and Spencer's on Oxford Street, you know, and they asked me to taste it . . . Oh acting. Acting, sorry. Um. Oh, *Lloyd George*, *All in the Family*, *Gathering Seed*, two Dennis Potter plays. I auditioned for all of those. D-d-d-didn't get the part . . . Oh sorry, what, what might you have seen me in? Oh you might have seen me in, oh, *To Serve Them All My Days*. You know, the school thing? I had a very nice cameo role in that and, um, it was a very important scene at the station actually and John Thing, you know the main man, he's, um, meeting a woman off the train, the train pulls in, do you see, and he's kissing this woman or something – and right at the back of the shot there's me half on half off the train with my coat caught in the carriage door! Which my friend said looked an absolute hoot, you know. It really lifted the scene apparently. Of course I was in

---

81 In the early 1970s GD and JW were both members of a mobile theatre company in Liverpool called Vanload.

82 Originally Keele.

83 The BBC news and current affairs programme was axed after fourteen years in August 1983 in the same month VW introduced this character.

hospital for quite a long time after . . . The train, you know, did sort of drag me quite a long way . . . Um yes, sorry, yes I think I'm very ambitious, oh yes. I mean there's so many roles I'd love to play. Oh, um, oh Dolly. Dolly in *Emmerdale Farm*. Yes it's very moving to me . . . Um, sorry, have you any objection to working in the nude? Oh well not if it's valid, you know. In fact at the Edinburgh Festival in 1978 I was the first nude Major Barbara.[84] Sorry, would I work nude for this? What, if you offered me this job would I work nude? Oh. Oh. Would I work nude for a dandruff commercial? Yes. Yes, I would.[85]

SPEECH TO LAUNCH THE
LUCKY BAG SONGBOOK

Now I haven't given many speeches of this kind. In fact, I've only ever given one speech, twenty years ago – school debate, informal debate. This House believes that Elizabeth Wilkinson is a big fat nit and never gives you a wine gum. I opposed the Motion – I think now I was wrong – I bumped into her last autumn and she *is* a big fat nit and she *didn't* give me a wine gum. So I'm not giving a speech – I don't feel I talk enough; I'm just going to give a talk.

No, because my book – you see I'm mentioning it right away instead of creeping up to it – is a song book, so I thought I'd talk about writing songs, and what a very hard and painful life it is, and how I'd like to stop doing it, and then perhaps take a collection and go to the Bahamas. I've been writing songs since I was about fifteen – I wrote an end-of-term show at my school, Bury Grammar School. I just remember one song from it which was a commercial for Cupid's Kiss cornplasters:

---

84 Play by George Bernard Shaw, premiered in 1905, about an idealistic young woman from the Salvation Army whose father is a wealthy manufacturer of munitions. In a later version of the sketch it was changed to 'the first nude Wendy in *Peter Pan*, which was jolly exciting. The flying was a little bit awkward.'

85 In the original draft she says no she wouldn't. In a later version dandruff was changed to Bovril and she said, 'I'll let you know.'

With a Cupid's Kiss cornplaster
You have feet like alabaster,
Be a Mrs, not a Miss
With a Cupid's Kiss.

Now I never said it was funny. I only said I remembered it.

Apart from the little things I wrote at school, I only usually wrote music; never lyrics. I had a boyfriend – I was lucky to get him because I had terrible acne, I had a face like Dick Whittington's hanky – and he'd won the Observer Poetry Competition,[86] so he used to write lyrics to my tunes. So when we weren't rolling about on the carpet going, 'Shut up, I think I heard my dad's car,' we were at the piano, collaborating. And I hated it but I couldn't say that to him because I thought he might ditch me, and I didn't see much chance of getting another, what with the glasses covered in insulating tape, so I stuck with all this songwriting. It was a terrible process, trying to write a song, all the scribbling and humming and playing bits over, and it's even worse watching someone else do it.

Well, four years and about three and a half songs later, we did split up.[87] I remember it was the time of flared trousers, and the day we split up I was sewing triangles of material in the bottom of his jeans to turn them into flares – a stylish and economical tip there in case the fashion ever comes back – and he said he'd fallen in love with somebody else and he was leaving, and would I please finish his jeans and post them on. Which I'm sorry to say I did. If it happened now, I'd choose another place to insert triangles of material, but I was more docile then.

By this time I was at Birmingham University, reading drama. Well, I wasn't reading it so much as avoiding it, ignoring it, and being told I was very bad at it. So I thought I couldn't act, and I thought nobody

---

86 In fact, her boyfriend and songwriting partner Bob Mason won a verse-writing competition in the *Daily Mirror*.
87 In reality there was more than one break-up, and VW started writing songs by herself in her first year at university. Some of them were break-up songs.

loves me, and I did what any person would do under the circum-
stances: I entered the Pub Entertainer of the Year Contest. I don't
know why. I never went in pubs, and I certainly wasn't entertaining.
I entered myself in one of the London heats and I wrote three songs,
the details of which escape me, but they were all along the lines of
'My Man Done Left Me and Where There Used to Be Two Bowls of
Knorr Packet Tomato Soup on the Kitchen Table, Now There's Only
One'. It was a pub near the Victoria Palace, and I stood and looked
up at the theatre. And, do you know, a few years later, I'd still never
worked there.

I had this idea that my ex-boyfriend would turn up at the pub, see
me singing these brilliant songs at the piano, winning huge amounts
of money, and be pig-sick. I thought, 'He'll really kick himself,' which,
of course, he didn't. Good job, because people kicking themselves in
flared trousers can create a terrible draft. Anyway, he never turned
up and I came third to a trio of girl singers in hot pants, and a man
dressed as a skeleton, who climbed out of the cardboard coffin and
sang 'Tain't no sin to take off your skin, and dance around in your
bones'.

I didn't give up. I went straight into another talent competition,
came third, then gave up.

But I was playing the piano at a party one night. There was a
crowd of people around me, they were saying things like, 'You hit
her hands with the poker, and I'll lock the lid . . .' It was a party
for the people who worked at the BBC Pebble Mill.[88] Hard-working,
creative, intelligent people who liked to relax, let their hair down, fall
out of windows . . . One of them, a TV producer, came up to me;
he'd had a few drinks. You could have sniffed the lapels of his jacket
and had a tooth extracted quite painlessly. He was so drunk he gave
me a job on television, singing songs.[89] It was a folk programme about

---

88 Opened in 1971, the same year VW arrived in the city as a student, Pebble Mill
Studios ceased operating in 2004 and was demolished a year later.
89 To make a better story, VW conflated two BBC figures here: the producer who saw
her in the pub introduced her to the director John Clarke, who commissioned her to
write songs for *Springs to Mind* and music for other programmes until 1976.

spring, it was called *Springs to Mind*. Not a very good title, and the show went downhill from there. But I did a lot more programmes for them, and they used to commission songs – they'd say, 'Write a song about money' – and I'd write one about lonely girls who go out with older men because they're rich. 'Write a song about food' – I'd write a song about lonely girls who eat too much because they can't find any older men.

I loved writing them. I used to sneak into the University Music Department practice rooms; tiny cubicles with just the piano and the sign up, NO SMOKING, NO SYNCOPATING. I'd go in with a carton of milk from the milk machine and before the chill had gone off the cardboard, bang! I'd have written a song. Three verses, two choruses. Terrible, but fast.

And I wrote songs for tons of programmes after that, and the most famous one was *That's Life!* It wasn't a live programme, but it was recorded about an hour before it went out, which meant you could go on, sing a song, and by the time you got home you were already unpopular. Because it was a topical show, they liked to leave it as late as possible before giving me a subject to write a song about. The programme was on Sundays, and they'd ring me up on Fridays and tell me what they'd decided. Now the sensible thing would have been to write it on Friday evening, rehearse it Saturday, take it in on Sunday morning. I was so nervous about it, I couldn't work on it. I never started work till midnight on Saturday night. I used to set the Baby Ben for 2am, and try and finish it before the alarm went off. Couldn't do it now. If I start writing a song now, I set the alarm for Boxing Day.

But it's very odd being told what to write a song about, writing three verses and two choruses about something you know absolutely nothing about. The phone rings on Friday night – it's Esther Rantzen – 'Oh, hello, Wednesday's *Guardian*, page seven second column, piece on divorce laws, do something about that, OK? Bye!' What? Wednesday's *Guardian*? I didn't even have Tuesday's *Bunty*.[90] So I'd get on my bike, pedal round to my friend's house, get Wednesday's *Guardian* out of their dustbin, brush the wet tea leaves off, set the

90 See note 106.

alarm and get going. DIVORCE, COURSE, HORSE, FORCE, HP SAUCE . . .

They weren't really songs. The ability to make feeble remarks and play the piano simultaneously doesn't make you Noël Coward. I used to turn up on Sundays for the show with some would-be hilarious song about the Sex Discrimination Act or the Raising of the School-Leaving Age, and I'd look at the running order and find I'd been placed directly after an item on fatal plane crashes or mugged pensioners. Never got any laughs; I'd feel quite pleased if anyone in the audience stopped crying.

It was after that I was asked to contribute to a topical revue being put on at the Bush Theatre in Shepherd's Bush – it was called *In at the Death* – which gave the critics lots of scope when they hammered it, quite rightly.[91] It was all about death, this revue; it was a bundle of laughs, and we were all asked to contribute items based on a particular week's news – as long as the items were to do with death. So for the first time I wasn't being told exactly what to do, I was able to look through the papers and write about things I actually cared about, and was interested in.

One of the stories was about a man whose wife was dying, and he'd helped her to commit suicide. He'd been in court and been acquitted. I didn't want to write about that incident, I wanted to do something about an ordinary man's feelings for his wife, and how he feels when she dies. It's called 'Love Song' (it's in the book). I didn't set the alarm and I really wrestled with this song all night, trying not to be clever or put in complicated rhymes to show off, but to say what I wanted to say as simply as possible, and I kept on until it was as good as I could make it.

I realised that decent songs can't be dashed off in two hours; it's going to take a lot more time, a lot of crossing out and crumpling up, and throwing away. So when people ring up now, and say, 'We need a song about what Scotsmen wear under their kilts for St Andrew's Day and we need it tomorrow morning, and we'll pay you £12,' I say, 'I'm sorry, I've broken my pencil, I'm not well . . .'

---

91 In fact, it had mainly positive reviews.

I wrote a play with songs called *Talent* and that was practically the first time other people performed my material.[92] Doing your own stuff is easy; you write it yourself, sing it yourself, accompany yourself, tell yourself you're marvellous, there's no problem . . . Somebody else does it – it's like having a baby and standing by while someone else rams sweets in its mouth. Apart from the fact you loathe the way they're performing it, because it doesn't sound like you, you notice all the places where it doesn't quite scan unless you gabble, or the feeble line you covered up with face pulling and the loud pedal. And actors always want to discuss everything. So you learn to make everything you write totally logical, actor-proof and discussion-proof: 'She says that on page eighty-two because he comes in on page seventeen with a jam sandwich, so shut up and get on with it.'

I don't think writers should appear in their own plays really. You spend all the rehearsals interfering, and prompting anyone who stops to breathe in, and then when it comes to the performance, you miss all your cues because you're counting the house and working out seven and a half per cent of 280 quid. I mean, half of you is acting away, finding your light, projecting to the back of the circle; the other half of you is thinking, 'God this is boring, did I really write this?' creeping behind the other actors and saying, 'Get a bloody move on.'

Seeing a play of yours that you're not in can be even worse. A musical of mine called *Good Fun* was done at a small theatre in London, and it wasn't a very good production. They got their biggest laugh when a lighting bar broke loose from the ceiling and fell into the audience. They called out from the stage, 'Don't panic. We'll carry on with the show.' The audience was saying, 'No, honestly, we'd rather panic, please don't go on with the show . . .'

So I don't really act in plays any more – I do my own show – it's called *Lucky Bag*. I wrote it myself, it's only me on stage, there's no script, which means if I go blank one night, I'm lumbered. No one can prompt me, or cover up for me. If I dry badly, and there's a silence, and you can hear the stage door keeper doing the *Daily Mirror*

---

92 As previously noted, only one of her songs written for *In at the Death* was performed by other members of the cast.

quizword, I pretend to have a coughing fit. I take a drink, and that gives me a chance to look at these little prompt cards I have stuck on the piano. Last week I launched into a great fusillade of coughing and then found I was staring at a card that said, '2 lbs sprouts, collect cleaning . . .'

But it's a strange life, driving round, doing shows. I used to do a show called *Funny Turns*. I was one turn, and the other turn was a magician, the Great Soprendo. We did a double show, it was quite jolly, because we were married as well – which means you come off stage and there's always someone to say, 'God, you were good tonight, darling,' and, 'God, it annoys me when you leave the plug in the washbasin.' It's nice to have someone with you when you die the death, as I sometimes do.

[I did one show in] Scotland. They didn't laugh. It's a lino town, Kirkcaldy. There's something a bit humorous about lino. They were deadly silent, no laughing, didn't like me. As they got up to leave, someone was heard to say, 'I don't admire her dress sense.' Don't blame them, I'm not very fashion-conscious. As long as it's this year's gravy spilt down the front, I'm happy.

When I did *That's Life!*, I thought you had to wear dresses to be on the television. I had just one – a smock thing from Laura Ashley – there was a tablecloth that went with it. It was a huge thing – the sort of thing you'd throw over your bubble car in the cold weather. I used to turn up for jobs and managers would say, 'When are you getting changed?' I'd say, 'I am changed.'

When we did *Wood and Walters*, the TV series here at Granada, people used to get very incensed because we wore suits. 'Dear Virginia, you look like Harold Wilson.' Surely I'm taller? 'You are too bulgy for trousers, I see you in a kaftan.' I see you in an oxygen tent.

Or people write with scripts. 'Perhaps you can use this in your TV series' (which you've just finished). 'A woman comes in with a hoover, she hoovers up the baby by accident. She shrugs and walks away.' 'Dear Janice, I don't feel television is ready for this sort of material.'

People send me songs. When I was first on TV, I was sent songs by a man called Norman A. Wass. I've kept a look out for his name, but he doesn't seem to have hit the big time yet. They were nice songs

– he'd written them specially for me. One was called 'Two Ton Tessie', and the other was called 'Every Day Is a Guzzling Day For Me'.

People write and say, 'We're having a concert in aid of our scout hut, please can you send me your entire act as I would like to perform it? We cannot pay but please find enclosed a padded envelope.' 'Dear Mrs Bloggs, you must be a lunatic, please find enclosed a padded cell.'

Well, everyone can buy the book and do all the songs now; I don't care. It's the first time I've ever seen the piano parts written out. I just got the book the other day, flicked through – so that's moderato molto, is it? Blimey, what a lot of black notes, I can't play this. But they tell me, these Methuen people, that somebody will be able to play it, and when I've found out who it is, I'll get them to teach me. OK? Thank you.

As a second-year student, in early 1973 Victoria made a splash singing songs before and after a production of *Loot*. She pasted this memento into her scrapbook.

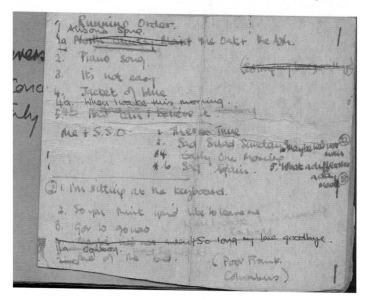

27 June 1973: the setlist from her first ever gig. The 'S.S.O.' was a scratch band grandly dubbed the Silver Screen Orchestra.

Robert Howie and Chrissie Poulter perform 'Do You Want to Know What I've Got in My Pocket?' written at speed by Victoria in 1975.

Joining the cast of *Wordplay* in 1975 with (from left) Lindsay Ingram, Roger McGough, Andy Roberts and John Gorman 'felt like being an early Beatle'.

'I shall probably never be picked as a contestant on *The Price Is Right*.' Victoria enjoyed
oking about the likes of gameshow host Leslie Crowther, and yet in 1975 she worked with
him in *The Summer Show*. 'They didn't really know what to do with me in this sketch show
because I was fat – so there was always a problem about my costumes.'

Lill Roughley, who caught Victoria's eye doing an end-of-the-pier job in Morecambe in 1977, became a regular in her comedy gang.

Almost famous: Swansea, February 1977.

At the Bush Theatre in 1978, Victoria Wood and Julie Walters perform together for the first time. 'What happened?' 'A duvet fell into my shopping bag.'

Alone at her desk in Morecambe, Victoria crafted two stage plays, three television dramas, a sketch series, her first stand-up show and countless lyrics.

'It is a wonderful job – like most things it has its low points.' Victoria and Julie join a Christmas shoot for the *TV Times* in 1981.

'We never did that in Delhi!' A glimpse of 'Comedy Ration Book', Victoria's spoof of Forties radio comedy discarded from *Wood and Walters*.

'I wrote it myself, it's only me on stage, there's no script, which means if I go blank one night, I'm lumbered.' Backstage snap from her personal album.

A publicity still for 'Driving Test', one of the very few photographs of unused sketches from *As Seen on TV*. The instructor is Roger Brierley.

7

AS SEEN ON TV SERIES ONE

Victoria wrote the first series of *Victoria Wood As Seen on TV* in the first half of 1984. It was nearly three years on from her previous experience of crafting comedy for television but *Wood and Walters* cast a long shadow. On a practical level she knew that, without commercials, she would need to come up with five minutes' more material per half hour on the BBC, on top of which Geoff Posner, who was to produce the series, recommended an added surplus of five minutes per episode. So she spent several months at her desk writing sketches and songs as if stocking a larder.

The selection process began at home. Of the sketches Victoria wrote, some were never submitted. With those she did submit, she was sensitive to her producer's opinion: 'She was her own worst critic,' he says, 'and all I had to do was go "umm". Thank heavens she usually agreed.' Often it was the lack of a killer punchline that did for a sketch even if what went before was strong. Some sketches would be typed up for filming at the end of a week's rehearsal, and across the week it might be felt that an actor wasn't quite nailing it: 'Vic would try to rewrite them in the hope that somebody might pull something out of the bag but in the back of our minds we thought this may or may not go well.' After they were shot, the two of them would independently draw up a list of what to include and what to drop. They tended not to disagree.

Victoria's primary objective, of course, was to parody the micro-absurdities of television but many of the shorter sketches known as quickies, often little ten-second exchanges to fill in between longer items, stood apart. Several had generic settings – at the doctor, in a department store, in the library – and while some were used, more were not filmed. 'We felt we didn't want to create too many building blocks we'd have to keep to,' says Geoff Posner. 'Quickies were very useful for pace changers, but tended to be a lot of work assembling a set and cast just for ten seconds of material. They are the hardest thing to get right since you have so little set-up time and each of them has to end in a punchline.' He doesn't recall her even showing him half a dozen such miniatures set in a dry-cleaner.

But it was not simply a case of sorting wheat from chaff. Although for the first time it was her name alone in the title, Victoria's instinct was to minimise her appearances and showcase other performers. It was in this series that she started to recruit a loose company of actors whose talent for comedy, and capacity to learn and deliver her lines as she'd written them, would serve her work so well for the next fifteen years. Not just the big four, but a wider gang – some of them adept at playing stock types (establishment figures, vacuous blondes, stolid blue-collar workers, etc.), others clever shapeshifters who would be unrecognisable from one sketch to the next. However, Geoff Posner insisted Victoria put herself at the centre of her own show. This did not protect her every appearance from the chop. Sometimes there was a toss-up between two sketches and they agreed on the one that produced the better audience reaction on the night of the recording.

The order and content of each episode of *As Seen on TV* was finalised only after the material had been filmed at the BBC. In those studio sessions there might be two episodes of *Acorn Antiques* in one evening (they were recorded without an audience and shown to the audience on large TV monitors), and three sketches involving a particular actor who had been booked for the week. So this group of unseen sketches – and the collection from the second series and special – has been put together much as Victoria ordered the sketches in *Up to You, Porky* and *Barmy*: interleaving longer sketches with shorter ones, and separating out sketches with the same setting. But it also attempts to capture the rhythms of an *As Seen on TV* recording.

Victoria opened every episode with three minutes of stand-up. None of that material ever went unused – indeed much of it had been recycled from her *Lucky Bag* set. Instead, we begin as *As Seen on TV* never did, with an announcement.

CONTINUITY

Well, we certainly seem to have lots of goodies for you in our new
season. For lovers of TV magic, and there can't be many, there's a new
series of 'I crack the jokes round here', comedy magic from all over the
world. And the series opens with the Magic of – someone I've never
heard of. Looks quite a bumptious little prat from the photograph.[93]

MAGIC SHOW

Magician and lady volunteer.[94]

Magician: OK. So you picked a card, I didn't see it, there was no way
I could have seen it. You signed it, you put it in the envelope, I
didn't touch it, you covered it with paraffin, the lovely Sandra
set fire to it with this kind gentleman's lighter. You took the
ashes, sprinkled them onto the studio floor. I was handcuffed,
blindfolded in a sealed milk churn, we picked a lady at random,
she hoovered up the ash, you took out the Hoover bag – I was
nowhere near it because I was suspended twelve feet in the air
from a burning rope in a straitjacket. We sent the Hoover bag to
a scrap metal yard in an old Ford Prefect – came back as thus –
Shows small cube of metal.

---

93 It can be confidently stated that this was not a conjugal attack but, married to the
Great Soprendo, VW was certainly steeped in the world of magic.

94 The magician was played by Patrick Barlow in a cape. Since 1980 he had been one
half (alongside Jim Broadbent) of the National Theatre of Brent, which specialised in
attempting to tell epic stories with only two terrible actors. Their version of the
Messiah had been shown on TV the previous year. In the first series of *ASOTV* Barlow
also played Sir Dave Dixon, a grandiose theatre director staging a musical version of
Bessie Bunter in 'Whither the Arts?'. In the second series he was the master of ceremo-
nies frothing with polysyllables in VW's parody of *The Good Old Days*.

Would you just like to tap that on the table, nice and hard?
She does so, cube falls open, rolled-up card inside.

Will you unroll the card please, I'm not going to touch it, is there a signature on it?

Woman: Yes.

Magician: And I'm just going to ask you – is that your card?

Woman: I'm not sure if it is actually, I just can't tell. It might be, it probably is.

DEPARTMENTS: CHINA AND GLASS

Very posh old shopwalker and rough-looking woman.

Man: May I be of assistance, madam?

Woman: I don't know if I'm in the right place, but I want a present for my husband. I'd really like a 3D winking Chinese girl, preferably in the form of a sink-plunger, or a pigeon-timer.

Man: I'm afraid I don't think I can help you, madam.

Woman: Oh blimey.

Man (*displaying horrendous article*): We only have the winking Chinese girl as part of the squirting lavatory Y-fronts.

VIDEO BOX 3[95]

Thirteen-year-old public schoolboy.[96]

Boy: Well, I did watch it though I'm not a great television fan. I have

---

95 The 'Video Box' scripts that VW numbered 1 and 2 were used in the first series. One featured Gerard Kelly as a punkish Glaswegian fan of Toyah Willcox; in the second Rosalind March played a coy middle-class woman speaking of the fashions she'd like to see on TV. 'We wanted a much more real performance than a lot of them gave,' says GP. 'When you record in front of the audience people behave differently, especially if it's a solo to camera. A lot of them looked acted and that was a no-no.'

96 Possibly channelling the ethos of the BBC children's programme *Why Don't You Just Switch Off Your Television Set and Go and Do Something Less Boring Instead?*, broadcast between 1973 and 1995.

shares in a television company, so I feel I should click it on
occasionally. I felt that one had rather seen it all before, but it
was very possibly a repeat, so perhaps one had seen it all before.
I don't really want to add anything else, I feel hobbies are a
slightly more constructive way of passing the time. I collect
seventeenth-century violins, and I would highly recommend
it, it's quite fascinating. Thank you for your time, and good
evening.

VIDEO BOX 4

Liverpool teenage girl.[97]

Girl: I just think there should be more jokes about the Government
because there haven't been any jokes about the Government,
I mean, like, it costs more than twenty quid to get your hair
streaked now, and television personalities ought to be saying
things like that, and not just be doing sketches about people
always. So – just more Government sort of jokes, really. OK?
Ta.

FIRST NIGHT[98]

*A theatrical dressing room. Clara, an ageing actress in a glamorous dress-
ing gown, is pacing up and down in hysterics. There is knocking at the
door, she speaks over it.*

Clara: Go away and leave me alone, the lot of you. Make an announcement, give them back their money, I'm too upset to go on.
I've been in this business thirty-two years, and I've never been

---

97 *W&W* featured two bored Liverpool truants of a similar stripe in 'Girls Talking'.
98 Written for CI and Jim Broadbent. VW was fascinated by the popularity of Cice-
ly Courtneidge and Jack Hulbert, two stalwarts of the English stage who married in
1916 and were still touring in ropey plays that she caught at the Alexandra Theatre in
Birmingham. They died in, respectively, 1980 and 1978.

treated so badly, not even in the provinces. There's no champagne, no chaise longue, no jacuzzi ... Alright, fetch Jack. You can fetch him right now but I'm not going on. You can bring up the curtain, you can play my music, but I shan't be there!

She collapses in tears. Knock on the door.

Jack (*OOV*): Clara? Clara, it's Jack.

She arranges her hair to make it look more dishevelled.

Clara: Come in then, but I shan't change my mind.

Enter Jack, an old theatrical knight in a cravat.

Jack: My darling, if you never set foot on another stage for the rest of your life, after what I saw you do in that dress rehearsal, I shall die happy. You were incandescent. In can bloody descent.

Clara: How can you say that? I was ghastly this afternoon. I'm just too bloody old ...

Jack: Old? You'll never be old, Clara. You were born with magic in your eyes, and I'll never leave you till the day you die.

Clara: The magic's gone for me, Jack. I used to be able to hold an audience in the palm of my hand, but since I lost my Bobbie ...

Jack: And God we miss him. There isn't a single morning I don't wake up and shake my fist at the bloody heavens that they took Bobbie away.

Clara: And such a senseless accident.

Jack: You weren't to know he'd learnt how to open the door of the tumble dryer. God he was a clever little dog. Won't you go on tonight, Clara, for his sake?

Clara: I can't, Jack – it's my voice, it's gone.

Jack: Gone? Gone? That voice is angel-given, Clara, and they're not ready to take it bloody well back. You could recite the ingredients of a packet of bread sauce mix, and I'd get a lump in my throat.

Clara: They don't want me, Jacky. I'm too bloody old, this isn't my world.

Jack: It's grey, it's grubby, it's a sad little has been of a world, but my God it needs you, Clara. Those poor zombies out there wouldn't know a champagne cocktail from a bucket of Brobat.[99] They're starved of glamour, Clara. Good God, there are people out there who've never seen a cravat! Show them, Clara! Bring back the magic – just for a few sparkling evenings before some soulless senseless bureaucrat blows us all to kingdom come!

Knock on door.

VO: Five minutes, please. Five minutes.

Jack: Clara?

Clara: I'll go on, Jack. After all I'm an actress and I have a duty. To my director, to my public, and to my talent. Could you please pass my costume, darling, please?

Jack brings over panto animal skin: golden goose or similar.

Thank you, Jack.

Jack: Give them hell, my darling.

DRY-CLEANER'S 1

Assistant hands over crumpled garment.

Assistant: Three pounds fifty pence.

Customer: It doesn't look any different.

Assistant: Think yourself lucky. (*Chucks washleather onto counter.*) That were a suede jacket when it came in.

DRY-CLEANER'S 2

Customer: But this is ruined! I want compensation.

Assistant: We're not liable.

Customer: Course you are.

Assistant: Not if it's purple.

Customer: What?

---

99 An early brand of bleach. GD: 'Vic loved the word. She privately gave the name to a cleaning lady we employed: Betty Brobat.'

Assistant: Purple at your own risk.
Customer: Where does it say that?
Assistant: On the back of the ticket.
Customer (*looks at ticket*): Where?
Assistant grabs a microscope wearily, fixes the ticket on a slide, and shoves it over to the customer.
Assistant: There!

DRY-CLEANER'S 3

Assistant: Do you want special finish or standard?
Customer: What's the difference?
Assistant: Special, we make sure the dog doesn't lick it.

ADVERT

Supermarket check-out. A black cashier rings up total.[100] Woman is dismayed.
Woman: Oh dear. I can't afford my pre-soaker, my powder and my fabric conditioner. I better put something back.
Cashier: Put them all back – and just take one of these.
Cashier hands over small white pill.
Woman: What's this? A revolutionary new breakthrough in washing care?
Cashier: No, it's acid. It stops you worrying about stupid things like fabric conditioner.
Woman: Thank you.

---

100 This is a first in VW's sketch-writing. She clearly wished to underline the whinge-ing customer's sense of privilege by having her served a dose of reality by a woman of colour.

AFTERNOON TV 1: TAKE ME SERIOUSLY[101]

Interviewer (*CU*): Good afternoon. This may be 1984, and women's liberation has I hope come to stay, but has it gone far enough? Are women genuinely taken on their own merits or are they still being treated as sex-objects first, and people second?

Camera pulls back to reveal she is wearing plunge neck dress, uplift bra, fluorescent arrows pointing to bosoms etc.

With me is the actress Melissa Kent, perhaps best known for her role in *Get Nurses' Knickers Off.* Do you find that people look at your body first and your acting talent second, Melissa?

Melissa is just wearing a bra covered with fairy lights and a bow tie on each nipple.

Melissa: Well yes I do, Penny. And it's infuriating – I'm a trained actress, I think I do a damned good job, and yet constantly producers will say 'can we see your legs?', 'what do you look like in a wet T-shirt?', and it's very demoralising.

Penny: It has been known for a well-endowed actress to use her body to get on, even in television – I've even been accused of getting this job because of my chest or whatever.

Melissa: I would never draw attention to my body in any way. I am an actress, not a pair of boobs.

Fairy lights light up.

The way women in the theatre are treated is sickening, Penny. I'm a serious actress. I want to play the classic dramatic roles, but I can't get casting directors to take me seriously.

The bow ties spin round.

I'd like to do some committed feminist theatre, but I just can't get the jobs, Penny.

---

101 In pencil VW wrote 'Vic & Celia' at the top of the typescript. According to GD, VW was fond of it and mourned its loss when it was deemed too technically challenging to create a bra that lights up like Piccadilly Circus, all in the service of a slightly underwhelming pay-off.

BRITISH RAIL

A train.

Tannoy: Ladies and gentlemen, we are now approaching Crewe, please make sure you have all your belongings with you – train due to arrive Crewe at 19.26.

Station platform. Train pulls in, people get on. Everyone on platform dressed in 1926 clothes, period chocolate machines, newsboys announcing General Strike etc. etc. Modern people getting off the train mildly puzzled.

DEPARTMENTS: SCHOOL UNIFORM

Posh mother, sulking teenage girl. Middle-aged assistant.

Mother: Hello, I'm fitting Dorinda here out for school. I have a list.

Woman: Yes, madam, which school?

Mother: It's Rigby Hall, you know, the, er, experimental establishment . . .

Girl: Oh Mummy!

Woman: Rigby Hall, madam.

She pulls out from glass drawers immaculately pressed holey vests, torn jeans, filthy long-johns, bits of cloth, ripped sweaters, hair-gel etc. Mother is delighted, Girl is bored sick.

Woman: Three of each, madam?

Mother: Yes please.

Woman: We do have a second-hand service available if madam . . .

Mother: Oh no, I think it's nicer to have everything new, don't you, Dorinda?

Girl: I'm not actually bothered.[102] All uniforms are foul . . .

---

102 The grumpy teenager Lauren, whose catchphrase is 'Am I bovvered?', first appeared on *The Catherine Tate Show* twenty years later.

THE LIBRARY 1[103]

Old Man: Last week I had out a book with tomato soup all over the
cover. Now this one here had fried egg in the middle.

Librarian: Yes.

Old Man: Now, what I want to know is, have you got any with trifle
on?

THE LIBRARY 2

Old Lady: Have you got any books about seventy-five-year-old
women who lure men to their lonely basements, poison them
with a rare undetectable poison, pawn their belongings and
spend the money on Marmite?

Librarian: No, we don't, I'm sorry.

Old Lady: So my autobiography might sell, then?

LOCAL NEWS[104]

Tim: Hello, welcome to Tuesday's edition of 'Reports Local' and here's
Sally Batstead to tell us of some rather startling developments
in the world of farming.

(*Film.*) *Messy girl in huge anorak, snowstorm, red nose, shouting voice.
She holds up an egg.*

Sally: Hello! Ever wondered where these came from?

The sound goes, she carries on talking, gesticulating, holding up chickens etc.

---

103 Two quickies set in the library made it into the series.

104 Another of these unused sketches was published in *Barmy* under the title 'Reports
Local'. The characters were played in the studio by CI and DP, but on the typescript of
this sketch VW pencilled the names 'Celia and Greg'. Gregory Floy, who had been in
GF at the Sheffield Crucible and *W&W*, was not available to film any of *ASOTV*. VW
was Sally Batstead.

Tim: Well, we seem to have lost sound on that report from Sally
     Batstead, we'll get back to it as soon as possible.

Fiona (*writing, casually*): Let's just scrap it, shall we? She's really pretty
     appalling.

Tim: OK, let's forget it. And here's Fiona with the local news.

Fiona: Oh, nothing's happened really, not worth talking about. Tim?

Tim: Well – we don't have anything happening in the studio really,
     just that thing on under-age drinking.

Fiona: Oh no – that really is boring.

Tim: Yes. Let's just not have a programme tonight, what do you say,
     Fiona?

Fiona: It's up to you, I can't get my car out of the car park yet anyway.

Tim: We could have a drink.

Fiona: OK. I'm just going to the fifth floor to get my shopping.

Tim: G and T?

Fiona: Yes, slimline.

They leave in different directions. Sally rushes in.

Sally: Hey – did my film come out OK?

She realises she is alone and backs away, silently.

DEPARTMENTS: COFFEE SHOP

Two very posh old ladies. One showing flip top bin to other.

First Lady: I bought this for my nephew Philip. What do you think?

Second Lady: It's a rubbish bin, isn't it?

First Lady: Is it? I thought it was a computer. I thought it was jolly
     cheap. At least one's found out what a litter bin looks like.

DEPARTMENTS: PERFUMERY[105]

Woman: I'd like some perfume.

Girl: Something summery, something sexy?

Woman: No, nothing sexy. I don't go in for all that.

Girl: This one's quite attractive.

Woman: No, I don't want to be attractive.

Girl: This one's fairly pleasant.

Woman: I'm unpleasant, you see. Have you nothing nastier?

Girl: There's this: it's actually for putting in the cistern of a lavatory.

Woman: Oh yes, he'll hate this. And do you do it in a bath-cube?

COUNSELLING

Vague abstracted woman sits behind a desk. Girl comes in.

Woman: Hello, come in, make yourself comfy. It's Bunty, isn't it?

Girl: Patricia, Smith.

Woman (*puts* Bunty *down, picks up paper*):[106] Sorry, that's my comic. Yes, now, Patricia. What can we do for you?

Girl: I just want to go on the Pill.

Woman: The Pill. That's double 'L', isn't it? And, er, why do you want to go on the Pill, Patricia?

Girl: Well, I'm sleeping with my boyfriend and I don't want to get pregnant.

Woman: I see, I see. You think intimacy without contraception would, might, result in pregnancy?

Girl: Well, yes.

Woman: I see, Pat. Have you considered stopping?

---

105 A different perfume sketch from the Departments series was used featuring anti-mugging spray.

106 VW was an avid reader of *Bunty* in her childhood and hung on to her collection. *ASOTV*: 'Typical hotel, they had delivered me the wrong newspapers. There was no *Exchange and Mart*. No *Bunty*.'

Girl: Beg your pardon?

Woman: We've found, of the women who come to our clinic, Pat, those who don't have any sexual contact with men rarely get pregnant and we are looking into this . . .

Girl: I don't want to stop.

Woman: No, I understand. You've started, and you don't want to stop. So. Yes, I see . . .

Girl: I mean, we are in love.

Woman: Are you? You're sure? It's not just the way he knots his bootlaces?

Girl: He doesn't wear boots, actually.

Woman: I'll leave that out, Pat, no sense in alerting the footwear authorities too early . . . Er, right, so you've been having sessions on a regular basis, everything alright there?

Girl: Yes, fine, I just—

Woman: We have a booklet, The Joy of Bedmaking. Deals mainly with sheets and so on, tucking in, but there may be possibly something about what you're doing.

Girl: It's just the contraception I came about, really.

Woman: Yes, what current method are you using? Withdrawal?

Girl: No, that's not very safe, is it?

Woman: It can be, withdrawing early enough is quite effective. If one of you leaves as soon as you're introduced, it's reasonably safe. But we at the Clinic, we're not very fond of, we don't recommend that you use a Li-Lo.

Pause.

Girl: I just want a prescription for the Pill. I wanted to discuss which type would be best.

Woman: There's more than one kind, is there?

Girl: Yes?

Woman: I see. And some are better than others.

Girl: Yes, depending on your age, and if you smoke, and all those kind of things . . .

Woman: Yes, a lot of these medical opinions are overrated.

Girl: Yes, but, smoking's bad for your health, isn't it?

Woman: Not really. I think getting run over is more dangerous. But, then, it's cheaper, so – make your own mind up, Pat. So you're fixed on having this pill, are you?

Girl: I think it seems the best method for me.

Woman: As I say, it's a new one on me, the Pill. Well, just take this note through to the doctor, it just says that you have had contraceptive counselling and I think you're entitled to a pair of boots, some calamine lotion and ten Benson and Hedges.

Girl: I think you're a bit mad.

Woman: Yes, I am, though only on a part-time basis at the moment, till my son does his A levels, then I hope to be mad all the time. Though I daren't count on it, with these terrible cutbacks.

Girl: I'll see the doctor through there, shall I?

Woman: Yes, that's right, just knock first, give him time to get his water-wings on, OK?

LOCAL ADVERTS 1[107]

Large and uncomfortable man in tight collar and new suit, standing in front of a slide of his shop, reading with difficulty off an idiot board.

Man: Hello. I am Derek Didsbury of Derek Didsbury's Flue Linings and Boiler Repairs. If you want your flues lined or your boilers repaired, don't go to just any old one, come to me, Derek Didsbury. We will line your flue or repair your boiler the Derek Didsbury way, properly.

He gives a thumbs-up sign.

Remember the name – Derek Didsbury, because lining flues and repairing boilers is our job. We are proud to call ourselves Derek Didsbury Flue Lining and Boiler Repairs for that reason

---

107 Inspired by the cheap ads VW saw on Granada TV after she moved to Morecambe. 'She particularly loved one for a carpet shop,' says GD, 'in which the owner had clearly decided to do the job himself rather than paying a celeb. He couldn't cope and her final stage direction perfectly describes its closing seconds. The thumbs-up comes from a Pontin's ad that Vic also loved.'

and alone. That reason alone. So be it linerless flue or faulty boiler, rest assured that Derek Didsbury can do the job properly. The Derek Didsbury way – properly.

Gives the thumbs-up and stays frozen to the spot, eyes moving sideways.

DEPARTMENTS: BEDS

Young couple looking at bed with duvet on it, with assistant.

Assistant: Would you like to try it out?

Couple: Yes, thanks.

They get under the duvet and roll about as if asleep, tugging the duvet from one to the other.

Girl: Get off!

Man: I'm bloody freezing, you cow!

Girl: Get stuffed, Martin!

They stop.

Girl: Not bouncy enough, is it?

They look at the next bed. He pushes her on it.

Man: And if I want to stay out till three o'clock in the morning, I will do!

She throws herself face down, having a tantrum.

Girl: Get out! Get out! Get back to your precious Barbara! (*She sits up.*) I like this one better, don't you? How much is it?

CONTINUITY

And later on we have a tribute to Charlie Cook, the comedian who died last week aged ninety-four. Famous in the later years as the voice of 'the disappointed potato' in the frozen food commercial – I don't remember that – Charlie made his name of course in the war, in one of those incomprehensible radio shows.[108]

She stares off at the monitor in doubt and puzzlement.

---

108 See 'Comedy Ration Book', p. 73.

LOCAL RADIO[109]

Angela sits on a bed in a tiny bedroom with a card table covered in papers and tiny cassette recorder and microphone. She is wearing a Radio Sycamore Crescent T-shirt and stickers with the same logo are stuck around the room. She plays a short snatch of music on the cassette player.

Angela: Hello. This is Angela Andrews wishing you a very good morning on Radio Sycamore Crescent, Britain's newest commercial radio station. It's eight o'clock and time for the news. I'm afraid we don't have an awful lot of national news this morning as the dogs chewed up the paper, but I did hear one of the neighbours saying something about the government so no doubt something happening there as per usual.

Abroad – Marbella[110] is very hot but food not up to par, that report now from Ken and Olive, and we'll be having full details when they get back from their holiday.

Local news, two underskirts were taken from a tumble dryer at the Sycamore Washeteria last night. Witness Mrs Rose Morgan said, 'It was all over in a flash, I was trying to fold a fitted sheet, and when I looked round they had just vanished.' The police say Mrs Morgan is not helping them with their enquiries, she's just making a nuisance of herself.

---

109 VW was a director of Red Rose Radio, based in Preston and launched in 1982 as Lancashire's first independent local radio station. In a letter to Jane Wymark dated 6 January 1984 she described attending a board meeting: 'I am really hopeless and never say a word. Spent all afternoon doodling on a page of figures . . . only to find at the end it was all confidential financial information. I had to hand it back in. I am treated very much as the barmy celebrity so not much is expected of me.' In the same letter she announced that this was her first week writing scripts for her new TV series. It seems safe to assume that Red Rose Radio and Radio Sycamore Crescent were related. GP wondered whether it was quite right for *ASOTV*: 'I said to Vic, "This is a radio parody but can it fit in a show which is a parody of bad TV?" I also thought there's nothing much I can show in a sketch which is her sitting in the front room. Vic agreed.'
110 More or less the only holiday destination that ever crops up in VW's sketches and stand-up. It's always pronounced to sound like fella.

And finally, sport. There will be sport all over the country this Saturday, depending on the weather. Local resident Mr Harry Ramsbottom is expecting to play darts this dinner time but he may be prevented by Mrs Ramsbottom.

And it's 8.03 or something. I'll have to get glasses or they'll have to move the Town Hall clock a bit nearer, and I'll give you the rundown of today's programmes after this pause for thought.

Pause.

Right. That did me a lot of good. At nine o'clock we hope to be playing you some records, I just have to find my Boots token and pop down there . . .

She looks out of the window.

Oooh – some traffic news just in – slight delays may be expected at the north end of the Cromwell Avenue as Anthea Parkinson is having a driving lesson – police warn you to approach with caution and on no account slow down to look.

At ten o'clock we'll be having our usual magazine programme, I'll be reading from our usual magazine. Mrs Piper from next door will provide the cookery item, she'll be telling us how she deals with children who are fussy eaters, and she'll also be giving us an amusing account of her tussles with the NSPCC. We'll have Beauty Hints from Lorraine, who'll be telling us which eye shadows look best under streetlighting.

What? And we've just heard from our reporter in the lobby that Albert Wellington, Anthea Parkinson's eighty-two-year-old grandfather, is out of the bathroom. Mr Wellington went into the bathroom yesterday evening and refused to come out. The dispute is believed to be over some pork scratchings allegedly found in Mr Wellington's turn-ups.

And it's still round about five past eight, and I'll be back right back after the break.

She plays the music.

I'm afraid we still haven't acquired any commercials yet on Radio Sycamore Crescent, so for the moment I'll just say, I did go past Freeman Hardy & Willis yesterday and quite liked quite a lot of their shoes, especially those brown ones with the toe-cap. Er – Bootses is having a summer sale, I noticed their cool-bags were half price, quite a few colours, the handle did come off of ours quite soon on, but that may have been the dog . . .

Oh yes, Doreen, Sycamore Crescent's foremost hairstylist, has asked me to remind you that her front door will be open for business as usual this affie. She says the rumour that she cuts your hair with greasy bacon scissors is totally untrue, they are well wiped, and it's all a pack of lies from Mrs Finney at number thirty-two, who as we all know has got hair like the inside of a Hoover bag.

Puts glass to wall.

But now, we change to a rather more serious mood, with an in-depth discussion between Mr and Mrs Andrews of this address. The starting point will be, should Mr Andrews have used Mrs Andrews's wooden spoon to stir creosote with, but if there's time it is hoped to broaden the discussion into other areas such as who never puts on a new toilet roll, we haven't been out of the house since the shed caught fire, and why can't Mrs Andrews's mother keep her pigging nose out?

(*Shouts off*) Alright, dad, hang on! Well unfortunately that's the end of our broadcasting on Radio Sycamore Crescent for today, due to power supply problems. It is coming on foggy, and Mr Andrews needs the batteries back for his rear light. So this is Angela Andrews saying goodbye, God bless and we'll be back tomorrow morning with our very popular phone-in, and do please be patient because it does take a few moments for the butcher to come over and get me. Bye!

CONVERSATION PIECE

Modern flat. Woman, taking off her coat, sees strange-looking object in man's room.

Woman: Oh – what's that?

Man: It's a conversation piece.

Woman: Oh (*can't think of anything to say*).

PAUSE FOR THOUGHT 1

Smart young woman in pinafore dress, holds up appallingly made prop, detergent packet labelled 'MORALS'.
Music.

Girl: Hello. Heard about the new products? Yes, brand-new improved 'MORALS'. They don't cost anything, but they don't come cheap. Impress your friends, break the ice at parties, satisfaction guaranteed or your old morals back.

She puts the box down, laughs.

You can't really sell morals in a cardboard box; we can't wash our souls whiter than white by buying a product over the supermarket counter. We are lucky, each human comes with a free delivery of morals, we don't have to lug them home from the corner shop, we can simply pop out in our spiritual housecoats and pick them up off our soul's doorstep. That's an over-simplification, but you know, we have all got morals, and as the ad says – use them or lose them. They don't have a date stamp, but still last forever. They don't have preservatives, but still never go mouldy. Or to put it a bit more simply – they don't have flavourings, but . . .

The music drowns out and the lights fade.

DOCTOR DOCTOR

Patient: My hair keeps falling out, doctor. Can you give me anything
      for it?

Doctor hands over a Tupperware sandwich box.

SNOOKERED[111]

Ken (idiotic northern comedian) with contestant Cath. They are stand-ing by a huge snooker table with enormous balls and different categories (Spelling, Affairs etc.) on each pocket. Margery, the other contestant, is sitting in a pink foam rubber chair shaped like an enormous brain.

Ken: You're doing well, you're doing well, Cath. You've got the pen and pencil set, the table mat and the packet of envelopes, those are safe, we can't take those away, understand?

Cath: Yes.

Ken: She's getting to like it now, I can tell. What is it to be, Margery?

Margery: Potpourri please, Ken.

Ken: Potpourri is what she wants, Cath. Ooh, that's good isn't it, asking you to pot potpourri and we've not given you a cue. Patti, may I have the cues please?

Hostess places two billiard cues, one real, one foam rubber, into his hands.
So Patti's placing the cues into my hands, I'm swapping them round, which is it to be Cath, left or right? Take your time.

Audience call out 'left' and 'right'.
Time is up.

---

111 Inspired by *Bullseye*. The darts-based game show, first aired on ITV in 1981, was invented by the comedian Norman Vaughan. He did a summer show in Margate that same year with GD in which he revealed how put out he was, having hosted the pilot, to have been overlooked as presenter in favour of his warm-up man Jim Bowen. 'Norman's self-esteem took a serious battering at the news and he talked of little else,' says GD. VW heard all about it and gave some of Vaughan's resentment to the continuity announcer: '. . . Then at five thirty, it's our very own quiz show *Snookered* with the very popular Ken Burrows. He's not very popular with me, but I suppose working-class people find him amusing.' The original continuity typescript ends at this point, but after 'Snookered' was dropped VW added an extra joke: 'Anyway, here's a preview now . . . Oh there isn't. I beg your pardon . . . Thanks very much, Nobby.' This snark at an off-camera producer had a private subtext: Nobby was the nickname of an old boyfriend of VW's who worked in television. She uses the name more suggestively in *We'd Quite Like to Apologise* (see note 45). 'Snookered' wasn't used but VW salvaged a gag for her stand-up show: 'I got very depressed the other day. I did. It was really bad. It was my own fault. I should never have watched *Bullseye*.'

Cath: Well I've been lucky with left, so I'll stick with left, I think, Ken.

Ken: Sticking with left, she says. Sure?

Cath: Yes.

He brings out the foam rubber cue. Groans from audience.

Ken: OK. OK. What am I going to do with you? What has she picked?

Audience: A wobbly cue!

Cath (*one second later*): A wobbly cue.

Music.

Ken: Never mind, do your best. Margery, the potpourri question is 'What is a magazine?' 'What is a magazine?' You get thinking about that, Margery, while Cath has a go at . . .

Audience: Potting the Purple!

Fade.

ONE HUNDRED YEARS YOUNG[112]

Old folks' home. Tiny old lady, surrounded by home helps, birthday cards, cake etc.

All (*sing*): Happy one hundredth birthday to you!

Enter excited nurse.

Nurse: Mrs Collins! Mrs Collins! This telegram's just arrived for you!

Mrs Collins: A telegram?

Nurse: Shall I open it for you?

Mrs Collins: Oh no, I'll open it.

Does so, watched in anticipation by the others.

Nurse: Well?

Mrs Collins: I've been waiting for this for a long time.

Nurse (*winking at others*): Who's it from, Mrs Collins?

Mrs Collins: It's from Yamaha – my motorbike's ready.

---

112 'We got an actress in who couldn't say the word Yamaha,' says GP. 'She kept saying Yamaha.' As a result, it didn't work in the recording and was dropped.

DENTIST

Efficient-looking man approaches a high-tech dentist chair, holding a tube of toothpaste in its box.
Man: Now I'm not a dentist…
Woman OOV: Then beggar off and let's hear from someone who is.
Man shrugs and leaves.
Woman OOV: That told him.

AFTERNOON TV: THE SOUSAPHONE

Set in a Pebble Mill at One type-studio with a window on to the street.[113]
Presenter (*male*): Not so long ago, the sousaphone had rather a dull image, a bit of a flat cap brass band down market sort of image, that is – until Geraldine Fox-Talbot decided to change all that.
He strolls ineptly over to Geraldine, be-ribboned hair, frilly frock and gleaming pink sousaphone.[114]
Well, Geraldine, how did it all begin?
Geraldine: Well Bob, I'm classically trained, and when I left college, I got a job in an orchestra.
Man: Well done.
Geraldine: I found I didn't have very much to do, and I didn't like the people who sat either side of me, and so I put my thinking cap on.
Man: Did yourself some thinking.
Geraldine: Did myself some thinking; I thought rather than give it up altogether, because I'd had all my doors widened by this time.

---

113 In the early 1980s VW made occasional appearances on the lunchtime magazine show filmed live in front of a studio audience at the BBC's Birmingham home. In 'Brontëburgers', which stayed in her *LB* set for nearly two years, she would add a gag about it: 'In days of yore those elderly persons did tend to give up and die that little bit more easily with not having bingo or *Pebble Mill at One* to give them a purpose in life.'
114 A lapsed trumpeter and veteran of the Bury Military Brass Band, VW clearly wrote Geraldine for herself to play.

And rather than move to another orchestra and find myself sitting between two more people with personality problems and body odour; why not?

Man: Why not indeed? But not as easy as that, presumably.

Geraldine: Well the repertoire for the solo sousaphone is very limited, well it's only three tunes actually, and two of them are jolly difficult.

Man: Tubby the Tuba's one, presumably?

Geraldine: I beg your pardon?

Man: Tubby the Tuba is one of the pieces you mention?

Geraldine: No, it isn't. So I be-think me a little more thinking, and I thought why not get into easy listening music, wear nice dresses, and try to cash in?

Man: So you bought your pop music and started rehearsing?

Geraldine: Yes, very hard work.

Man: You'd rehearse every day?

Geraldine: No, every week or so, I'd have a little tootle.

Man: Then you wrote to the Ritz, and Claridge's?

Geraldine: That's right, Bob.

Man: And they said, do come and play in our restaurants.

Geraldine: No they didn't, though I had some very sweet letters. But I do have a job now, I play at Victoria Coach Station, every morning between six and eight thirty, and I may possibly be given a spot near one of the escalators at Heathrow.

Man: Something I've always wondered, Geraldine, is it a problem getting that great thing from place to place?

Geraldine: Not really, Bob. You see I'm quite promiscuous and I make sure that they're always pretty brawny chaps that I sleep with, with big cars, so . . .

Man: Right, well, best of luck in your new venture, Geraldine, and you're going to play what?

Geraldine: I'm going to play 'Annie's Song' by John Denver.

Man: Geraldine Fox-Talbot, thank you very much.

Applause. As she begins to play two women come and press their noses against the glass.

HAIRDRESSER'S

Very drab girl in chair. Male hairdresser behind.[115]
Girl: I'd like a style to go with my personality.
Hairdresser: I think you've got it.

COMPULSIVE EATING

Psychiatrist: How long have you been a compulsive eater, Miss Macdonald?

Girl: Since I was seventeen. I was involved in an accident, when a pizza lorry shed its load on the M62.

Psychiatrist: What flavour?

Girl: Quattro Formaggi.[116] I was buried. I had to eat my way out.

Psychiatrist: I see.

Girl: Then I buried myself and ate my way out three more times.

Psychiatrist: And now do you find that certain events will trigger off an attack of over-eating?

Girl: Yes, if I have a disappointment at work, or if somebody says hello to me, or if I'm awake . . .

Psychiatrist: Could you perhaps describe a typical day for me?

Girl: My teasmade wakes me about half past seven, it's not actually a teasmade, it's a specially adapted mobile chip shop. Then I go downstairs and eat whatever I can find in the kitchen, fish fingers, calendars . . . At work I have quite a long lunch break and if anybody's away I have their lunch break as well. At coffee time we all have cakes, mine's usually a three-tier wedding cake . . . At home, for supper, I'll perhaps

---

115 CI and DP.

116 VW enjoyed the comedy value of this pizza topping. In *ADB*, JW plays a shop saleswoman who boasts of her rich cultural hinterland. 'Do you know Vivaldi?' she says to her dim assistant played by VW. 'Int he the Four Seasons?' 'Well, I prefer to think of them in the original. The Quattro Formaggi.'

defrost a sheep, then I'll take a couple of loaves up to bed with me.

Psychiatrist: What about crumbs in the bed?

Girl: Yes, I eat those. I eat everything.

Psychiatrist: And your boyfriend?

Girl: He's in hospital.

Psychiatrist: You didn't, er, consume any vital parts of him?

Girl: No, he slipped on some gravy. This compulsion is ruining my life.

Psychiatrist: Have you tried treatment before?

Girl: Yes, I was with Professor Imrie.[117]

Psychiatrist: What went wrong?

Girl: I ate him.

Psychiatrist: I see. Well I'm afraid our time is up. Are there any questions you would like to ask me?

Girl has eaten the couch.

Girl: Do you have any mustard?

DRY-CLEANER'S 4

Assistant checking garment.

Assistant: It'll be three pounds altogether if you want creases.

Customer: How much without creases?

Assistant: Six pounds because somebody'll have to iron it.

---

117 VW had an ear for the musicality of names – Petula Gordeno, Betty Comstock, Margaret Mottershead, Tracey Clegg, Nicola Battersby and so on. But occasionally she simply borrowed names from people around her. There was usually a backstory when she did. In *Talent* the main character, who was inspired by VW's first experience of working with JW, is called Julie and is engaged to a man named Walters. *W&W* has a sketch about a soprano called Celia Wynn Owen, who shared the surname of VW's second-year Birmingham flatmate Jane Wynn Owen, then an aspiring opera singer. 'Just an Ordinary School' (*ASOTV*) featured two posh girls called Ceal and Babs. Stanley, the handyman in *DL*, shared his name with VW's father while Dolly Bellfield takes her surname from a schoolgirl at Bury Grammar. 'Professor Imrie' may be a not especially kind joke: VW used to tease her friend about the number of books she'd read; a more overt reference was included in *Val De Ree (Ha Ha Ha Ha Ha)* (1989). CI has since published five novels and a memoir.

DRY-CLEANER'S 5

Customer: Do you think you can get this stain out?
Assistant: We'll have to test it first.
Customer: OK.
Assistant cuts out the stain with a razor blade.
Assistant: Harry!

GOING PRIVATE[118]

Nervous woman enters reception area of private hospital, holding over-night case. Receptionist picks up phone.
Sonia: Oakview Private Hospital – can I charge you? Putting you
　　　　through. Have your name please?
Mrs Robinson: Mrs Robinson.
Sonia: Won't keep you a moment, Mrs Robinson.
Mrs Robinson looks around and sits down.
　　　　Have you paid for sitting down? Seventy-eight pence for the first
　　　　fifteen minutes, then one pound for each subsequent quarter,
　　　　any minute over the quarter to be counted as a whole quarter, or
　　　　there's a bus shelter over the road which I believe is free.
Mrs Robinson: Right.
She picks up a magazine.
Sonia: Sorry, which one is that?

---

118 VW and GP came to the conclusion that the sketch's three minutes contained really
only one joke. She would boil that joke down to a line in 'Today in Hospital', in which
a nurse asks a patient lying unconscious on a trolley for the number of his Access card.
A longer scene in which a hospital administrator unveils schemes for raising money
('bring your own anaesthetic, though we have to charge for corkage') was cut, though
it was included in *Barmy*. In the script of 'Going Private' VW pencilled names in the
typescript against characters as they appear: 'Vic' for Sonia, 'Celia' for Nurse, 'Julie'
for Sister, 'Rog B' for Doctor. Roger Brierley was VW's go-to establishment figure in
Nearly a Happy Ending and *W&W*. Following his death in 2005, VW gave his name to
Nella Last's GP in *H49*.

Mrs Robinson: *Woman's Realm.*

Sonia tings cash register.

Sonia: Twenty-six pence, don't pay me now. I'll pop it on your bill. (*Into intercom.*) Nurse Winthrop, I have a Mrs Robinson for you. She won't keep you a moment.

Mrs Robinson: Thank you. I'm a bit nervous. I've never had an operation before.

Sonia: Really. Now would you like me to put you at your ease?

Mrs Robinson: Yes.

Sonia: OK. (*Tings cash register.*) Long or short message? I'll do short, it's on special offer. (*Reads.*) There's absolutely nothing to worry about, you're in the best possible hands heme, sorry, here, you'll soon be fit and well again.

Enter Nurse, wearing miniature cash register instead of watch on apron.

Nurse: Mrs Robinson. Now have you brought everything on the list?

Mrs Robinson: I think so, two nighties, face flannel, tissues . . .

Nurse: No, the other list, dear, cheque book, cheque card, bank statements, savings book.

Mrs Robinson: Oh yes.

Nurse: Lovely. Would you like to come this way?

Mrs Robinson: Yes.

Nurse: Or would you like to come the back way, by the bins, which is cheaper?

Mrs Robinson: Actually, do you think I could have a wheelchair? I do get so tired.

Nurse: Sonia, do we have any wheelchairs?

Sonia: We don't, I'm sorry. I'm almost sure we sold the last one this morning. We're expecting some more in on Friday . . .

Nurse: The lady's feeling tired and doesn't want to walk, you see, Sonia.

Sonia: Oh dear. Well, as I say, they have promised us some for Friday, I should pop back then.

Mrs Robinson: Could you perhaps take my bag?

Nurse: Course. (*Tings cash register.*)

They walk and stand outside a door.

Oh, here's Sister coming to let you in.

Nurse leaves, enter Sister.

Sister: I'm Sister Drew (*checks list*). Mrs Robinson, you're in the Geoffrey Howe[119] Room. (*Takes out hotel-type key with kidney bowl as tag.*) It was a room with bath, wasn't it?

Mrs Robinson: That's right.

They go into bare room with just a bath in it.

Mrs Robinson: There's no bed.

Sister: Did you want a bed?

Mrs Robinson: Well, yes, I'm ill.

Sister: Oh, you're ill, are you? So you may need nursing care as well as a room?

Mrs Robinson: Well, yes.

Sister: And do you think you might die? Only we don't do dying here. I think our Manchester branch does, I'd have to check. Ah, here's Doctor.

Enter Doctor.

Doctor: Mrs Robinson, how are you? Opulent, well off, or just comfortable?

Mrs Robinson: I earn six thousand a year.

Doctor: I'm sorry to hear that.

Mrs Robinson: Look, I have pains here, I'm very sore here, I get very tired, and my doctor thinks I should have an exploratory operation.

Doctor: What does that sound like to you, Sister?

Sister: It sounds like about two and a half thousand pounds, Doctor.

Doctor: I'm inclined to agree. Are we running the operation instalment plan this week, Sister?

Mrs Robinson: You mean I could pay in instalments?

Doctor: No, we operate in instalments.

Sister: That was last week, Doctor. This week's special offer is Startling Reductions on Intravenous Drip Stands.

Doctor's bleep goes.

---

119 Chancellor of the Exchequer in the first Thatcher government. After the 1983 election he became Foreign Secretary. It was quite unusual for VW to joke about politicians in sketches. They would appear more frequently in her stand-up.

Doctor: Right, I'm on overtime now, do you want to carry on talking?
Mrs Robinson: No.
Doctor: Splendid. Well, Sister will explain the details of the operation. You can go for standard or splash out for deluxe and have an anaesthetic.
Cardiac arrest lights and sirens go. Sound of running feet. Sister and Doctor run out.
Mrs Robinson: What's happening, is it a cardiac arrest?
Doctor: No, an overdraft!

VIDEO BOX 5

Hip young male executive.
Man: I realise that the BBC don't really have any choice about using women these days, and fair enough, they've lumped the whole quota into one programme, but surely they could have used better-looking ones? I mean they're hardly stewardesses, are they? And my second point is that we'll probably all be dead quite soon, with this nuclear thing, so why have humour at all? Why not show blue videos? Or use the money for drugs? I mean I don't really do drugs, I just like to have something to do with my nose, in social situations . . .

VIDEO BOX 6

Jolly middle-aged Birmingham woman.
Woman: Now I haven't seen them all, because I've been in hospital, quite bad. And they don't have it in intensive care. I suppose they can't spare the socket – but – since I been home, I have been watching, and I think they're having a good try, I'm not trying to do them down, it's a jolly good attempt, but I haven't laughed. I've tried, I've had my mouth open specially, but not so much as a chuckle so far. I may have smirked,

but for me, no one's bettered Mr Pastry, comedy-wise.[120] Sorry.

PRIVATE LIVES[121]

A couple in evening dress on a chaise longue, smoking with cigarette holders, dressed in the style of a Thirties Coward play.[122]

Giles: Nervous, darling?

Bunty: Quakingly.

Giles: After this is over, let's go away together. Where shall it be? Sorrento, Marrakesh, Rome?

Bunty: Oh, Marrakesh. Those dear little men in their fezzes or fuzzies or whatever they're called. Let's sit in the moonlight and drink – champagne cocktails?

Giles: Sorry, I can't bear champagne. I had a sinus operation as a child, and I've never been able to bear things going up my nose since. I'll toast you in tea.

Bunty: Indian or China?

Giles: Indian, in the hope that they'll use the profits to improve their appalling railways.

Bunty: I adore trains, don't you? I'd rather travel by train than anything.

Giles: I prefer the bicycle. No one on a bicycle has to endure the miseries of a compartment full of ill-informed pipe-smokers. Your skin is unbearably beautiful in this light, Bunty. I want to cover it with emeralds.

Bunty: Please don't. Emeralds always remind me of a particularly unpleasing pair of green gym-knickers. But diamonds with everything.

---

120 Walrus-moustached slapstick character played by Richard Hearne (1908–1979), first on stage in the 1930s, later as one of the early stars of television.

121 GP argued against this on two counts – that the series shouldn't have too many sketches that rely on a reveal, nor sketches about the world of theatre.

122 CI and Alan Rickman. This was a prescient piece of casting by VW, as Rickman would play the role of Elyot in *Private Lives* in the West End and on Broadway, where his performance was nominated for a Tony Award.

Giles: Shall it be a necklace, a ring or a bracelet?

Bunty: Why, a necklace of course, darling. So useful if one's hotel bathroom is missing a lavatory chain.

Giles: It's almost time to go.

Bunty: But this is madness. I feel I don't know the least thing about you – do you prefer your potatoes sautéed or in their jackets?

Giles: Oh jackets, provided they're not double-breasted?

Bunty: Favourite flower, author, sport?

Giles: Lily, Dickens, and fishing for tiddlers. I'm a size nine shoe, I loathe fretwork, and I love you, love you, love you!

Knock on door. Man pops his head round.

Man: Would you care to come this way?

They clasp hands and follow him.

Cut to:

Set of Mr and Mrs. [123]

Hostess: And the next couple to play *Mr and Mrs* are Giles and Bunty Petherbridge of Knightsbridge, in London . . .

PAUSE FOR THOUGHT 2

Music. Scottish nun in chair, in shortish skirt and cardigan.[124]

Nun: Faith's a funny word, isn't it? (*Pause.*) Just say it. (*Pause.*) Faith. (*Pause.*) Let's try it with another word. (*Pause.*) Adam. (*Pause.*)

---

123 Daytime TV game show in which married couples were tested on how well they knew each other. It was shown in various ITV regions from 1964, then a network version was broadcast from 1972 through to 1988. It was revived twice in the 1990s, and a celebrity series was broadcast from 2008 to 2016.

124 VW wrote 'Celia' on the typescript. Although they had been friends since the mid-1970s, VW cottoned on to CI's comic gift only after she saw her in a Scottish sketch show called *81 Take 2*. 'Vic was constantly delighted by her outstanding array of Scottish accents,' says GD. She liked these jokes on the word 'faith' enough to resurrect them for another sketch in the *ASOTV Special*, which was also dropped. See pp. 171–2.

Adam Faith.[125] Remember him? (*Pause.*) But there's another
sort of faith. (*Pause.*) Faith Brown.[126] (*Pause.*) She's an impressionist. (*Pause.*) Life's marvellous really, isn't it?

---

125 British teen idol in the early 1960s. His real name was Terence Wright.
126 Impressionist. She and VW were often clubbed together, alongside Marti Caine
and Pamela Stephenson, in articles about the new wave of funny women as they started
to appear on British television. The two of them were on the same bill only once, a
tawdry Granada year-end variety show called *There Goes 1980*. Brown, co-hosting in
a shiny gown, introduced VW: 'Our next guest is a young lady who's had a terrific
year . . . Ladies and gentlemen, a big welcome to Victoria Wood!' VW sang 'Fourteen
Again' from *Talent*. Faith Brown closed the show mugging along to Cleo Laine, Kate
Bush, Dolly Parton and Barbra Streisand. Over the closing credits VW, ever the pro,
consented to lean against her piano, smile and wave at the camera.

8

SONGS

In 1986 Victoria took some of the songs from *As Seen on TV* out on the road with her. But feeling her audience deserved a constant supply of fresh material, she composed new ones too. Each had a certain role to perform within the set. A high-energy show opener such as 'If I Hadn't Been Here Tonight' needed to bid a cheerful welcome. 'Little Hands' and 'Photo Booth', the latter inspired by memories of her first boyfriend, provided a change of pace from the relentless tempo of stand-up. Then there were the character songs. 'I Work in a Salon' (unveiled on her autumn tour in 1984) is in the voice of a trainee hairdresser and written in the declamatory style of Marvin Hamlisch – you could imagine her nervously telling her story in *A Chorus Line*. Victoria's untitled Brecht song, composed in the cabaret style of Weimar Germany and sung in the sultry manner of Lotte Lenya or Marlene Dietrich, was a rare parody of music outside the English or American tradition. 'I hope it alienates you enormously,' she said as she introduced it. 'It's my tribute to Bertolt Brecht who had a very sad life when we think about it. He did die before he could collaborate with Andrew Lloyd Webber.'[127]

---

127 Unlike TS Eliot. *Cats* had been running in the West End since 1981. During the lifetime of the song – VW introduced it in her 1986 spring tour and was still perform-ing it at her Christmas shows in Cardiff at the end of the year – *The Phantom of the Opera* opened, adapted from the novel by Gaston Leroux. But this joke may also have

'Carry On Regardless' was Victoria's attempt at an audience participation song. It was initially used as a final encore in 1987 then redeployed in 1990 when she decided to try ending the first half on less of a downbeat note, as had been her habit up until now.

In this fertile period Victoria wrote more than she needed. In her archive there are lyrics for songs for which there is no record of performance. 'One Day' (not to be confused with the song of the same name in 'Whither the Arts?') was written in 1987. From the same year is an untitled song which, although no melody survives, is clearly written in the same up-tempo rhythm as 'Feeling in the Mood Tonight'. Both songs were tried out and discarded.

---

been a dig at Richard Stilgoe. Having covered roughly the same beat as VW as a topical songwriter, he had written the lyrics for *Starlight Express*, which opened in 1984, and would write the book for *Phantom*. This gave her a gag for the Cardiff shows: 'The song I'm going to sing is from the latest Richard Stilgoe and Andrew Lloyd Webber musical, which is called *Twats*. This musical hasn't opened yet but it's already completely sold out for the next two years. In fact, they've made so much money they're not even going to bother to write it.' It wasn't her first joke at the expense of Stilgoe. 'Somebody's told me that Richard Stilgoe does a thing in his act where the audience call out words,' she said before the interval of *LB* in 1983, 'and during the interval he goes away and he writes a song incorporating all these words. So what I thought I'd do is I'm going to sing a song and I'd like you to incorporate all the lyrics into your conversation.' In the section VW cut from 'Today in Hospital' (see note 57), there was a final *Cats* gag: 'I'm looking at the figures now – the waiting-list situation – fifteen months for a tonsillectomy, three years for a hip replacement, and five years for two seats in the Upper Circle for *Cats*.'

I WORK IN A SALON[128]

Hello my name's Karina
And I work in a salon
Hanging people's coats up and stuff
It could be worse.
I don't do perms or tinting
Cos I haven't been there long enough
But I'm doing shampooing
And I'm training to converse.

And I say[129]
Do you use conditioner?
Or does it make it greasy?
Or do you not use any?
Beg your pardon sorry what?
And I say these towels are awful
They ought to be more tufty
Is the water comfy is it not too hot?

Sometimes a stylist says Karina
Fetch us a cheese and chutney sandwich
Or twenty Bensons
And I quite like the walk.
Once I went out for bias binding[130]

---

128 This was performed on TV twice, once on *Pebble Mill at One* in December 1984
just before the broadcast of the first series of *ASOTV*, then just after on *Aspel and Company* in February 1985, with the house band providing backing. The song ended with
comic abruptness, which the Pebble Mill audience didn't pick up on, obliging VW to
announce that it had finished. These performances have rarely, if ever, been repeated.
129 The chorus was spoken rather than sung.
130 Tape used to enclose the raw edge of a neckline, armhole or hem. VW's mother

But I couldn't find the right colour
But when I'm doing shampooing
We're sort of obliged to talk.

So I say
Are you going away this year?
Venezuela, lovely
I'm prob'ly going to Douglas, you know, the Isle of Man.
Or I say
Have you done your Christmas shopping?
I haven't done my Christmas shopping
I'm getting my mum a wok thingy
It's a sort of pan I think I don't really know.

I'm getting quite good at sweeping
And brushing hair off people's shoulders
And saying excuse me your three o'clock lady is here Vaughan
Things like that.
But clients are like different
Cos you have to like relax them
By doing shampooing
And sort of keeping up the chat.

So I say
A-are you going somewhere special
Oh just just not you're not you're not are you not you're not going
I'm not going out this evening I'm stopping in
No I did have a sort of a boyfriend but we had this argument in
    Boots cos he doesn't really like Wham
He were called Bryn.

So I just say things like that really
And sometimes I sterilise a comb

Helen Wood made all her daughters' clothes when they were young so she was used to
the terminology.

Then I give everybody their coats back
And then I put mine on
And then I go hooooooooome.

IF I HADN'T BEEN HERE TONIGHT[131]

I'm a very philosophical person
And I do a lot of thinking about things oh yes
Hardly a day goes by without me thinking about something
I'm just a very intellectual person I guess.
And one of the things I been thinkin' about – quite hard about
I just keep my brain quite reasonably busy alright
I been thinking about all the things I coulda been doing
If I hadn't been here tonight.

Coulda been on a drinking spree
Lurched about going hee hee hee
Could have ended up in casualty
If I hadn't been here tonight.
Coulda been in a right old state
At me bingo night with my best mate
Saying I only needed a thirty-eight
If I hadn't been here tonight.
Could have gone to a hunting do
Saying hunting's fun, you know that's true
And I think the fox enjoys it too
If I hadn't been here tonight.

It's a nice idea, but I I I I prefer it here
Could have gone to dinner full of greed
Has everyone got all they need?

---

131 VW experimented with the length of the song, cutting or moving sections around.
This is a longer version.

Do dig in, there's piles of swede
If I hadn't been here tonight.

Could have been a funny poetess
Been ever so nice in a bit of a mess
Written terrible poems in a pinafore dress[132]
If I hadn't been here tonight.
Could have seen a rock show, could have gone
Screamed and cried and carried on
Could have thrown me knickers at Elton John
If I hadn't been here tonight.

Things I've never done, but I'm hav- I'm hav- I'm hav- I'm hav- I'm
    having fun
Could have organised a slimmer's tea
Saying Dorothy Bloggs you're twelve stone three[133]
I said Ooh I know it's buns with me
If I hadn't been here tonight.

Could have gone nightclubbing down the docks
Seen celebrities in their party frocks
Talked politics with Samantha Fox[134]
If I hadn't been here tonight.

Things I've neeeeever done, but I'm hav- I'm hav- I'm hav- I'm
    hav- I'm having fun
At a nudist camp I can't say where

---

132 A marginally more coded reference than usual to Pam Ayres.
133 One pound up from the weight which makes Dolly shudder in *DL*: 'Do you *want*
me to be twelve stone two?'
134 Page Three topless model, began appearing in *The Sun* at the age of sixteen in 1983.
In *ASOTV* VW predicted she would marry Prince Edward: 'They'll have three sons, all
of whom will go into the navy and none of whom will be able to button their uniforms
up.' In 1986 Fox embarked on a career in pop but that didn't stop VW. In her 1990
show she imagined wife-swapping as 'something invented by the tabloids and blown up
out of all proportion. You know, like Samantha Fox.'

Could have strolled around completely bare
Excuse me, who cuts your pubic hair?[135]
Things I've never done, but I'm hav- I'm hav- I'm hav- I'm hav- I'm
    having fun.

Could have done aerobics, joined the pack
Work that body, don't be slack,
My leotard's crept oop me crack
If I hadn't been here tonight.

But aaaanyhow, I'm hap- I'm hap- I'm hap- I'm hap- I'm happy
    now
Could have watched TV, my favourite vice
It's always fun it's always nice
It's always bleeding Anneka Rice
Why isn't she here tonight?

Could have fed the ducks and made them quack
Seen a nasty man in a filthy mac
Said very nice now put it back[136]
If I hadn't been here,
If I hadn't been here,
If I hadn't been here tonight.

135 VW would often revisit the subject of pubic-hair management in her forties. From
her 1996 show: 'The real trouble is my pubic hair. It's all over the place. It's spreading
and it's joining and clumping up. It's like some bloody rockery plant. I look like one
of those fawns in *Fantasia* that play the flute.' Then in *At It Again*, during an extended
account of her hysterectomy, she decided that with tweed knickers she'd resemble the
bewhiskered racing tipster John McCririck.

136 This is a light-hearted recollection of being flashed at as a teenager. In one of the
compositions written for *The Camera and the Song* VW sang, 'And the man in the funny raincoat is coming to chat me up/I think I'll keep on moving round the park.'

LITTLE HANDS[137]

Take my little hand, let's hold hands
Let's calm down we're both like rubber bands.
No one's winning why not pack this in halfway
Loving me loving you love today.
Smile a little smile call a truce
Take ten minutes for an orange juice
Let's remember just before the start of play
Loving me loving you love today.

Why do people scream and bawl
At people they love best of all?
It's senseless when love is defenceless
You always hurt the one you love
So why not use a boxing glove?
It's stupid
What happened to Cupid?
Well let's not be fools
Let's change the rules.

Take my little hand, let's not shout
I've forgotten what this row's about
Why hurl cruel words when one of us could say
Loving me . . .
Let our little feet march in time
Save the cross talk for the pantomime

---

137 A merry, sauntering melody.

Let's be Startrite kids[138] and not be Cassius Clay
Loving me loving you love . . .

Why do people scream and bawl
At people they love best of all?
It's senseless
When love is defenceless
You always hurt the one you love
So why not use a boxing glove?
It's stupid
What happened to Cupid?
Well it's no one's fault
Let's call a halt today.

Wipe that little tear, let's not cry
Let's peel onions for an alibi
Let's cheer up because we're basically OK
Loving you, loving me love . . .
Oh let one little kiss blow my way
I'll still love you when you're old and grey
I will help choose a style for your toupée[139]
Loving me loving you love today love today love today.

---

138 Early on in their professional careers VW and GD would refer to themselves as the
Startrite kids after a 1930s advertisement for children's shoes. Previously she composed
a confessional song about their rows called 'I Love You' that she sang in *W&W*. It
concludes:

I lose my library ticket
Nearly every day
My lenses drop out
On the motorway
I make you apoplectic
But I do hope you'll stay with me,
I love you.
I love you.

VW did once lose her contacts one night when they were driving home from a gig.
139 GD had long since started to lose his hair.

PHOTO BOOTH[140]

Found your picture the other day
Memories took my breath away
Made me smile, made me cry a bit
What a stupid git you were.

When we met I was so naive
All you told me I'd just believe
Said you'd written half of *Abbey Road*
What a lying toad you were.

Couldn't believe you'd asked me out
Though we only mooched about
Cos I'd never had a proper boyfriend before
When we kissed we bumped our lips
And you bought me pie and chips
And I was really happy, happy.

In the flicks well I had some qualms
Holding hands with my sticky palms
I found love in that smoky shade
With my Orange Maid, and you.

You took me home to your mum and dad
Sunday tea oh it makes me sad
Tinned fruit salad and condensed milk
Oh and Acker Bilk[141] and you.

---

140 VW's albums are full of photobooth snaps, most of them with one or two friends
crammed in. They don't include any with her first boyfriend Bob Mason, who is the
inspiration for this mid-tempo song.
141 Popular clarinettist (1929–2014).

Posing in that photo booth
Trying to look relaxed and smooth
Trying to look as if we hadn't been snogging at all
I wouldn't let you go too far
But you half undid my bra
And it felt really daring, daring.
Wrote your name with a dopey smile
In felt tip on my history file
Phoned you up nearly every day
What did we say? It's a blur . . .

You ditched me or did I ditch you?
Some old girlfriend came out the blue
You were seen, and this wounded me
Outside the TSB, with her . . .
Found your picture the other day
From that booth all those years away
Chips and kisses and tears and joy
What a lovely boy you were
Yes you were
Yes you were . . .

BRECHT SONG[142]

I knew a girl a lonely girl
Who could not get her hair to curl
Who'd never had a man
She vonted a man
And every night she'd take her pill
Put on zat stuff called Clearasil
And plan herself a little plan.

---

142 Performed in a drawling German accent. The lyrics on the last verse were rewritten
two years into the song's life.

And she would say please
I vont a lover
Someone to cover me with kisses
Till I've had my fill
He must be gentle
And sentimental
And he must possess a Black & Decker drill.

God sent her Villiam from Vembley
He was into self-assembly
He put wardrobes up for fun
Not my cup of tea
He would laugh with her and cry with her
He went to MFI with her
Vot more could he have done?

But she said no
I vont a poet
Whose love will show itself to me
Whose vords will make it clear
He must be arty
No Russell Harty[143]
And he must come out in paperback this year.

God sent her Tom an intellectual
In bed quite ineffectual
Not even very bright poor Tom
Not only was he not erect
He wrote monologues in dialect
And read them out aloud all night.

So she said please

---

143 The broadcaster (1934–1988) met VW in the early 1980s and was hugely supportive
of her. She appeared in his Christmas show four years running.

Send someone hunky
He must be chunky with a tan
And sexy deep blue eyes
Let muscles ripple
From knee to nipple
And I think I'll let the rest be a surprise.

God sent her Dave whose vonderful physique
Resulted from a six-day veek
At the Vy Emm Cee Ay
You know vot they say
He'd stay the night but all he'd show
Was Judy Garland on the video[144]
Ven morning came she sadly valked avay.

That lonely girl came off the pill
Gave up that stuff called Clearasil
Is that don't you agree quite sad?
But she's OK she gets along
She tells a joke she sings a song
Ah yes, because that girl voz me.

LOVE YOU LIKE I DO

I've got this feeling now – it's really good
I want to tell you 'bout it
I feel that things are going the way they should
I couldn't do without it
It took me so long to choose you
I couldn't bear to lose you

---

144 VW enjoyed the comedy of women falling for men who turn out to prefer men.
See also 'It Would Never Have Worked':
  I like big hunky men, and so do you, dear
  Things would never have worked.

Baby, baby.

No matter what I did it would still be the same
I wouldn't be snappy with you
It could be different rules or a different game
I'd still be happy with you
And it is my impression
No matter what profession
I'd still love you like I do.

If I had a corner shop I'd say . . . 'ello
'Ave you any loaves left? Sorry no
See that notice have you read it
We don't give change we don't give credit
But I'd still love you baby like I do.

If I was house proud I would smell of Vim
My toilet would be fresh right round the rim
Into your bedroom I'd manoeuvre
Not for sex but just to hoover
I'd still love you baby like I do.

I could form a brand new party
I could ever form a queue
But whatever I did I bet you a quid
I'd still be nuts on you.

If I was an announcer I would be
The softly spoken sort on Radio 3
Now Delius A Walk in the Paradise Garden
Ach tch ptfth[145] I beg your pardon
But I'd still love you baby like I do.

If I was Miss World I wouldn't look my age

---

145 The sound of expectoration.

I'd say there's a lovely friendly atmosphere backstage
I'd have a luscious bod you'd die to hug it
A brain the size of a chicken nugget
But I'd still love you baby like I do.

I could take the morning service
I could even take a pew
But whatever I did I couldn't get rid
Of what I feel for you

If I was a next-door neighbour I would say
Second time that milkman's been today
Curtain's drawn, the lights are dimmed
He's never popped back with a semi-skimmed
I'd still love you baby like I do

And if I was on the switchboard I would coo
Thank you for calling this is Melody speakin' how may I be of
    service to you?
Puttin' you through to Mr Mold
He's masturbatin' can you hold?
I'd still love you baby
But I'd still love you baby
But I'd still love you baby like I do.

CARRY ON REGARDLESS[146]

When the skies are turning black
When you hear the thunders crack

---

146 When VW first introduced 'Carry On Regardless', which was her only stab at a
clapalong song, she pretended to be coy about it: 'I do know one more song but it's a
rather personal song. I don't normally sing it in front of the public. But I don't consider
you a normal public, so I think this is alright. It's rather a difficult song. It expresses a
lot of my own personal philosophy of life.'

When they say you must turn back
You must not go-o-o-o-o-o-oo
Do not trudge that rocky road
Do not take that heavy load
Leave the portable commode
You tell them no-o-o-o-o-o-oo.

You carry on regardless
Because you're raving mad
It's not accidental
It's fun to be mental
When lunacy waylaid me
I promised not to stray
Being mad has made me
What I am today.

When you're set to lose the match
When your team's not up to scratch
When you drop the vital catch
The crowd go o-o-o-o-o-o-oh
And the batsman's skill departs
When the cry comes from their hearts
You could have told them it was darts
You tell them no-o-o-o-o-o-oo.

You carry on regardless
Anyone can join
You may be small as Toulouse[147]
And still have a screw loose
No one can dissuade us
From our barmy way
Being mad has made us
What we are today.

---

147 The French painter Henri Toulouse-Lautrec (1864–1901) was five feet tall.

When the guns light up the sky
When the mud and bullets fly
When no matter how hard you try
Morale is lo-o-o-o-o-o-ow
When your men have taken flight
They say run don't stay and fight
We'll go to Tesco's another night
You tell them no-o-o-o-o-o-oo.

You carry on regardless
We need more lunatics
We're misrepresented
Because we're demented
It's very hard to spot us
In fact there's no good way
Except that it has got us
Where we are today.

ONE DAY

One day the man who reads the news will say
The old age pension was increased today
David Owen[148] to much surprise
Has teamed up with Ernie Wise
And Ronald Reagan's gone grey
Mrs Thatcher and the head of the NUM[149]
Said their affair was over, when we spoke to them
They said they were woebegone
Too lacquered to carry on

---

148 Former Foreign Secretary in a Labour government, but by now the leader of the
Social Democratic Party, which entered into an alliance with the Liberal Party. Hence
the joke about forming a double act with Ernie Wise.
149 Arthur Scargill. The miners' strike of 1984–85 was a fresh memory when the song
was composed.

And please don't condemn.

Trying to be an optimist
Making up this hopeless list
Dreaming all these dreams that just can't come true
Maybe some
Just a few.

One day the front-page headline has to cry
We are not interested in Charles and Di
That story we chose to run
Drugged vicar was sex-change nun
That was a lie
Our Page Three model will of course remain
But now in keeping with our new campaign
Here's Winnie aged sixty-four
Posed here by the pantry door
Sluicing her drain.

Trying to be an optimist
Proving that they do exist
Dreaming all these dreams that may not come true
Or perhaps they're just – overdue.

One day I'll read the latest health report
Cottage cheese gave slimmer penile wart
It's healthy to drink and smoke
Ryvita was just a joke
It's not what we thought.

We now know chocolate tends to lower stress
Maltesers will be free on the NHS
Our cure for arthritic hips
Two sausages beans and chips
Has been one huge success.

Trying to be an optimist
Feeling that I must persist
Dreaming all these dreams that may not come true
But they cheer me up
And I hope that they cheer you up too.

UNTITLED

It comes to me in starts and fits
That life is full of know-all gits
And most of them have sat on my settee.
It started when my friends were small
None of us knew bugger all
But they all knew more bugger all than me.

I do not lie, I do not steal
But other people make me feel
Like some acned and inadequate trainee.
However brave, however bold
It always leaves the others cold
There's always someone much more brave than me.

I never know what life's about
My grasp of it has just conked out
I seem to have mislaid my guarantee.
I scour the press, I watch the news
I know some things, I have some views
But the inside story never comes from me.

You buy a house, you buy a flat
You think how nice, and that is that
You close your own front door and turn the key.
But this myself I do not find
I do not have such peace of mind
Cos people never leave enough for me.

It comes to me in starts and fits
That life is full of know-all gits
And most of them have sat on my settee.
I only hope next time they come
A spring pops up and gets their bum
And nobody will be more pleased than me.

9

AS SEEN ON TV
SERIES TWO AND SPECIAL

The second series of *As Seen on TV* incubated in Victoria's imagination for a great deal longer than the first. The show was recommissioned early in 1985 and she planned to start writing in the spring, but a delay that was beyond her control meant pausing until January 1986.

When she came to sit down, she had slightly less time to get it all done, as there was a month-long tour in her calendar for which she also needed new material. As a result she was more economical. But she had also learnt from experience what would and wouldn't be needed. Thus the surplus for the new series included almost none of the quickies she had written the first time round.

In the longer sketches she looked for settings where comic misunderstanding was likely to occur – a careers office, a marriage-guidance session, a driving test. Two of the unseen sketches ('Tupperware Party' and 'Call Girls') visit a favourite subject of Victoria's – the British awkwardness around sex, confronted here more forwardly than ever. Sex is also the punchline in 'Christmas'.

Because the pause between the second series and the special was much briefer, there was a certain porousness between the two. The concept that Victoria came up with for a single episode broadcast at Christmas 1987 was more ambitious: to knit an entire set of television parodies together with links. Among these would have been 'Lady Police Special', her spoof of the BBC police drama *Juliet Bravo*, which had been filmed for the second series. It was held over for the special, then dropped from that too in favour of newer material. Its ghostly presence was alluded to in an advertisement for 'Television Classics' voiced by Duncan Preston. 'Now you can have in your very own home, to view and view again, the very best of Fifty Years of British Television! Classic programmes such as *Doctor Who*, *Juliet Bravo*, and *Coronation Street* . . .' At the foot of the typescript Victoria wrote: '(Followed by *Coronation Street* ep one, *Juliet Bravo*, *Doctor Who*.)' She would have more success threading such a structure through later Christmas specials.

As for the rest of the episode's cast-offs, while 'Clancy – Interior Decorator' was never recorded, it would not suppress Victoria's itch to parody TV detective drama. Having already taken Coward's *Private Lives* as a template for the unused sketch written for the first series, she now tried again in 'Balcony Scene'. As before, the comedy was in the distance between a suave 1930s milieu and the real world. The longest sketch to be axed was 'Travel Agent', in which she made considerable cuts to the dialogue in the shooting script to pare it down. But that Christmas there was no more room at the inn.

SERIES TWO

ADVICE

Careers office. Middle-aged woman and lumpy girl.

Woman: So, Sara, have you thought what you'd like to do when you leave school?

Sara: Eat chips in the street.

Woman: We're talking about careers here, Sara. I take it you do want a career?

Sara: Don't mind.

Woman: What jobs do your parents have?

Sara: Out of work.

Woman: So that's always a possibility to fall back on. OK – what would you like to be, Sara?

Sara: Not bothered.

Woman: Right – well I'll just fire away with a few suggestions. Are you creative at all?

Sara: How do you mean?

Woman: Can you draw, or—

Sara: Oh yeah.

Woman: Ah. Now what sort of things?

Sara: Two Mexicans weeing into a biscuit tin, four Mexicans weeing into a biscuit tin . . .

Woman: What about writing? Are you good at essays?

Sara: Not really. In first year we had to do day in the life of a two pence piece, and mine was in a till.

Woman: And did it get given in change and have lots of adventures?

Sara: No, it didn't.

Woman: Do you like the idea of travelling and meeting lots of different people?

Sara: Don't mind. Been to Minorca.

Woman: Did you like it there?

Sara: No, the flip flops were rubbish.

Woman: And what impression did you have of the Minorcans?

Sara: Don't know. Everyone in our hotel was from Derby.[150]

Woman: Cooking, catering, that's quite a growth area.

Sara: Yeah.

Woman: Suppose you had five pounds and had to make a nutritionally balanced meal for six people what would you do?

Sara: Borrow a tenner off my dad and go down the chippy.

Woman: Do you cook at home?

Sara: Well, I defrost, you know.

Woman: What about – nursing, police-work, the armed forces?

Sara: I don't want to do anything where you have to wear a belt.

Woman: I meant jobs where you're in contact with the public, helping people. Do you like people?

Sara: Which ones?

Woman: Any.

Sara: Not really. I quite like that girl on *Tomorrow's World*.[151]

Woman: Well what about a career in the media – do you think you'd suit that high-powered, high-pressure sort of environment?

Sara: Might do.

Woman: Do you thrive on being in charge, making your own decisions, snap judgements?

Sara: Erm . . .

Woman: Right. Look, I have one vacancy for a job, you're one of two hundred applicants. Convince me you're the girl for the job.

Sara: I'm the girl for the job.

Woman: No, convince me.

---

150 This may have been the germ of the stand-up sequence from the 1987 tour, later featured in *AVW*, in which VW goes on holiday to Spain with Betty Comstock and a gaggle of girls from Derby.

151 BBC programme about developments in science and technology that ran from 1965 to 2003. Judith Hann was its longest-serving presenter.

Sara: I'm the bloody girl for the job, you cow!

Woman: So, you don't want to travel, you don't want pressure, variety, or adventure; you want something uncreative and dull where you don't have to be decisive, self-reliant or tactful, and it helps if you don't like people.

Sara: Yes.

Woman: Careers advisory service?

HOLD UP

Silent poor-quality black and white video of interior of post office. All one shot from the high angle of a remote-control security camera. A masked armed raider pushes the door and runs in. He goes to the head of the queue. Little old lady at the front reprimands him and he goes meekly to the back of the queue, stands shuffling his feet and looking at his watch. Normal business continues.

CONTINUITY

And now it's time for that very popular programme *Gardener's Year*, and we're now up to the month of November. Well, they couldn't think of anything to film for November, except a man in thick fog tripping over a watering can, so here's an episode of our lady police serial. So it's over to Blancashire, to see what's happening to tough but vulnerable inspector of police, Blotley division, Elizabeth Deckchair.[152]

---

152 This continuity announcement was to cue up VW's *Juliet Bravo* spoof 'Lady Police Serial'. Indeed, they are stapled together in a bunch of papers collected as 'provisional scripts for Programme Three'. When the sketch was dropped from the episode, this went with it.

CALL GIRLS[153]

Bar/lounge of provincial hotel. Businessman sits alone. Porter brings a drink on a tray.

Porter: Gin and tonic, sir.

Man: Keep the change. Er – is it usually this quiet in the hotel?

Porter: It was pretty noisy last night, sir.

Man: Oh, what happened?

Porter: I had a cough, sir, I kept coughing.

Man: Pretty quiet tonight though.

Porter: I've got some cough mixture tonight, sir.

Man: Do you get many girls in this bar, as a rule?

Porter: Not in the bar, sir. We have the Old Age Pensioners Whist Drive in the ballroom, they're mainly female.

Man: I meant young girls.

Porter: I think if you're a young girl, they don't let you be an Old Age Pensioner, sir.

Man: You know this town pretty well, I expect.

Porter: Lived here all my life, sir.

Man: You know what goes on, you have a lot of contacts . . .

Porter: Sir?

Man: For guests' – requirements.

Porter: Oh yes, sir. If you needed a – what shall we say – a half-price puncture repair outfit – I could point you in the right direction.

Man: Good – and you're not averse to providing a bit of 'Room Service'.

Porter: Pleasure, sir. Cheese and tomato, egg and tomato, chicken and tomato . . .

Man: Anything else?

Porter: Ovaltine.

Man: I'm thinking of something 'extra'.

---

153 In the *ASOTV Special* the idea of a man paying for sex in a hotel would resurface in another form in 'The Mayflower Hotel'. As in that sketch, DP was to play the punter.

Porter: You could have a tomato with it, sir, we've got loads.

Man: Can you get me a girl?

Porter: I don't know what you mean, sir.

Man (*laying money on porter's tray*): Any wiser now?

Porter: No, I've been as stupid as this for years, sir.

Man: It's a lonely life on the road – what's your name?

Porter: Gerald, sir.

Man: It's a lonely life on the road, Gerald, and a man like myself needs female companionship. With me?

Porter: Sir.

Man: I don't have time for taking girls out in the normal way . . .

Porter: No, sir.

Man: So I tend to call on girls whose job it is to – be called on. Do you know any of those sort of girls?

Porter: No, sir.

Man: Have you ever had a massage, Gerald?

Porter: Couldn't do that, sir.

Man: Why not?

Porter: Ticklish, sir.

Man: Well – ever had a sauna?

Porter: Yes, sir.

Man: And while you were there – were you ever offered anything else?

Porter: I was offered a mentholated lozenge by the man on the next shelf up.

Man: Look – Gerald, I need a woman. Scout round, could you? Find one who's not averse to a bit of fun, a few games – there'll be a few bob in it for both of you.

Porter hurries off.

Man (*calling after him*): Preferably two, if you can! (*To himself.*) Those twins in Wolverhampton – dear me – I was finding little bits of chocolate between my toes for weeks.

Porter back, leans over man.

Porter: That's all sorted out, sir. Two women as requested. They don't usually stay up this late but they'd appreciate the extra money.

Pull back to show two old dears settling in at man's table with pack of cards.
Old Dear: Right. You shuffle, Ida, and I'll dig out the butterscotch.

ACCESS TV

Nervous man in empty studio.
Man: Hello. Are you relaxed, outgoing, with your own transport
and interested in waste-paper baskets? We're looking for new
members to join the Henley Park Waste Paper Basket Club.
We're all very friendly and meet once a month in one another's
homes. You don't have to have access to your own waste-paper
basket, a photograph or even a rough idea of what they look
like will do. We're not a big club, we're not intimidating, and
we don't dress up. In fact casual clothes are a positive advantage
because we do tend to spend rather a lot of time on our hands
and knees. As you may know, next Monday sees the start of
Wicker Week, so we'd particularly welcome any wicker buffs;
though later on in the year we'll be having a Pedal and Flip
Flop day, so you can see we do cater for everybody. Oh, and
we don't want any alcoholics or divorced people. Thank you.

TREASURE HUNT[154]

Studio.
The competitors, Julia and Steven, poring over book-covered table.
Compère at bookcase, Wincey at the back of the set by a large map. The
atmosphere in the studio is frantic.[155]

---

154 *Treasure Hunt*, presented in the studio by the patrician former BBC newsreader
Kenneth Kendall, with Anneka Rice wearing an assortment of jumpsuits in the field,
began broadcasting on Channel 4 in 1982. The team was joined in the third series by
TV-am weather girl Wincey Willis. VW didn't bother to change her name in the script.
Willis would subsequently be a guest on *AVW*.
155 Steven was played by Christopher Hancock, the compère by Desmond Carrington,
the actor and host of a weekly BBC Radio 2 show who was quite a casting coup. VW

Steven: OK, Ronnie, back to the helicopter please.

Ronnie (*VO*): Back to the helicopter, right you are.

Steven: And hover please, Ronnie.

Julia: We're looking for something like an abbey or a ruined church, by a river.

Ronnie (*VO*): An abbey or a church, I see.

Film. Cut to a field. Ronnie and her pilot leaning against the helicopter, having a fag, rolling her eyes.

Julia (*VO*): We think sheep may have something to do with it . . .

Ronnie makes yap-yap-yap gestures with her fingers.

Cut to studio.

Compère (*taking a book out of his pocket with a marked page*): Ah, this may be it – Sheepscote Abbey.

Steven: Right, Ronnie – head north-west to Ampleford and just before the bridge you should see Sheepscote Abbey, a ruined abbey.[156]

Cut to film. Pilot reluctantly finishing his Fab. Ronnie still leaning.

Ronnie: Right, we're heading north-west now.

Julia (*VO*): How long will it take to get there, Ronnie?

Ronnie: I'll just ask Keith. (*She doesn't, just flaps her mouth.*) About a minute and a half, so we might just make it.

Ronnie climbs into the helicopter.

Cut to studio.

Wincey: Steven and Julia, you have two minutes.

Julia: And Ronnie – when we get to the Abbey, we want some kind of a gate – it might even be a kind of sheep pen—

Steven: Or perhaps a cattle grid.

Cut to film. Helicopter blades are rotating but it's only a few inches off the ground. Ronnie takes her headset off, fusses with her hair.

Julia (*VO, tiny tinny voice*): It's definitely some animal connection . . .

---

was Wincey and Julia was played by Rosalind March, a former flatmate of JW's and a VW occasional who remembers 'being in a studio and poring over a great big table full of books and Victoria standing at a great big map on the wall'. Ronnie was played by CI. 'My first and only time up in a helicopter,' she says. 'It was very fun being Anneka for the day.'

156 These plausible-sounding locations were made up.

Cut to studio.

Compère: You should be just above over the Amplesfore Gorge, Ronnie – is it very spectacular?

Ronnie (*VO*): Yes, it's absolutely breathtaking, Michael.

Compère: So I believe.

Cut to film. Interior helicopter. Ronnie reading a magazine.

Ronnie: Oh and the sun's just come out at last, it's shining on the water, the effect is really spectacular, gorgeous.

Cut to studio.

Wincey: Julia and Steven, you have one minute left.

Julia: Are you nearly there, Ronnie?

Cut to film.

Ronnie: Yes we're just landing.

Nods to the pilot.

Cut to studio.

Steven: Is there a gate, Ronnie? It may be near some ruins—

Julia: Or rocks, can you see any rocks?

Wincey: Julia and Steven, you have forty-five seconds left.

Cut to film.

Helicopter lands on exactly the same place (all their things are still scattered on the grass. Ronnie climbs out of the helicopter, she is filmed from the back in the usual way. Her boiler suit is very elaborate and has 'Don't Look At My Bottom' written on the back of it in sequins.)[157]

Ronnie: Quick, where am I going?

Picks up her handbag from the grass.

Cut to studio.

Julia: Some sort of gate, or fence, oh gosh . . .

Compère (*taking piece of paper from his pocket*): Ah, this may be it, I think you'll find we're looking for the old sheep dip.

Julia: Is there anyone around, Ronnie? Ask for the old sheep dip!

Steven: Hurry, Ronnie!

---

157 As she was often seen running with the camera in hot pursuit in *Treasure Hunt*, Anneka Rice's jumpsuit-clad bottom became a tabloid obsession. When she replied to my email about making the sketch, CI changed the subject field to 'Re: The bum shot'.

Wincey: Steven and Julia, you are getting overexcited.

Cut to film. Ronnie runs across the field to a pub garden full of customers who take no notice of her.

Ronnie: Oh gosh, I can't see anybody. Hello? Anybody there? Oh please, there must be somebody, oh there's someone!

Runs in circles round a table. The pilot sits down.

      Where's the old shim-dim?

Cut to studio.

Julia: The old sheep dip, Ronnie, sheep dip!

Cut to film.

Ronnie: The old sheep dip.

Pilot points to a bottle of lager, she nods, he goes to get them.

(*In silly voice*) 'It's over there.' Over there? Thank you very much, I can see it! I can see it!

Cut to studio.

Steve: The treasure should be on some sort of cross-piece, please hurry, Ronnie!

Julia: Or a cross-bar!

Wincey: Steve and Julia – you are beginning to smell.

Cut to film. Pilot brings drinks back to table.

Ronnie (*panting*): I'm at the old sheep dip.

Steven (*VO*): Look for a cross-bar, Ronnie!

Ronnie: Oh God, I can't see anything, this is awful, what's the treasure like again?

Cut to studio.

Julia: Gold! Something gold, Ronnie – on a—

GONG.

      Oh . . .

Wincey: Steven and Julia, you are out of time, and you have not located the treasure.

Compère: Bad luck both of you, and well done, Ronnie.

Steven and Julia ad-lib mumbled thanks.

Cut to film.

Ronnie: I feel so awful, I feel dreadful – but I really couldn't have run any faster.

Compère (*VO*): I'm sure you couldn't.

Ronnie (*pulling face*): Well, I'm truly sorry, Steven and Julia, I shall
     have a rotten night thinking about how we only just missed
     finding the treasure.
Pilot does knife and fork acting. Ronnie nods in agreement.
Steven (*VO*): Oh it wasn't your fault . . .
Ronnie pulls off the headset and has a drink.

FABRIC SOFTENER

*Supermarket. Two women standing by soap powder/fabric softener sec-
tion.*[158]
Wendy: Haven't seen you for a long time, Sue – how did you get on
     with that Fabric Softener?
Sue: Well I stole it as you suggested, Wendy.
Wendy: That's good.
Sue: And they searched me on the pavement and I've just come out
     of Holloway.
Wendy: Not so good.
Sue: But I tell you one thing, Wendy, I had the softest mail bags on
     the whole wing. Bye!
They part laughing.

DRIVING TEST[159]

Examiner: Right, Mrs Jones, that concludes the first part of the test,
     would you just like to tell me what this sign means? (*No Entry.*)
Mrs Jones: I think it's pimples. I beg your pardon – no pimples.
Examiner: And this? (*Countdown to level crossing.*)
Mrs Jones: I've seen that before, but in a different colour. Does it

---

158 This sketch was an unused sequel to one in which Wendy (JW) recommends that
Sue (CI) shoplifts her fabric softener.
159 This is one of only a tiny handful of the unused sketches for which some publicity
stills were shot. They reveal VW as Mrs Jones with Roger Brierley as the examiner.

come in another shade? Ee, you're a Dismal Desmond, you. I know you're not supposed to chat but you could have helped with that crossword at the traffic lights. Yes – I've seen this in blue, it's our Christine's jumper – it's a skiing sweater, but she never went, because she banged into a litter bin at Ringway Airport.[160] It's baby blue and the lines go across like this.

Examiner: Suppose you saw it on the road?

Mrs Jones: I'd pick it up.

Examiner: What would you expect to see?

Mrs Jones: I'd expect to see Christine tootling along to the launderette with a worn-out washbag.

Examiner: At thirty miles an hour, what would your stopping distance be?

Mrs Jones: It would be before I hit something.

Examiner: How many yards?

Mrs Jones: Us? Just one, at the back. We're thinking of having tubs and creating a patio, but tubs don't grow on trees, do they? Trees grow in tubs though. My dad told me that. He's dead now. Fatty Hart. That's my maiden name, Hart.

Examiner: Well that concludes your driving test, Mrs Jones, and I'm sorry to have to tell you, you have not reached the required standard.

Mrs Jones: Never expected to, Desmond. First time I've been in one of these.

Examiner: In a Metro?

Mrs Jones: In a car. It was my sister's test, and she said, you go Cath, I've got a headache.

Examiner: That wasn't your driving licence?

Mrs Jones: No, I can't have one, because of my fits.

Examiner: You mean you can't drive?

Mrs Jones: Let's have a shufti. (*Grabs form.*) No, I can't, can I? Failed on everything. Not looking in the mirror – that's not fair – how do you think I did this lip-line? What's this – failure to control the vehicle?

---

160 The original name of Manchester Airport.

Examiner: That's when you swerved onto the wrong side of the road.

Mrs Jones: Well I couldn't believe what they were charging for those kitchen units. Reversing round a corner, I did that. Well, it wasn't a corner, more of a traffic island, wasn't it?

Examiner: I'm not permitted to discuss the test.

Mrs Jones: Fair enough. I'll let you off then. Right, now, how are we going to get off this roof?

MARRIAGE GUIDANCE[161]

Woman: Sit yourselves down. Now – first time at Marriage Guidance?

Jane: Yes.

Andy: Yes.

Woman: Jane – why are you here?

Jane: We just seemed to be growing apart, I needed to talk about it.

Woman: Andy?

Andy: My wife thought I should come.

Woman: That's interesting. Jane – quickly – what's your idea of an ideal evening?

Jane: Oh – dinner party, salad, intelligent conversation.

Woman: Andy?

Andy: Ten or twelve lagers, game of arrows, blue video.

Woman: How do you feel about blue videos, Jane?

Jane: I find the idea of them very upsetting. I don't like sex on television, and I'm very disturbed by the number of commercials for biological washing powder.

Woman: How about sex in the marriage? Jane?

Jane: I used to be a nymphomaniac and compulsive eater.

Woman: Was that a problem?

Jane: I think my sexual enjoyment was spoilt by crumbs in the bed. Now I find it difficult to let myself go, to be exuberantly demonstrative.

---

161 There was a sketch with a similar set-up in *W&W* which may have counted against this.

Woman: Do you regret that?

Jane: Well, it means I shall probably never be picked as a contestant on *The Price Is Right*.[162]

Woman: Andy – how do you feel about your sex life, or lack of it?

Andy: Well, I have got a few longstanding extramarital affairs, like – a girl at work, a widow in the next street, and one of the waitresses from our wedding reception.

Woman: Do you feel anger about that, Jane?

Jane: No.

Woman: Have you ever been unfaithful yourself, Jane?

Jane: Once. Usual thing. Man came to sharpen the scissors . . .

Woman: Did you know about this, Andy?

Andy: Me? No.

Woman: What were your expectations of marriage in the beginning – Jane?

Jane: A meeting of minds, a sharing of souls.

Woman: Andy?

Andy: Regular sex and interesting sandwiches.

Woman: Look – I'm going to have to say this – you don't seem to be remotely compatible – I don't detect any aura of friendliness or intimacy – you really seem like strangers – Jane and Andy – tell me – what made you marry each other?

Andy: We didn't.

Jane: We just came up in the same lift.

Woman: That's interesting.

---

162 The game show had been on ITV since 1984, hosted by Leslie Crowther. VW worked with him in *The Summer Show* (1975) and makes reference to him in *Talent*: 'When I was eight I won five bob off Leslie Crowther at Southport for singing "Catch a Falling Star".'

HEADACHES

Ad.
Three women chatting over coffee at outdoor café.[163]

Kathy: What do you particularly like about this headache remedy, Barbara?

Barbara: I think the shape, Kathy, it's very easy to swallow.

Anne: And of course the new pop-out foil packing makes it very handy to carry.

Kathy: That's right. And they've improved the flavour.

Barbara: Mmm, no bitter aftertaste.

Anne: I agree.

Kathy: And what do you think about the new regulations governing the import of confectionary and soft drinks from Israel and its surrounding borders?

Barbara: I don't really know anything about it, Kathy.

Anne: And I don't feel I could contribute any kind of particularly informed opinion.

Kathy: Shall we talk some more about this new remedy for women's headaches then?

Barbara: Yes let's.

Anne: I'd rather do that, I must admit.

They carry on discussing it earnestly.

CHRISTMAS

Christmas tree. Wife hands husband a small present.
Wife: Merry Christmas, John.
John: Thanks, Christine. (*It's three pairs of socks.*)
Wife: They had navy and black, but I thought grey was probably the safest.

---

163 Kathy was played by VW, Barbara by CI and Anne by JW.

John: No, grey's dead right. Three pairs, great.

Wife: That's alright.

John: Now, I was a bit stuck for what to get you, Christine.

Wife: Oh, you always say that.

John: And I seem to remember you weren't too thrilled with the cutlery drainer.

Wife: No, it was very nice.

John: And I know you girls like Christmas presents that make you feel feminine and alluring.

Wife: Well—

John: Something a bit out of the ordinary. Well, I felt a bit of a fool blundering round the department stores.

Wife: Oh John.

John: Half the assistants looked at me as if I was some kind of pervert, and of course I got into a terrible muddle about sizes.

Wife: Did you?

John: But I managed in the end. I got what I wanted. (*Drags out large square gift-wrapped box from behind the settee.*) Merry Christmas.

Wife: What is it?

John: It's a sewing machine table.

Wife's reaction.

John: I thought we could have sex on it.

CONTINUITY[164]

And later on, I see we have a ballet from Ballet North, a new work based on the Stanley Holloway[165] monologue 'My Word You Do Look Queer'. So that's something to look forward to.

---

164 The details are lost in the mists of time, but this seems to have been inspired by a ballet on an earthy northern subject that VW and GD saw on television. It was a prophetic script too, as she would be even more tickled by clips from a 1989 ballet version of *Hobson's Choice*.

165 Popular entertainer (1890–1982) now best remembered as the father of Eliza Doolittle in the film of *My Fair Lady*. His comic verse monologues, delivered in a Lancashire accent, were a fixture in the Wood household when VW was growing up. See p. 276.

CRUISE

Dance floor of cruise ship. Couples dancing to organ and drums. Man and woman, forty-fiveish, tanned and upper class.

Man: Is your husband enjoying the cruise?

Woman: He was enjoying it tremendously – then he fell overboard; are you with me? And from what I could see of his face in the water as we pulled away, he didn't seem to be enjoying it quite so much, I thought.

Man: Did you have him picked up, at all?

Woman: No, I mean, don't misunderstand me, I liked him enormously, he had very good taste in slacks.

Man: Yes, didn't he, my word.

Woman: But I'm a little bit of a Buddhist – do you see, and I thought if he's meant to be bobbing up and down in the middle of the Indian Ocean, so be it.

Man: So you're more or less a widow.

Woman: Yes, I suppose I am.

Man: Shall you go into black?

Woman: I would doubt it. If you're a turquoise sort of a person – why fight it? Where's Bettina?

Man: In the cabin.

Woman: Queasy?

Man: I should say more sleazy than queasy, she's giving a private strip show for C Deck cabin staff.

Woman: How marvellous. I always feel I should do more charity work.

Man: To be frank – she has a drink problem.

Woman: One had noticed. Though, credit where it's due, not many women could drink a yard of Martini.

Man: I married beneath me. My wife worked in a dry-cleaner's.

Woman: Really?

Man: It was a marriage of convenience. She needed financial security and I needed a same-day alteration on a pair of trousers.

Woman: Now I was very poor when I met my husband. He was a twenty-five stone millionaire.

Man: Good heavens.

Woman: I married him, put him on a strict diet, and I'm so glad I did.

Man: Why's that?

Woman: Because it made it so much easier to push him through the porthole, do you follow?

Music stops. They applaud the band.

MARATHON

Film.

Ad. Windy busy city.

VO (*male*): Why do people eat chocolate?

Office Girl: Well, I'm in a really boring job, right, and I like to get out of the office, cos everybody hates me, and they say I've got BO so I just go and get a bar of chocolate, yeah.

Spotty Boy Student: Why do I eat chocolate? Well I'm on a student grant and it's one of the cheapest ways I know to get acne.

Businessman: I like it, it's satisfying, it makes me feel good, it's a nice break in the middle of the day and after I put my clothes back on I like to have a bar of chocolate – yes.

TUPPERWARE PARTY

Living room. Mixed bunch of women of all ages helping themselves to coffee off a trolley and settling down. Kath stands up nervously.[166]

Kath: Now if everyone's got coffee, perhaps we can all get going. I'd like to welcome you all to this Wendy Winters Marital Aids Party – I'm Kath – please don't feel obliged to buy anything, but if you do go away without buying anything, perhaps you could all chip in for the quiche – could you? It's not the pastry, it's the broccoli . . .

---

166 Kath was played by JW, Denise by VW, Woman by CI and Husband by DP.

I've never actually given this type of party before – let alone a
Wendy Winters Marital Aids Party[167] – the doctor was all for it
– my husband and I haven't – well, not for a long time – I can
remember taking off my midi skirt. Now I've got the brochure
– 'Wendy Winters says sex should be fun' – you see, coffee is
not half drunk and we learnt something already. The box came
this morning and Denise has undone it for me – it was quite a
hairy piece of string and I didn't like to touch it; if I read them
out could you hold them up?

Denise rustles in the box.

Right. (*Reads.*) 'You will definitely feel good vibrations and
ease any aches and pains with this handy battery-operated
personal massager.'

Rude cries of 'Whooo!' from the women.

'Batteries not included.'

Denise holds up a Tupperware drinks container. Kath keeps reading.

'Used with your partner, it can bring new dimensions of pleasure to your love-making.'

Kath takes it – sees nothing amiss.

Lovely – battery is in here – then brum brum away you go.

Puts it down on the end table.

'Tired of winceyette nighties and nylon housecoats? Give him
a bedtime thrill as you parade sexily in these – made from
sensual oriental fabric.'

---

167 In her live show in Cardiff that Christmas VW returned to sex toys when introducing 'The Ballad of Barry and Freda': 'When I used to sleep with people – this is before
I got my Holly Hobbie vibrator.' The following year she added an aside: 'it's better
than the My Little Pony one . . .' In her 1990 show she imagined one wife-swapping
couple arriving at the house of another with a gift: 'We didn't know whether we should
bring a bottle. Anyway we've brought this. And these are the batteries for it.' From her
1993 show: 'If she had a vibrator it would be because she had a stiff neck.' In *DL* Dolly
denies owning one:

Dolly: Just because I have a full sex life.
Jean: Oh yeah? Then what's that appliance I found in your underskirt drawer?
Dolly: It's for stiff necks!

Denise holds up two joined oven gloves[168] *in a quilted pot holder.*

'This really is lingerie with a difference.'

Woman: How do they fit on?

Kath (*draping them on the obvious places*): Like this I imagine. Quite erotic, the gingham. 'And Hubby likes to pose too – you'll both enjoy everything he has to offer as he slips into a pair of these—'

Denise gets out two plastic egg cups.

'In smooth polyvinyl for true sensual comfort.'

Kath takes one.

Mmm – we're all a bit excited already perhaps, are we?

Silence – she hots up the pace a bit.

'Well, ladies, love-making does sometimes have its problems – how often have you said if only it would last longer?'

Agreeing groans from women.

'Now it can last all night long.'

Cheers.

'Keep this under the pillow, and if Hubby starts to flag, rub him ever so gently with this marvellous product.'

Denise gets out four-sided cheese grater. Groans from women, some leave.
Kath begins to panic.

'Perhaps Hubby is losing interest – rekindle his desire with this aphrodisiac perfume. Spray it everywhere you'd like to be kissed.'

Denise brings out other spray.

Woman (*leaving*): That's oven cleaner!

Kath: No – it's very aromatic, it's a bit like Charlie![169]

Snatches the box from the knees as the rest leave, waves a pastry wheel.

'And just run this over your skin' – oooo – it's quite a tingle. (*Sink plunger.*) 'And it's party night with this little attachment – a spray of this and you're all set . . .' (*Sprays on the oven cleaner. Enter husband.*)

---

168 This was around the same time VW composed 'The Ballad of Barry and Freda' in which Freda pledges to wear 'stilettos and an oven glove'.

169 Jean in *DL*: 'Can you smell my Charlie?'

Husband: Hello, Kath – who were all those – my God, what's that
      smell?

Kath (*deflated*): Oven spray.

Husband: It's fantastic. (*Leaping on her.*) You smell wonderful. (*Holds
      out the oven gloves.*) And put these on, darling, put these on . . .

FIRESIDE TALES (IRISH)

Cosy hearth, man by fire in fisherman's jersey and pipe.[170]

Man: You've heard me tell of the little town of Ballycumlately, so you
have, and my old friend Donal O'Flaherty, who did nothing very
much at all.

Well, one fine day, Donal O'Flaherty was standing by the pump
in Ballycumlately, and it was a fine pump so it was. And up comes a
stranger from another town altogether. What sort of a town am I in?
says the stranger. Ballycumlately, says Donal.

And what sort of town might that be? enquires the stranger.

A very fine town indeed so it is, says Donal, scratching a bit of
mashed potato from the knee of his corduroy trousers.

Do you have a grand theatre? says the stranger.

We do not, says Donal.

Do you have a magnificent ballroom? We do not, says Donal. Do
you have an F.W. Woolworth? Well, we do, says Donal, but it's after
being closed temporarily while they deal with the asbestos. And can I
help you any further? says Donal, leaning back against the Ballycumlately pump. Yes, says the stranger – I'll have six gallons of two star.
And he did. Stay warm.

---

170 Bryan Murray, best known at the time for *The Irish R.M.*, which had run for three
series on Channel 4. As with the actors in the Scottish and Welsh editions of 'Fireside
Tales', he was not cast in other parts of *ASOTV*. He later played Cousin Shifty in Carla
Lane's sitcom *Bread*.

AS SEEN ON TV SPECIAL

CLANCY – INTERIOR DECORATOR

Film.
Hard-hitting cop-type music. Car speeding along. CU of grim-faced tough guy. He screeches the car to a halt and runs into a deserted-looking house.
Caption: CLANCY.
He bursts into an empty room by kicking the door in. Terrified woman cowers away.
Caption: INTERIOR DECORATOR.
Clancy: My advice is lose the pelmet and go for a heck of a lot of ruching.
Cut to:
A fabric shop. Clancy contemptuously throwing down rolls of material – terrified salesman.
Clancy: You can tickle my china and call me Pussy but if you hold that to a window I think you'll find it's lavender.
Cut to:
Rich living room. Sobbing woman on sofa, Clancy looking down at her.
Clancy: I did warn you, Lady Marcia. Watered silk is deliciously effective, but it won't take jam.
Reprise of caption: CLANCY. INTERIOR DECORATOR.

CONTINUITY

(*She's staring into space.*) Sorry – I was just wondering which tights to wear tomorrow. Erm, yes, well the pace is really hotting up in the Innsbruck International Skating Gala. As you know, the British pair are currently lying twenty-ninth, let's take another look at the routine that's put them in that position. Here's Barbara Conway and Gregory Smith skating to the music they've made so much their own – the theme from *Coronation Street*.

SKATING[171]

Two skaters dance slowly and pompously together to the closing bars of the music from Coronation Street. *They are dressed in the skating equivalent of Shakespearean costumes. They finish spreadeagled on the ice. Scattered applause from empty stadium. They skate to the side, kiss their trainer, large woman in fur hat, hold bouquets and kiss each other and wave to the camera.*

Commentator (*VO*): Perhaps a little disappointing, that performance from Barbara and Greg. That was rather a nasty fall Barbara sustained in the opening bars, in fact I can see they are still mending those particular seats, and I felt too, that Greg's performance lacked a little of the brio we've seen in training, Robin?

Robin (*VO*): Well, unfortunately I have to agree, David. I see he has thrown the cigarette away now, but for me, skating and smoking just don't go together.

David: Ah, here are the marks for technical merit.

They flash up above the skaters' heads.

0.0 0.0 0.0 0.0 0.0 0.0 0.9 0.0

And that 0.9 is from the British judge.

Robin: I think they're hoping to pick up on artistic impression, David.

Score flashes up 0.0 0.0 0.0 0.0 0.1 0.0 0.0

---

171 VW had already taken the mickey out of underwhelming British skaters via the continuity announcer in the second series: 'And in the skating the British pair will be waving and smiling and coming thirteenth.' Here their performance is even more calamitous. The joke about British figure skating was out of date thanks to the gold medal won at the 1984 Winter Olympics by Jayne Torvill and Christopher Dean, but VW found ice dancing irresistibly comic. Torvill and Dean later surfaced in *The Library* (1989) as a punchline that was hastily written in the rehearsal room when filler dialogue was needed: 'Weren't they a lovely couple? And they never did it. Mind you, she spent so much time lying face down on the ice, I'm not surprised.' Twenty years later on *MLX* the stars of *Dancing on Ice* guested in 'Beyond the Marigolds: What Mrs Overall Did Next . . .'. To complete VW's portfolio of skating gags, in her 1996 stand-up show she mentions a friend who has a boring sex life with a skater boyfriend: 'Every night it was the compulsories followed by the short programme.'

David: And they won't be pleased with that.

They carry on smiling and waving and drinking orange juice.

No, they don't seem to mind. They're obviously pretty stupid as well as being hopeless skaters, would you go along with that, Robin?

Robin: I think that's fair comment, David.

David: Their coach seems quite happy as well, Robin, I find that rather surprising.

Robin: Well, she's on a bottle of brandy a day, David, so not too worried, I would've thought . . .

David: OK.

BALCONY SCENE

Two adjoining hotel room balconies abroad – evening – see Noël Coward's Private Lives *– sound of waves, distant palm court orchestra in the background, elegant man strolls out with a cocktail, he is wearing a white dinner jacket; he stands admiring the view. Unseen by him, an elegant girl[172] in an evening dress comes out onto the adjoining balcony, she too stares out, then they catch sight of each other.*

Man: Amanda. How this Mediterranean light becomes you, you have all the shimmering translucence of an orchid.

Girl (*in raucous tones*): Oh hiya, Derek. Our shower's buggered, is yours? (*Sniffs armpit.*) I feel right skunky. (*Calls back into room.*) I'm coming! (*Goes in.*) See you at Naked Limbo. Ta-ra.

Man thinks.

---

172 This was rehearsed and shot with Jamie Ripman and Georgia Allen, who played several airheads for VW. She appeared as Ceal, one of the haughty schoolgirls in 'Just an Ordinary School', then Fiona in the *Doctor Who* spoof. Finally, there is her leotard-clad glamour model Sally Ann in *Mens Sana Thingummy Doodah*. 'I mean if you read a book, Victoria,' she says, 'that's not going to make me more intelligent, is it?' 'I wouldn't have thought so,' replies VW.

CONTINUITY[173]

(*Over still of anoraked man from the back.*) And now our try anything once reporter turns his hand to the making of a pop video as Keith Mackilveny goes 'Making a Mess of It'.

TRAVEL AGENT[174]

Rowena comes in. Tired man behind the counter glances at his watch, looks up and smiles.

Man: Can I help you?

Rowena stares back in silence. After a moment he carries on with what he's doing. Barry comes in, tidying himself up. He stands next to Rowena.

Rowena: Barry. Barry. He's been talking to me.

Barry: Did you talk back?

Rowena: No, I were waiting for you.

Barry: Shall we go to the counter?

Rowena: Lean up or just stand?

Barry: Lean up.

Rowena: OK, Barry. Hey, Barry.

Barry: Oh yes?

Rowena: I love you. You're right alluring.

Barry: Oh that's right.

---

173 This was to have cued up the song 'High Risk Area', which mocks contemporary pop videos with gauzy white sheets draped around a candle-lit set. At the top of the lyric sheet there is a caption: MAKING A MESS OF IT. 'Over intro,' it then says, 'a hand removes the anorak that's on the piano.' In the chorus the script calls for backing singers to pop into shot at a window, and for a woman to open a door, apologise and withdraw. Although the song is wonderfully dotty ('I've got a certificate saying I can swim two lengths of the bath'), in the end the video plays it straight, apart from the moment the music flies off the grand piano in a puff of wind.

174 This was filmed in the studio, with VW as Rowena, Jim Broadbent as Barry and DP as the travel agent.

They approach the counter and hang over it.

Barry: Have you got any holidays?

Man: Yes.

Rowena: Have you got one for two people?

Man: Yes.

Rowena: Is one of them us?

Man: Yes it can be.

Rowena: If the other person drops out can you let us know?

Man: Sorry?

Rowena: We're not on the phone but the grocer'll bang on the scullery.

Man: Shall we start again?

Rowena: Alright. I was here and you were outside the shop, Barry.

Man: No hang on, it's alright. Do you want to go abroad?

Both (*wildly enthusiastic*): Yeah!

Man: How do you want to get there?

Rowena (*as they both launch into a jolly synchronised walk*): Like this!

Man: What country would you like to visit?

Barry: Throw some, throw some.

Man: Right. Spain, Italy, France, Greece.

They watch him intently.

      Malta, Belgium, erm . . .

He begins to slow down.

      United States, Canada . . .

Rowena: Russia.

Barry: Oh yes.

Man: You want to go to Russia.

Rowena: No, I were just saying another country, I thought you were
      stuck.

Man: Look – give me an idea of what sort of things you like to do.

Barry: This is like to do as opposed to not like to do, is it?

Man: Er yes.

Barry: I'll just chip in here I think, Rowena.

Rowena: Chip away. Chip chip chip. I'm having a lozenge.

Barry: My fiancée and I have just got married.

Both: Whoo!

They pull ecstatic faces and wiggle their hands.

Man: So you're looking for a honeymoon?

Both: Whoo! Yes. We. Are!

They do it again.

Man (*looking at his watch and lying*): We actually only do one honeymoon.

Barry: Oh lovely. We only want one honeymoon.

Man: It's a five-day package in Paris.

Looks through leaflet.

       Half board, champagne breakfast, shopping, five-star hotel.

Rowena: Do they do burgers?

Man: I don't know. Read the leaflet, I'm closing, alright?

They study it intently.

Rowena: They do do burgers. Look, Barry, burgers.

Barry: Oh that's right.

Rowena: What sort of burgers are they? Are they French burgers,
Barry?

Barry: Oh ask him.

Man is tidying up his things.

Man: I'm closing.

Rowena: Sorry. What sort of burgers do they do? See where it says
burger?

Man: That's not burger. That's Folies Bergère. It's a—

Rowena: Looked like burger. Looked like burger. Barry – it looked
like burger.

Man: The Folies Bergère is a Parisian nightspot, a sophisticated place
of entertainment.

Rowena: Do they do burgers?

Man (*getting up*): No they bloody don't. They have showgirls and
dancers. They wear feathers (*putting on his coat and hat*) and
sequins and skimpy brassieres.

Barry: Steady.

Man: They parade. (*He parades.*) They dance. (*He dances then stops
defeated.*) Good God, you must have seen them.

Rowena: What d'you think?

Barry: Oh I'm keen.

Rowena: Shall we do it now?

Barry: The dancing?

Rowena: Yeah. Shall we do it now, Barry?

Barry: Oh yes.

Rowena: D'you want to dance?

Man: Do I want to dance? At half past five on a lousy Friday afternoon with a splitting headache, after a week of fending off morons, ditherers and certifiable cretins? Do I Want To Dance?

Rowena: Yeah.

Man: I should say. (*Switching on tape deck.*) Get in the middle.

To the strains of luscious French music, they link arms and launch into a perfect high-kicking routine.

THE EPILOGUE[175]

Vicar and nun side by side on swivel chair.

Vicar: Hello.

Nun: Hello.

Vicar: You may be wondering what in the 'hello' we're doing.

Nun: That's droll.

Vicar: But joking very much aside, Sister Kirkcaldy and I are going to put our inter-denominational cards on the table tonight and talk about – well ladies first, Sister, we're talking about . . . ?

Nun: Faith. Hello. It's a funny word – faith.

Vicar: And rather like soap powder, there's more than one sort of faith.

Nun: There's Faith Brown, the impressionist; she's awfully clever.

Vicar (*a bit lost but gamely carrying on*): But there's another sort of faith.

Nun: Oh aha. Adam Faith. Remember him? Impressed us very much

---

175 This was an expansion on the epilogue written for CI in the first series (see note 124), conflating her Scottish nun with John Nettleton's vicar. It may have counted against the sketch that CI played another Scot in 'McConomy'. Also, it feels too long to have been tacked on to the end of the episode, which finished with the continuity announcer clearing her desk and turning off the lights.

with his performances in 'Budgie'. And a lovely script by Keith Waterhouse, well done Keith.[176]

Vicar (*moving hastily along*): There's the sort of faith that says if I'm a jolly good boy when I die I'll pop straight through those Pearly Gates and twang away on a harp to my heart's content.

Nun: Like Mary O'Hara.[177]

Vicar: Or there's the sort of quiet belief that cushions one from life's little bumps and knocks like a sort of 'no prescription needed' tranquilliser.

Nun: I'm one of those. Hello!

Vicar: Or there's the sort of blind faith that says to heck with what you chaps believe – I'm jolly right and I'll do what I jolly like. That's one dangerous thing—

Nun: And the other dangerous thing is drinking cough medicine and then attempting to operate heavy machinery.

Vicar: Faith's rather like our granny's old pot plant, isn't it—

Nun: And you're rather like someone I met in Inverness twenty years ago. He offered me a Sherbet Dab and I reported him.

Vicar: Yes granny's old pot plant. (*He kicks her chair, which is on castors and slides out of shot.*) Get out of it. She didn't water it for months on end.

Nun (*sliding back sideways and cannoning into the Vicar*): And she didn't wash either, if she's anything like the people I've met.

Vicar: Well I must go. But just before we do – (*holding up a card that says CH_ _CH*) – take a look at this word and see if you can tell me what's missing.

Pause. Music.

Yes. U. R. Toodle-oo.

Lights dim.

Nun: U. R. – that's pathetic. Where d'you find that, the *Beano*?

Vicar: You're not the only nun in this region, bear that in mind.

Nun: I'm not a nun at all, I'm a cloakroom attendant but my ears get cold.

---

176 The author and columnist (1929–2009) had become a friend of VW's.
177 Singing Irish harpist.

10

CHARACTERS ON TOUR

Before *As Seen on TV*, Victoria's greatest success as a stand-up had been at the King's Head Theatre, with a capacity well under two hundred. When she toured in the spring of 1986, the average venue held more than two thousand. These huge audiences were hungry for new material, including character monologues.

The first of these was Wendy Morpurgo, a cheerfully naive singleton who is clearly a forerunner to Kimberley's friend. To come on in the second half Victoria invented Margaret the Usherette, who holds the fort while the star nips to the chippy. By the time Victoria reached the London Palladium in the autumn of 1987, Margaret had been ousted from her post-interval slot by Kimberley's friend but her ghost would linger on for years in the form of a joke about Mavis, the patron saint of knackered usherettes.

When she created a new live show in 1990, Victoria was determined to use fewer songs, which meant she needed characters to provide variety. Having enjoyed rich returns from the Haworth Parsonage tour guide in *Lucky Bag*, now she imagined herself on a bus tour of a northern city in the incapable hands of Corinna the City Bus City Tour guide. Although she didn't do the character in costume, Victoria pictured her 'dressed in very traditional Lancashire costume. Shawl, clogs, Littlewoods tracksuit. She's got really really long nails. She's the sort of person who could pick the nose of a woman living three streets away.' Corinna speaks in the sing-song delivery of tour guides everywhere, blithely mispronouncing random words.

For the same tour Victoria invented an overweight roadie she called Susan, who wanders out on stage to test the microphones. A sound engineer, whose interventions have to be imagined, acts as an unseen feed. She has a thick Lancastrian accent and feels like a raucous forerunner of Twinkle in *dinnerladies*. By the time the show reached the Strand Theatre in the autumn, she too had been ousted by Kimberley's friend.

The third new character in the show was a calamitously bad orator. Victoria was tickled by the idea of a woman addressing an audience of women despite possessing no gift for public speaking. The first stage monologue she ever wrote and performed, in Leicester in 1977, was in the character of a woman sharing the results of a sex survey with a branch of the Women's Institute (later included in *Wood and Walters*). She returned to the idea in *Lucky Bag* with a sixth-former addressing the debating society on the subject of school uniform. The most talentless speaker of all – who doesn't have a name – turned up in the second half of her 1990 show. She is breathless with nerves as she attempts to argue that 'Life Begins at Forty'.

WENDY MORPURGO[178]

Hello. My name's Wendy Morpurgo.[179] And I've had an uplifting experience in the launderama. Shall I tell you about it? . . . Alright, I will do. Things were very busy in the launderama. And there was only one machine vacant. And that had a notice on it. 'Mechanics overalls only'. So I'd had to go out and buy some. When I came back all the seats were occupied so I take up a position on the flip-top bin provided. It's a very nice seat as long as you don't tip. And you get a lovely view of the laundry-bag dispenser. They're lovely, have you had one? I had one once. It was orange. I had one before. That was orange. Me friend's got one. I don't know what colour hers is.

Anyway, so me washing's in. But I'm not watching it go round because I'm not supposed to get too excited. And there was a bra chasing a dishcloth – I didn't know what it might do to it if it caught it up! But I'm alright cos I've got two tubes of milk gums and a *Woman's Weekly*. And I'm reading a knitting pattern and I've just got to the most exciting part, cast off, press flat, join up, and a shadow falls across the page and I look up – not too quickly cos I'm wearing my friend's contact lenses while she's on holiday – well, it's not exactly holiday, it's prison – it's an open prison – my friend says it's like Butlins – once you're in you don't have to pay for anything. So I look up, not too quickly because if you blink too much with a contact lens it slips round behind your eyeball and tickles your brains! Claire Rayner[180] said so. But she said the main thing was that if one did slip

---

178 To capture a sense of Wendy's speedy speech patterns I've gone light on formal punctuation.

179 Although Michael Morpurgo was already a successful children's author in the 1980s, it seems more likely that Wendy took her name from his brother Pieter Morpurgo, who was VW's director on *That's Life!*

180 The agony aunt (1931–2010) had been a guest on the second series of *ASOTV* in the spot-the-celeb game show sketch 'Say Who You Are'.

behind and tickle your brains you weren't to worry about it. But I do worry about it – cos I'm quite ticklish. I don't let it hamper me but I can't wear elasticated trousers.

So I look up, not too quickly, there's this man looking a bit agog at me ski pants. Now I know what you're thinkin'. They *were* elasticated – but I took the elastic out. And they fell down. But it was only in the reference library. So now I wear braces. And they're not men's braces, they're ladies' braces. They must be because they're made out of sanitary belts. It said on the packet I could be fully confident while I was wearing them. But I'm not. But I was a bit worried about these ski pants anyway cos a girl in the shop had talked me into them she said get into those I said alright. I said what colour are they please because all the cubicles were full and it was a bit dark where I was trying them on under the counter. She said they were hot mustard. Well it looks nice on a sausage. Wasn't so sure about it stretched over a bee you emm. Well she talked me into buying them she said go on buy them I said alright. But I'm a bit worried about my thighs in them because a man had once asked if I'd had them lagged for the cold weather.

Anyway, so I look up and there's this man looking a bit agog at me so I remember what we said at Getting To Know You Club and I started to make conversation. I said, are you a burglar? He said no, he had an empty packet of Persil and he couldn't reach the bin cos I was sitting on it. So I offered to flip the top for him, and we just clicked. Like that. He said, what are you doing when your washing's ready? I said, I'm putting it in the dryer! He said, what are you doing when your washing's dry? I said, I'm foldin' it up! Then his nostrils went a bit white so I shut up. He said do you want to come to Jones the chippy with me I said I don't know I'll have to think about it he said go on come with me so I said alright.

So we got to the chippy. He says do you want to eat in or do you want to eat out. I said, well, I'd rather eat in because the last time I held chips against my chest I melted my body warmer. It was a man-made fibre. A man made it. So we sit down in the chippy and there's a lovely painting of pie and peas right next to my face. And he says it's not exactly a candle-lit dinner. I said no but there's a nice gleam coming off of the mushy peas saucepan. So you can see I was keeping my end up manners wise. He was a lovely man he had a lovely gap between his two front teeth. I specially noticed it cos he had a mushy pea stuck in it. He said can I take you home I said hang on I haven't finished my Tizer. So we get home he says can I come in for a coffee. I said I haven't got any coffee but you can come in for a Horlicks if you don't mind sucking your own lumps.

So we're sitting there and I'm just eating the froth off the top with a medicine spoon, and he says to me, you've got lovely dimples in your cheeks. I said they're not dimples, they're holes where I ate a kebab sideways. He said I'm feeling a bit romantic put a record on I said alright. After a few minutes he said I'm not feeling quite so romantic. I said, why, don't you like my record? I love it. It's by Linguaphone. It's called *Get By in Flemish*. I'm learning it in case I ever go to Flem.[181] I offered him a jammy dodger he said no ta he'd had seven, and how did I feel about nooky? Nooky. Have *you* heard of it? I bluffed. I said I didn't like it. I said I'd had it on a Ryvita at a running buffet. He said, well, there's not much point in me sticking around then, is there? I said there is, there's another jammy dodger I didn't get it out before cos it's cracked. He said it's not the only one.

But it's alright cos we're goin' out now, actually. We're in love. It's fabby. And he's just proposed to me and he's called Denis Hatchard – and last night he got down on one knee and he said, 'Wendy Morpurgo, will you change your name to mine?' I said alright. So now I'm called Denis Morpurgo.

MARGARET THE USHERETTE

Sorry, can we just stop talking? Sorry, I'm Margaret I'm one of the usherettes. I've just got a little bit of an announcement. I'm afraid we can't carry on with the show just at present. It's quite silly actually, all it is is that our stage door keeper Billy, he likes to have a bag of chips and a jumbo sausage round about now and of course he can't

---

181 This joke was too good to lose – VW would give it to Kimberley's friend.

leave the stage door unattended so Victoria Wood has very kindly offered to go to the chip shop for him. And apparently there's rather a long queue so we're just going to have to fill in as best we can till she gets back. It's rather silly actually because normally our theatre manager Mr Chinley, he goes to the chip shop for Billy, but he's hurt his back because Mary O'Hara was here last week and I think Mr Chinley must have strained it after helping her lift her harp out of the sidecar.

So Mr Chinley came straight to me and said, Margaret, you're totally reliable and superb in a crisis. I said, Oh! Ah! Me? He said, Can you go to the chip shop for Billy? I said, Well, no I can't, Mr Chinley, I daren't leave the theatre. I'm expecting a very important call from my friend Connie, she's getting divorced, she's going to court, it's all rather traumatic, and what's particularly upsetting is she can't find a handbag to match her shoes. I said, But why don't I direct Victoria to the chip shop? And it's not that complicated – once you've crossed the dual carriageway and the flyover and the underpass you're practically there. I said, And why don't we get old Billy, who's an old variety performer, to come up on stage and give a little bit of his old variety act? But unfortunately that's not possible. He says he hasn't got the euphonium any more and the chimpanzee's dead.

So Mr Chinley turned to me and he said, Meg. Most people call me Margaret but Mr Chinley sometimes calls me Meg cos that was his sister's name. She's not dead or anything, but she spent rather a lot of time in the Far East and she met this rather peculiar surgeon. Anyway, she's now in the merchant marine. And she's called Ken.[182]

So Mr Chinley turned to me and he said, Meg, I'm ever so busy cashing up with the other usherettes because we've had a heck of a run on tubs tonight. He said, Can you pop up on stage and explain the delay and then if we're still hanging on carry on chatting? I said, What shall I say? He said, Well just tell them a little bit about yourself, it'll be fascinating. I thought, Well, I'll take your word for it because he's quite a fascinating person himself, Mr Chinley, he collects doilies. So here goes.

---

182 By no means the only instance of gender reassignment in VW's comedy.

Anyway, I'm Margaret (*coughs*) sorry piece of popcorn. I'm Margaret, as I said, I'm married to Peter, he works for a double-glazing company, he sends the crew on ahead to fit the secondary windows as we call them and then he follows on to explain to the people how their own windows got broken. And of course it's rather a stressful job and he spends a lot of time on his hobby which is having electro-convulsive therapy. No, he's found a lovely place where they do it ever so cheaply, with jump leads. I've got two children. Cathy – she's a trainee interior decorator. She's hoping to combine this with some sort of welfare social work, perhaps provide an emergency twenty-four-hour curtain-making service or something like that. And then there's my son Nick – he's rather veered away from a career in English literature – he works on a newspaper. And then there's Peter's granny who lives with us. In fact, she does most of my housework for me. I do get a little bit annoyed with her actually because her walking frame does tend to chip the skirting board.

But it's quite a modern marriage, Peter's and I, it's quite swinging in its way. At one time we were very much involved in the wife-swapping thing.[183] I often found myself going upstairs with other ladies' husbands. I can remember once I was with Anthony Brown who has the DIY shop and he undressed and he said, Margaret, what would you like me to do? And I said, Well, really I'd like you to insulate the loft and lag the hot water tank.[184] But I've got quite a nice house, I like to think it sticks out from the others in the cul-de-sac because I've had a

---

183 VW first joked about swingers in *LB*, later revived in *ASOTV*: 'I went to one of those swapping parties where you throw your car keys on the floor. I don't know who got my moped but I drove that Peugeot for years.' In her 1990 tour she imagined a swingers party where British manners impede passion: 'Now steady on, mind the barometer.'

184 The conflating of sex and DIY runs through VW's comedy. *LB*: 'What a night . . . We put up shelving.' In the wife-swapping section of her 1990 show, she imagined a husband spotting mid-coitus with his neighbour that 'her central pendant needed rewiring', while a wife's erotic massage technique is akin to 'unblocking a sink'. In 'Offensive Old Man Dancing' from *Julie Walters and Friends* (1991), two men ask if they can watch the old man have sex with his wife: 'I said, "You betcha, boys." It's not like they were asking to sit in on me doin' something tricky, like planin' a door frame.'

Georgian porch added. It wasn't expensive – well, it was free actually. I think we just had to order a couple of extra pints and a yoghurt. But the living room's rather nicely decorated I think. I did it myself, it's light yellow with touches of green – I based it round a Marks and Spencer's broccoli quiche. And we've got a nice kitchen – it's all brand-new units, all stripped pine. We were going to strip down the old units but we were having such trouble sanding off the Formica.

Peter and I like to give little dinner parties where I do my speciality, which is something I do with liver that I don't think a lot of other people do. I bake it with a meringue topping. But of course if Peter's away I don't have dinner parties, I just have my girlfriends over for coffee like Connie and we sit putting the world to rights over a couple of Kunzles.[185]

She's quite a fascinating person actually, Connie, because she used to run a restaurant. Well, it was a caravan in a lay-by on the A597, but she was quite noted for her boiled onions. But I said to her, Connie, we have such a scream, we usherettes, because every so often the usherettes from this theatre and the usherettes from the cinema, we all get together and we all have a couple of gin and Kia-Oras, and we try and walk backwards, it's a scream!

Ooh, I'm getting a little message, I think we're just about ready to, yes . . . Can I just say, before I go, that we usherettes, we have little collecting boxes at various points around the theatre and if you would like to make a donation the money doesn't go to us, it goes towards our convalescent home for knackered usherettes, which is named after one of our members Mavis, Mavis House. Now Mavis dropped dead one day when somebody gave her the right money for a King Cone . . . Oh yes, I'm just coming . . . if I could just say, another little perk is if you've had an ice lolly tonight and you've got a lolly stick can you please leave it lying where it is because one of our little perks is that we collect all the lolly sticks together and we wash them and we sell them to a very nice man called Mr Barratt and he makes houses out of them.

Ladies and gentlemen, will you please welcome all the way from the Happy Haddock Fish Bar, Victoria Wood.

---

185 Period confectionary.

CORINNA, CITY BUS CITY TOUR GUIDE[186]

Good mornin.[187] I'd just like to welcome everybody to our City Bus City Tour this mornin taking you round this very ancient city of ours, fillin you in on a bit of knowhow and je ne says quat[188] along the way. My name's Corinna, I'm a fully qualified City Bus City Tour guide, havin undergone the very intensive City Bus City Tour trainin programme. And a very gruelling forty-five minutes it proved to be. I'm Corinna, as I say, I'm block-a-chock with info and like all the City Bus City Tour guides I should be handin out various juicy nuggets enn route. (*Makes thumping sound.*) Drive on, Denis. Denis . . . Denis!

We're startin our tour here in City Square. As you can see we have the town hall, the law courts and the municipal library directly ahead of us. These were all designed by one and the same person, I can't quite think of his name just at the moment but as we pass his statue you will see that he had curly hair and quite a long jacket. Movin along down the Broadway we pass the ancient medi-aye-evil banque-tin hall, scene for the secret meetin between Mary Queen of Scots and Queen Elizabeth the First. Whether this meetin actually took place or not we cannot askertain. But we can be fairly sure that they were not disturbed in their meeting by the bleepin of the pelican crossin as we are today. (*Laughs at own joke.*) They would of course not have needed a pelican crossin in those days, ladies and gentlemen, because they would have had the Belisha beacon and the zebra outside of Woolworths.

---

186 There are three extant recordings of VW performing the monologue across three consecutive shows in Birmingham. She fiddled with sections every night, adapting it to audience reaction. One bit she removed on the second night she reinstated on the third. This transcript elides those three versions.

187 As Corinna, VW pronounced words ending in 'ing as if the letter G had not so much been dropped as never actually existed in the first place. Hence the lack of apostrophes to indicate their absence. Occasionally she kept the G – it's not clear whether by mistake or design – and when she does I've left it in.

188 Pronounced, deliberately and suggestively, to rhyme with twat.

Stopping here at the north end of Silver Street – Denis, stopping (*stamps foot*) – this originally was the old Roman road out of the city – a beautifully straight highway leadin straight to Scotland. Or as it was known in those days, Wales. Remains of an old Roman camp or campus, to slip into the Latin for uno momento, remains have been found a few miles outside of the city and anybody wishing to set foot on the very spot where Agricola slew the leader of the north Britons just needs to head straight for the new Tesco's and stand by the macaroni.

Takin a left turn here we're passin City Park home of last year's international garden festival. Originally a typical urban wasteland, ugly, bleak and derelict, you can now see that twelve months after the garden festival is over it is much the same only with an ice-cream kiosk. Designed to boost civic pride and bring trade and employment to the city, the garden festival has been adjudged in government circles a great success. But the people who live here will tell you they're just as miserable only with more trees.

Takin a left turn now OK climbin up the hill and leavin the city centre behind us now on our right we have our very famous art deeco buildin the Gaumont cinema. This was for thirty years a bingo hall but has been recently reopened and refurbished as an arts centre. A very sad loss to the community. On the other side of the road we have our equally famous Mr Pickwick cake factory, home of those exceedinly good cakes made in the traditional manner by women in hairnets chain-smokin over a conveyor belt. And stoppin at the top of the hill now if you care to glance down you will get a lovely Panamanian visto. You will see that a lot of our architecture is post-war, the city centre havin been extensively bombed in 1940. This is particularly upsetting when it was later proved that most of the planes involved were British.

OK and we're stopping now outside 172 Cemetery Road. This is a typical Edwardian terraced house, totally unchanged from the olden days of its period, apart from the satellite dish and the mauve cladding. I expect you're wonderin why your City Bus City Tour has stopped outside this particular house. Has it perhaps some particular architectural or historical significance? Well, no, not really, but I live here so that's the end of your City Bus City Tour, ladies and gentlemen,

I'm gettin off now and you can find your way back, I'm poppin in for a salady-type lunch and Denis will be manning the cab with a cold saveloy. For your own comfort and convenience I advise you to leave the bus immediately as I believe Denis is planning to relieve himself into the glove compartment. Thank you.

SUSAN THE ROADIE

No one'll notice me . . . Cos I'm wearin black, aren't I? If you wear black under stage lighting an audience can't see yer. Have you never 'eard of Black Theatre of Prague?[189] . . . Prague! . . . Near Cardiff . . . Eh? Oh, I don't know what they do. Nobody knows what they do. Nobody's ever seen 'em . . .

You what? Int it? It's this speaker. One two one two . . . Bassy? Is it knickers bassy. It's trebly . . . What you got for ears, Y-fronts? It is trebly, Trevor. It has been trebly since that party. No, it were not me that done it. I only sat ont corner, it were Showaddywaddy's[190] roadie's cowboy boots going through mesh made it trebly . . . Eh, I tell you what, trebly – Trevor – somebody's cowboy boots gone through your mesh youda gone trebly. Eh? Eh? Do you get it, trebly 'igh voice, eh?

Eh, Trevor, I sent off me competition last night . . . Eh? No, I didn't mean it, I didn't mean Spot the Ball, no I don't think I were going to do very well with that, I went out on a bit of limb thur, I said it were on another page. No, this is a Win Jason Donovan for a Night competition. Yeah, it were in my *Annabel*.[191] No, I dint gerrit every week, I can't cope wi' two. Takes me a week to read *Motorbike & Sidecar*. Did you see it this week? Ooh, couldn't believe it, could you? Two whole pages of carburettors. Woo, what a buzz. No, this competition I had to say where I would tek him and why, right? . . .

---

189 A Czech theatre where optical illusions are achieved by lighting in a blackbox stage. Quite a specialist reference coming from someone who, despite her drama degree, often claimed to know nothing about Stanislavski.
190 Band formed in 1973 who dressed as teddy boys and covered oldies from the 1950s.
191 Women's magazine.

Hey, this is humming. (*Tests microphone.*) No, it's 'umming.

No, I wouldn't tek him there, it's too posh. I mean it's nice but what's the point of extra cheese? It only gets stuck to cardboard . . .

Hang on I'll shift it, is this better? B-b-b-b-b-b . . . Eh?

I've said I'll tek him to Flying Ferret . . . Yeah on a Thursday . . . Is it eck violent. Is it bugg'ry . . . Is it bugg'ry . . . Is it bugg'ry violent? Oh that, that were nothin', they weren't stitches they were only clips. I were alright soon as me 'air grew back . . . No, I've said I'll tek him to Flying Ferret because they 'ave Rolf 'Arris[192] ont jukebox . . . Well, and 'e's Australian int 'e? Like Jason Donovan. You what? Rolf 'Arris is not Welsh. Is it bugg'ry Welsh . . . Is it bugg'ry. You what, Green Green Grass of 'Ome, that's Tom Jones, you Y-fronts. You know Rolf 'Arris, him int overcoat wi' three legs . . .

You what, t'other mike, I've not checked do you want me to check it now? Alright, I'll go and get it, are you listenin'? Yeah, this is this one, right. ONE TWO ONE TWO B-b-b-b-b-b. ONE TWO. This is t'other one now. Yeah? B-b-b-b-. ONE TWO ONE TWO. I dint bring it out before cos it's got all chewy stuck to clip. Was it your chewy, Trevor? Grey wi' a fillin' in it? I'll put it int ashtray for yer.

And then I had to say like I like Jason Donovan because, right . . .

Eh, this is 'ummin', it's 'ummin'. (*Taps microphone.*) . . . It is, it's 'ummin' . . . now it's buzzin'. Now it's 'umming and buzzin'. Stopped buzzin' it's still 'ummin'.

I like Jason Donovan because, right? Well, I dint know what to put . . . Well, because I don't like Jason Donovan . . . He is *not* sexy . . . Is he bugg'ry . . . In the end I just put I like Jason Donovan in a dim light sideways on 'e reminds me of Mike Gattin'[193] . . . Nooo, I don't think I'll win, I'm not bothered. If I won I'd only have to go out and get new gear, wouldn't I, you know, get all dressed up . . .

You what? Wash these? What for? They're just right these. If I put 'em int washin' they'd go up me bum . . .

---

192 See note 294.
193 Cricketer. Not a flattering likeness. His name was mud in 1990 as he had just led a so-called rebel tour to South Africa, which was banned from international sport.

You wot, you reckon that mic's better? You want me to put this one back then? Yeah alright . . .

What did you say about slimmin'? Why would I need to go slimming? . . . I am not overweight. I am not, Trevor, overweight . . . I do know what I weigh and it's not overweight, right. You look in my *Annabel*, this week there's a little chart in there, right, height, weight, wi' lines on it, right? Well, I'm five foot five, right[194] – yeah, I'm goin', I'm goin' to put it back, listen – I'm five foot five, it says eight to ten stone acceptable, right – ten to eleven, overweight, right – eleven to twelve, fat, right – over twelve: obese. Yiss. I am obese . . . That doesn't mean I'm overweight, does it? . . . You what? 'Ealth risk? Is it Y-fronts an 'ealth risk. I'm right fit, me. I shifted that piano all by meself yesterday, dint I? Just got that little mark on where I had it under me arm. I shifted that piano all by myself, did I not, I went to an all-night party and I push-started a three-ton truck. Well, I were alright when you saw me next morning, weren't I? . . . That's what I mean, considering I were unconscious.

Eh up, we're startin' second half now apparently Victoria says. She says we should have done soundcheck before show – says it's more professional or some such bugg'ry. I said, oh yeah and miss *Emmerdale*? That shut 'er up. Anyway, bung level up, Trevor, she's comin'.

LIFE BEGINS AT FORTY

Ladies . . . no sorry. Madam chairman, ladi . . . oh no, sorry. Forget my hat if it wasn't screwed on. Lady mayoress, madam chairman, ladies, before I begin my speech proper, as 'twere – ha, as 'twere – I'm sure you'd all like to join me in thanking all the restaurant staff here at the Binley Moathouse for an absolutely delicious lunch. I must say I thought the soup was beautifully lukewarm and a very nice

---

194 VW's height, as she also sang in 'Baby Boom' (1996):

Well I'm five foot five

And I'm still alive

And that's all I want to say.

note to see in these conservation-minded days was paper serviettes obviously being used for the second time. The beef Wellington I can't comment on that – as a vegetarian I didn't have the beef I just had the Wellington.[195] But friends at a similar table to mine said after the first five minutes it definitely got easier to chew. The dessert, well that was truly edible, an inspired combination of dark chocolate, Benedictine and sago. Something for us all to think about there. Plus, coffee and mints, a truly fitting finish to a sumptuous spread. Has it not come yet, the coffee? Oh, I think there may be kitchen difficulties we know not what of. Of. What? Of what we don't know. No, it can't be easy serving a three-course luncheon to a hundred and seventy ladies, and I think our waitress did marvellous. Well done, Win. And what a splendid advert for your electric wheelchair. Finally, absences. Miss Thorne writes to say she's still bedridden, still busy with her soft toys and appealing for stuffing. Members donating all stockings or tights, could they please rinse through first?

Now, onto my speech proper. When Mrs Talbot drew my name out of the beret as this month's speaker, I don't mind admitting I panicked. Oh, and thanks to Betty Shawcross for quick work with the oxygen mask there. But once I'd calmed down – and that's one good thing about these long queues in casualty, plenty of time to ponder – I started to brood over that infamous saying, everybody has one luncheon club speech in them. What the flip was mine? There was no time to be lost, as Shakespeare so cleverly said in that uproarious comedy *Hamlet*, if 'twere done when 'twere done 'twell ter twon ti twenty twenty. Topics whirled through my head like confetti in a blender. What was mine to be? I am only an ordinary housewife. I am not a pop star like Madonna or Simone de Beauvoir. To be blunt, I am not even Chris Bonington.[196] Where on earth was my crevice? Then I hit on my theme. LIFE BEGINS AT FORTY.[197] So here goes.

---

195 VW was a vegetarian and had many demoralising experiences of being an after-thought on such occasions.

196 Mountaineer whose bestselling books made him a household name.

197 In handwritten prompt cards, VW put the phrase in capitals each time it occurred.

Life begins at forty. Life begins at forty! How often have we heard those words. Quite how often I don't know quite. But it is certainly a saying. Life begins at forty. But does it begin then, you ask, or earlier? Or later? But seriously I believe there is quite a ring of truth re that phrase. I am forty-seven, so if the sentence is to believed . . . to be believed . . . and life does begin at forty, then I am seven. Well, I am not seven otherwise I could not have had that sherry (*high-pitched laugh*).

Life begins at forty. We are hearing this from all sides these days. From doctors, health experts and, yes, even Miriam Stoppard.[198] And what a shining example Miriam is to us all. Holding down a good part-time job as well as writing serious plays and making her own jumpsuits. As well as Myriad, Miriam other names spring to mind. To use an old netballing expression, let me bounce a few onto the tarmac. Mother Teresa, Mary O'Hara, Rosalind Runcie:[199] what do they have in common? Yes, you're right, they have all visited Stockport. But more importantly they blew out their fortieth birthday candles many moons ago. But you don't have to be married to the Archbishop of Canterbury to have a more swinging lifestyle. Just remember life begins at forty and you will not go too far. Wrong. Too far wrong.

So yes indeed – life begins at forty, and that is the magical word. Life. And what is the meaning of life?[200] . . . I seem to have lost that part of my speech. If anybody sees it it's a blue card, it's got 'the meaning of life' written on it. Erm, I'll just carry on without it. Well, I may not *be* the pope, and thank goodness I am not as I suffer from vertigo and would go very queasy on that balcony. But poke or no pope, I do believe life begins at forty. And what a marvellous time the forties can be. The children are off your hands, the mortgage is all paid up,

---

198 Doctor and presenter of medical and scientific programmes. She had been married to Tom Stoppard since 1972.

199 Pianist and wife of Robert Runcie, Archbishop of Canterbury since 1980.

200 At this point VW rustled through her cards looking for the answer. In a hand-written script written on prompt cards she wrote: 'Well the question was answered once and for all by his Holiness Pope John Paul quite recently on *Woman's Hour*, but unfortunately I switched off after *Listening Corner* and missed it.' But she drew a line through it.

and sex is all over and done with. So many exciting opportunities have come my way in my fortieth decade I could not have imagined when I was earlier. You may think a divorce after twenty-six years of marriage would not be very nice particularly but I look on the bright side. I use much less milk and housework is halved in my bedsit.

So to sum up, life begins at forty. It certainly did began for me at that juncture. I took up windsurfing, stamp-collecting and, most exciting of all, armed robbery.[201] Yes, I was responsible for the unsolved Midland Bank case, the building society job and, most recently, just before our delicious lunch, the very safe here at the Binley Moathouse. So off I go here through the cloakroom window, with my shotgun, and if Betty and Joan would just like to untie all the waitresses I overpowered earlier, perhaps you'll all be able to finally have that coffee. Thank you.

---

201 In the handwritten script her hobby is 'safe breaking'.

11

ALL DAY BREAKFAST

When Victoria returned to sketch comedy in 1992, there were fresh developments in the landscape of television for her to feed on. *Victoria Wood's All Day Breakfast* was inspired by the rise of daytime programmes which packed their many hours of screen time with flimsy items. But there were too many new targets in her crosshairs – telethons, snazzy station ident graphics, the rise of the glamorous weather girl. Alongside an unused final scene for the Romany Roast coffee-ad series, all were consigned to the cutting-room floor.

There had also been a recent spate of period crime dramas, supplementing the regular flow of Agatha Christie adaptations, resulting in 'The Classical Detective'. The longest sketch to be cut was 'Video Diary', which parodied the new style of storytelling on TV in which members of the public invaded their own privacy with a handheld camera.

The only sketch to be excluded that didn't in some way reflect contemporary television was 'Tea Lady'. The show already had two other sketches in which a woman reveals herself to be more powerful or vital than she seems – Victoria as an undercover copper, Julie Walters as a self-pitying pensioner. Space demanded that one of them be sacrificed.

THE CLASSICAL DETECTIVE[202]

Some classy location, Victorian palm house, a country house herb garden, or similar. Classical music playing. Detective Inspector and Harrison stroll, deep in thought.[203]

Detective Inspector: Just suppose, Harrison.

Harrison: Sir.

Detective Inspector: Just suppose George Landerby isn't the brother-in-law, and that Lady Catherine didn't go to New Zealand, and that it was actually the housekeeper who left the answerphone message that sent Paul and Harry to the Riverside Gardens.

Harrison: That's amazing, sir. But what would that mean?

Detective Inspector: I don't know. Bugger.

Female VO: More classical music, with just a tiny bit of murder, on One.

WEATHER 1[204]

Drenched woman in a field.

Woman: Morning! Well, it's raining. (*Looks at sky.*) And I think it's going to carry on raining. That's what it said on the radio anyway.

---

202 There were plenty of crime shows set between the wars to choose from. The final *Miss Marple* starring Joan Hickson was broadcast two days after *ADB*. David Suchet began playing Poirot in 1989, the same year the BBC launched *Campion* starring Peter Davison as a gentleman sleuth who specialises in 'nothing sordid, vulgar, or plebeian'. Then in 1990 came the pilot episode of *The Inspector Alleyn Mysteries*, based on the novels of Ngaio Marsh and featuring a well-born, buttoned-down copper.

203 David Hargreaves and Richard Albrecht.

204 In 1989 *TV-am* employed Ulrika Jonsson, a half-Swedish twenty-two-year-old, as its weather girl. In 1992 she moved from meteorology to *Gladiators*. The weather girl was played by VW.

WEATHER 2

Windblown woman on roof of high building.
Woman: Hello! Well, it's very windy as you can see! But that's maybe
    because we're very high up here. It may not be windy down
    there.
Pause.
    I don't like to look.
Pause.
    Bye!

TEA LADY

Boardroom. Little old lady[205] in pinnie serving tea from wheel trolley.
Men queue up. They take their tea in turn and sit down.
Little Old Lady: There you go, Mr Richard, not too milky, two sugars,
    and I've kept you a bit of Swiss roll. Accounts were after it, I said
    no – black coffee, Mr Thomson, you want something sugary
    with that – these are nice – go on, you're too thin! There's
    your strong one, Alan, it's a bit full, don't slop it or we will
    be in trouble. Last again, Mr Buckeridge, it's all tannin is this
    now, never mind, live dangerously! Right – everybody happy?
    OK?
She takes off apron and sits at head of table.
    Now, we must thrash out this Canary Wharf takeover.

---

205 JW.

MINI-TELETHON

Female presenter[206] *in sports stadium or field, next to girl in wheelchair in tracksuit.*

Presenter: Yes, Gordon – the fun promises to be fast and furious very shortly, lots of things planned with jellies and buckets of water, all raising lots of lovely money we hope for poor poor people in wheelchairs. People like Daisy here – you're in a wheelchair aren't you, Daisy? – jolly good for you! Anyway, you look jolly cosy in there – well done!

SONARA TWO[207]

Same set as Sonara One, dim lights. Woman leaving, putting on coat, collecting her things etc.

Woman: I've told you about Sonara, the lighter, fresher towel for today's busy lifestyle. But now I've discovered Sonara Two – just as daintily effective, but now with a unique new feature – wings! Wings that cling cosily to your underwear, giving you that extra confidence.

Checks hat in mirror and turns to camera.

Sonara Two – the one with the wings.

She turns to leave and is lifted Peter Pan style to the nearest windowsill. She climbs down.

They don't suit everybody!

---

206 VW.

207 This was a companion to an ad that was used in *ADB* featuring an executive woman played by CI: 'I want a towel that's light, comfortable to wear, yet strong enough to withstand leaks no matter how much blue ink I pour into it.'

COFFEE 3[208]

Beautiful graveyard. Woman stands by gravestone, tears in her eyes. Amos, the older gardener, passes by with a wheelbarrow of leaves.

Amos: Mrs Beech.

Woman: Lovely bonfire.

Amos: That's right. It has the dark roast smoky aroma I associate with only the best filter coffee.

Woman: Oh don't.

Amos: You made him a good wife.

Woman: I don't know about that, but I made him a wonderful cup of coffee.

They stare down at the headstone. It says:

John Beech

1959–1992

He really appreciated the true smoky flavour of Romany Roast

Woman smiles as she takes off the top of her thermos.

Woman: Join me, Amos?

VIDEO DIARY

Scene 1.

Small, bright modern kitchen. Caroline is unpacking a big carton marked BBC GET WELL SOON SHOW! She is taking out scales, vitamins, bran, juicer etc., all marked with the GET WELL SOON logo.

Caroline:[209] Well, I'm Caroline and I'm taking part in *The BBC Get*

---

208 In the first of two ads edited together and shown in *ADB*, a couple played by Geraldine Alexander and Nicholas Pritchard meet in a doctor's waiting room and take a fancy to each other over a cup of Romany Roast. In Coffee 2 they are married but he is dying in hospital and taking his Romany Roast by intravenous drip. The ads parodied the saga of the couple in the Gold Blend ads that had been running since 1987. VW had only recently fronted an ad for Maxwell House.

209 Lill Roughley. VW first came across her in the summer of 1977 when she and

Well Soon Show; my husband and I have agreed to follow a low-fat, high-fibre diet, cut down on alcohol and take regular exercise for six weeks. Our surname is Fat, F.A.T., it's a bit of an unfortunate name, the girl at the BBC, Naomi, she's calling us 'The Fat Family', I find that a bit depressing, but – we're all for it, new lifestyle and et cetera, and I'm keeping this video account of how we go on. (*She looks to door.*) Are you coming in?

Derek (*OOV*):[210] Not till you switch that thing off.

Caroline: I'm just unpacking the carton.

Derek (*OOV*): Bully for you, I'm off out.

Door slam.

Caroline: That's Derek, my husband. He's quite stressed. He manufactures washing machine coin slots for launderettes – you know the kind that jam. But his real love is wing-nuts.

SCENE 2.

The bedroom. Derek in bed reading a Peter Alliss[211] book, Caroline on the edge of the bed in her dressing gown.

Caroline: Well, we've been on the plan for a week now – I've lost three pounds, I'm feeling much better; I don't think Derek's weighed himself yet.

GD were in an end-of-the-pier show in Morecambe. 'Lill was superb,' says GD. 'She caught Vic's eye and they renewed their friendship that Christmas when Lill and I were in *Dick Whittington* at the Duke's Playhouse in Lancaster.' VW gave her substantial things to do in *ASOTV* and several of the 1989 half-hour plays. In *Mens Sana Thingummy Doodah* she plays a woman who, like Caroline, is trying to lose weight. Although 'Video Diary' was cut, limiting her contribution to three smaller cameos, in the closing credits Lill Roughley's name was listed alongside the core regulars. Her most indelible performance came as a fiery mother in *DL*: 'Answer me one question, luv. Where's my Clint?'

210 DP.

211 Long-serving golf commentator, and the very embodiment of conservative Middle England.

Derek: No.

Caroline: We've been given a sex manual – a nice one – by the BBC
– to sort of see if we can enhance our sex life at the same time,
but I don't think Derek's too keen.

Derek: I'm not.

Caroline: I'd quite like to try something different.

Derek gives her a look.

Caroline: Put the romance back.

Derek: Romance – that was what you were after with the driving
instructor, was it?

Nasty silence.

Caroline: Well, anyway, I've lost three pounds.

Scene 3.

*Small BBC office. Naomi (twenties)[212] is pouring coffee for Derek and
Caroline, while muttering earnestly at Derek.*

Caroline: Week three, and we're here at the BBC because they're a
little bit concerned that Derek isn't cooperating with the
experiment – he's not doing the diet, or the exercise, and he's
broken the scales. They've had this very good idea about the
Fat Family, I understand that – it makes me feel about so high
but – but obviously they don't have money to splash around
these days – they're very keen that the project works out. How's
the discussion coming, Naomi?

Naomi: I think the problem is Derek doesn't really see the point of a
healthy lifestyle.

Caroline: But, darling, don't you want us to stay healthy and active
into our eighties?

Derek: No, I don't. I've nothing to live for, why would I want to drag
it out?

Caroline: Don't make me cry on video, Derek.

Derek: Crying has no effect on me, I'm afraid. Not since Harrogate.

---

212 Emma Bernard.

Caroline: I've told you, he was putting on calamine lotion!

Naomi: Perhaps if Derek could just try the exercise, and maybe keep the skins on the potatoes.

Derek (*getting up*): Yes, alright – I'll see you Thursday. (*He leaves frame.*) I'm off to Barrow.

Caroline: And will you see Audrey?

Derek: Hope so.

Caroline: She's no better than a prostitute.

Derek (*back in frame, putting his coat on*): Are you barmy? She is a prostitute. And you get a decent cup of tea after.

He leaves frame. Door bangs.

Naomi (*getting on phone*): So we'll book Derek in at the gym.

Caroline: Super, Naomi. (*Glumly.*) And I've lost another two pounds, and an inch off each thigh – I'm really feeling on top of the world.

SCENE 4.

The living room.

Caroline (*pedalling away on exercise bike*): Week four, and the good news is Derek has really taken to the gym in a big way and has made so many friends.

She gets off bike and goes over to the seating area where Derek is in the middle of a heavy discussion with a group of male friends.

Colin (*in midflow*): Sexual preferences you're born with – dealing with those preferences is a life choice.

Derek: I get you, Colin.

Martin: The door's there to be opened, Derek.

Derek nods thoughtfully.

Caroline: Anyone for a Diet Vimto?

Derek: So you can be gay and still make wing-nuts?

Colin: Oh, any kind of light engineering . . .

Caroline moves to dining table covered with remains of dinner.

Caroline: And the other good thing is we both love this new oil-free coleslaw.

Scene 5.

The kitchen. Most of the kitchen contents are in packing cases, some china still out to be packed. Teapots and biscuits on the table. Caroline is eating biscuits.

Caroline: Well, it's not been such a good week for me, food wise. There's been rather a lot to do with the sale of the house going through so quickly. I've been having a lot of those white sliced loaves, and the big pork pies with the hard-boiled egg in the middle. But they say smoking keeps your weight down, and I always have a gin and slimline tonic . . .

Alan, Derek's boyfriend, in with a couple of empty mugs.

Alan: OK, Caroline. Upstairs is clear – Derek's just packing the car – he's having the exercise bike!

Caroline: Yes, that's fine, Alan.

Alan: And you've got our address.

Caroline: The Old Bakery . . .

Ray, removal man, in.

Ray:[213] I can pack the rest of this china, yeah?

Caroline: Mm, do.

Alan: Anyway, we'll come and find you once the car's packed.

Alan out.

Caroline (*through biscuit*): Alan's macrobiotic. (*To man.*) Biscuit? They're opening a wholemeal creperie near Bury St Edmunds. I don't think Derek'd cross the road to stamp out a coin slot these days.

Ray: Not very jammy, these dodgers.

Caroline: I thought that. It'll be something to do with the Common Market.

---

213 Bryan Burdon. The sketch equivalent of a spear-carrier, he played half a dozen handymen and oddjobbers for VW. The fearsome Marion Clune removes his chewing gum on set in 'The Making of *Acorn Antiques*'. His best role was Jim in *Staying In* (1989), a miner turned painter of miners who can't do noses: 'That's why I paint welders.'

Derek enters in new enlightened clothes.

Derek: I'm off, then. Sorry we never managed to touch base on a fundamental level, I feel we must blame society's powerful conditioning for that one.

Caroline: Your pyjamas are in the tumbler.

Derek: I've let go, pyjama wise. I prefer the rough male kiss—

Caroline: Of the blanket. Yes, I know that poem.

Derek: No, of Alan.

Caroline: Oh.

Derek (*out*): Bye then.

Ray (*by BBC carton*): What have I to do with this, love?

Caroline (*breaking down*): I don't know!

Ray: Hey, cheer up. Have a custard cream; the crumbly texture of the biscuit base is a little disappointing but the filling has the tang of real vanilla.

Caroline eats it gratefully.

Scene 6.

The counter of CAROLINE'S COOKIES. Caroline and Ray side by side in bright red uniforms and little hats.

Caroline: Well, this is the last week of my video diary – Ray and I have opened this very successful homemade cookie outlet, with plans for seventeen more. I've put on half a stone, I'm ecstatically happy, and I have a very full relationship with Ray, all over the house.

Ray: Not in the kitchen.

Caroline: Oh no, we couldn't risk something dropping into the mixer.

Naomi comes in from the back, same uniform.

Naomi: The double choc chip are ready for testing. (*Goes back in.*)

Caroline: Two secs, Naomi. Naomi was fired from the BBC when the Get Well Soon project collapsed, in fact the BBC may have to close down, so much money was spent. So – (*calls*) – what do I do, Naomi, now – just switch off and send it back?

Fade sound.

Ray: I can pack it up.
Caroline: Of course you can, sweetheart.

STATION IDENTS

1.

An upright piano, beautifully painted in glossy pastel colours, including the keyboard. To sophisticated 1922 music, a Siamese cat walks along the keyboard, a breeze riffles the pages of the music on the piano, it blows open at a page saying 'BBC One'.

2.

As above, only another take, so the cat's walk and the riffling of the music are very slightly different.

3.

As above, but the cat is just sitting on the piano, head turned to one side. We hear the cat's voice (male).
Cat: Well, my friend's in *Coronation Street*, you know the cat on the
roof, well the producer on that – oh here we go, back along the
bloody keyboard.
He walks, the breeze blows the music to reveal the final credits.

12

SOUNDING OFF

Whenever Victoria spoke in public, her audience naturally expected to be entertained. What they also got, far more than when she was working as a stand-up, was a version of the truth. There was less of a requirement to misshape the facts of her life into an entertaining fabrication. Instead, she used such opportunities as came her way to tell her story and impart only the mildest top spin.

An invitation to give such a speech came in November 1989 when Victoria was awarded an honorary doctorate of letters by Lancaster University. She knew the city well. Having lived in the area for a dozen years, she had only just moved to London when she found herself returning to give a speech of thanks. Her parents were in the audience, as were the local press.

Victoria was then given honorary degrees by the universities of Sunderland (1994) and Bolton (1995). There is no record of the speech she gave at the former, while at the latter she wasn't invited to speak. In 1996 her own alma mater offered her an honorary DLitt. In her address she did not mention that she had left Birmingham University in 1974 with a pass degree without honours. She delivered the speech using four cards bearing notes. Under headlines in upper case ('LEOTARDS LOOMED V LARGE', 'HERE I AM, 43') she wrote further prompts ('tank top, 2.50 a week, Baby Belling', 'marijuana/

Victoria with producer Geoff Posner on location shooting the first series of *As Seen on TV*.

With fellow cover stars Susie Blake and Duncan Preston at a *Radio Times* reception in 1987.

Celia Imrie and John Nettleton pause for a thought about faith. There was no room for the sketch in the *As Seen on TV Special*.

Album snaps from 1987 . . .

. . . and 1990

'Parading around with a cushion on my head': Victoria receives an honorary doctorate of letters from Lancaster University in 1989.

'No one'll notice me . . . cos I'm wearin black, aren't I?' Susan the Roadie backstage.

By the time Victoria toured in 1993, she was relying on fewer new stage characters.

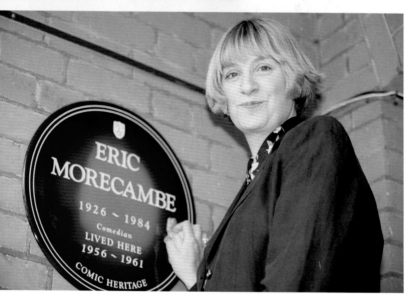

'He made you feel better about being on this miserable old planet.' Victoria unveils the Eric Morecambe blue plaque in 1995.

Dressing room, Sheffield City Hall, 1996.

With producer Jemma Rodgers on the set of *All the Trimmings* in 2000.

Kate Robbins was down to play a Geordie battleaxe in 'The House of Lolly Goggins'.

A group snap of (from left) Jason Watkins, Victoria, Christopher Dean, Julie Walters and Jayne Torvill during the shoot for 'Beyond the Marigolds: What Mrs Overall Did Next . . .'.

'And bang that was Whitney – in love.' In a photo booth at the wedding in 2013 of Jonny Campbell and Beth Willis, the bride had herself snapped with the author of 'Whitney's Wedding'. It was to be Victoria's last comic turn.

interesting conv'). The speech was subsequently published in the university magazine.[214]

A year earlier Victoria gave a slightly different sort of speech at the invitation of Eric Morecambe's widow Joan and their son Gary. The occasion was the unveiling of a blue plaque commemorating the comedian outside his old home in North Finchley. Victoria made reference to a museum of comedy in Morecambe that was in the planning but never came to fruition.

In 1997 she paid tribute to a less public figure. Geoffrey Strachan first published words by Victoria when a book commemorating *The Secret Policeman's Other Ball* came out in 1981. Together they brought out seven books, culminating in *Chunky* in 1996. To mark his retirement, Methuen invited authors and artists to contribute to a miscellany of tributes. Victoria submitted three verses which riffed on the spelling of her publisher's frequently mispronounced surname.

---

214 VW was given two more honorary degrees: in 1998 she was made a master of science by UMIST, the University of Manchester Institute of Science and Technology, and Manchester University made her a doctor of letters in 2007. She was probably proudest, in the same year, to accept an honorary fellowship from the Royal Academy of Music.

ON ACCEPTING AN HONORARY DEGREE AT LANCASTER UNIVERSITY

Your Royal Highness,[215] members of the university, lords, ladies and gentlemen, on behalf of Sister Aine, Mr Smith[216] and myself, I would just like to thank the university for the honour they've conferred on us this afternoon.

When I was coming up on the train this morning, I was trying to think about what I was going to say – it was a bit hard to concentrate with the usual frustrated broadcaster in the guard's van, and he had to be replaced at a moment's notice by Janice in the buffet who did a twenty-minute stream of consciousness about hot snacks cold snacks and please tend the correct money to oblige.

But I was thinking what a good thing it was to be parading round with a cushion on my head,[217] and what a funny job I've got anyway, and generally brooding and staring out of the window and thinking, Oh blimey, we're at Oxenholme.

You see, when I was at school I was advised by an English teacher not to be a performer but to go into journalism. If I'd taken any notice of her, I could have been sitting round the back with a notebook, getting everybody's names wrong for the *Lancaster Guardian*. They're very keen on advising people at school, aren't they? I was always being advised to do things like shut up, and go back and walk, and go out and stand in the corridor. I spent so much time in the corridor, when I was at a school reunion a couple of weeks ago, the only person who recognised me was the cleaner.[218]

---

215 Princess Alexandra, Chancellor of Lancaster University from 1964 to 2004.
216 VW's fellow graduands were Sister Aine Cox, the founder of a local hospice, and Robert Smith, a vulcanologist.
217 Part of the doctoral wardrobe, supplied by the university.
218 This joke made its way into her live set when she went out on tour a few months later.

Anyway, I didn't take the advice of this teacher because she was so old and out of touch – she was about thirty-two – because I wanted to go out and make people laugh. And it's great being an entertainer – I have that written in my passport – though I always worry one day I'll come through passport control at the airport, and the man in a peaked cap will give me a pitying look and cross it out.

But it is a wonderful job – like most things it has its low points – like being driven through the streets of London in a horse-drawn carriage dressed as Father Christmas sitting between Jeremy Beadle and one of the hostesses from *Sale of the Century*.[219] Doing a show in Macclesfield and finding that 87 per cent of the audience is Danish. Doing a cabaret as I did two nights ago in the Imperial War Museum, trying to fit the piano between a tank and an anti-aircraft gun. I couldn't concentrate – I kept worrying somebody might mistake a Polaris missile for a novelty ashtray.

But it has lovely high points too, this job – like spending a whole day filming a chocolate commercial. They said, 'You don't have to eat it every take, just a little bite and spit it out.' I said, 'No, you're alright.'

And I've been lucky so far with the people I've worked with, and we've picked up the odd prize along the way. But this degree today, it really came out of the blue. It was such a thrill when I read the letter – when I read it properly, I should say – I've not really had much to do with the university. I used to swim in the pool here and I thought perhaps they were letting me know I'd left my goggles in the ladies' changing room.

But I do appreciate the honour you've paid me today, and on behalf of Sister Aine and Mr Smith I can only say it again – thank you.

---

219 At a photoshoot in Covent Garden for the Christmas 1981 edition of *TV Times*, VW and JW were joined by – among others – Russ Abbot, Lionel Blair and the presenters of *Game for a Laugh*. One of them, Henry Kelly, would later play himself in 'Winnie's Lucky Day' (*ASOTV*) and *DL*.

UNVEILING THE PLAQUE TO ERIC MORECAMBE

I would just like to thank Comic Heritage for inviting me to do this. I've not had a very good week. I took part in a big charity show for VE night. Charlie Chester[220] refused to go on; he'd just found out the war was over. Gina Lollobrigida brushed past Raquel Welch in the wings and smudged the running order. And Virginia Bottomley[221] got into a padlocked milk churn in a tank of very cold water, so that was alright.

Before I talk about Eric, who is the one we're all thinking about today – today would have been his sixty-ninth birthday, not very old – I have met him. I never worked with him – he was never a barmaid in Birmingham.[222] I met him in the lift in the Midland Hotel, Manchester. That's before it was the Holiday Inn Crowne Plaza. They used to leave old bacon and eggs in the corridor outside the rooms and if you could get it off the plate you could have it. But I was in a lift with him and I did what I really love people doing to me – I said, 'It's Eric Morecambe,' and he went (nod) and got out.[223]

Anyway – I've been asked to announce the launch of a project to build the National Museum of Comedy, in Eric's birthplace – Morecambe – where I used to live. I say live – it was more a question of counting the hours till the chippy opened. The museum will be a celebration of everything to do with comedy. It also plans to build an archive to preserve all aspects of our comic heritage. The project is steaming ahead and they are applying for funding from the Lotteries Commission – hope they get in quick before it all goes on something crucial like Winston Churchill's Y-fronts.

I think it's a brilliant idea to have a comedy museum, and heaven knows Morecambe could do with a new attraction. The Winter

---

220 Comedian (1914–1997).

221 Secretary of State for Health in John Major's government from 1992. Two months after this speech she was demoted to Secretary of State for National Heritage.

222 VW worked as a barmaid in The Sportsman in Harborne Road in Edgbaston in the summer of 1973. It was her only job before she became an entertainer.

223 In another – and more plausible – version of the story Eric Morecambe did speak, if only to say, 'It's that girl!'

Gardens hasn't had a show for twenty years, both piers have closed down and the Colin Crompton Visitor Centre[224] has never really caught on. Morecambe does have one museum – the Wax Museum – which is three shop dummies labelled the Beverley Sisters and one black shop dummy where they've crossed out Muhammad Ali and written in Lenny Henry.[225]

Morecambe plans to erect a statue of Eric on the seafront – he'll be looking out to sea apparently in birdwatching pose, going 'Bloody hell, there is somebody with their own teeth in Grange-over-Sands.' And supporters of the comedy museum will get one of these eighteen-inch-high bronze miniatures in recognition of their help with the project.[226]

But if you want to know more about it all, there's members of the museum of comedy project around today. If you want to ask them any questions like, 'Are you barmy? Morecambe *is* a comedy museum,' you can't miss them – they're wearing revolving bow ties and going 'boom boom'.

But now I want to say something about the man that I think was one of the very best comedians this century. He had the perfect partner in Ernie Wise – they learnt the craft in the only way that works – performing night after night in front of a live audience – and we had the benefit of all that experience and invention and expertise in all those wonderful television programmes. I never saw Morecambe and Wise live, but Eric's complete mastery of the relationship between the performer and the camera, and the studio audience and the people at home, is an education to anyone like me who is struggling to do the same job.

He was so funny, and so clever, and so inspired, and he had that quality that all great comedians share – he made you feel better

---

224 VW's own stand-up routine about Morecambe, written in 1980 and performed until 1983, owed much to Crompton (1931–1985), a Lancashire comic who described the town as a place where 'they don't bury their dead, they stand them up in bus shelters'.
225 This joke was merely stating the facts. VW first used it in a comic verse for *W&W.*
226 The sculptor of the Eric Morecambe statue was Graham Ibbotson, who would go on to create the statue of VW that stands in Bury. It was unveiled in 2019 by Ted Robbins, who played the impresario Jack Hylton in *Eric & Ernie* (2010).

about being on this miserable old planet. Morecambe and Wise had viewing figures we won't see again unless the Queen Mother marries Max Bygraves.[227] He was loved by millions, really loved and really loved . . .

ON ACCEPTING AN HONORARY DEGREE FROM BIRMINGHAM UNIVERSITY

Pro-Chancellor, Vice-Chancellor, ladies and gentlemen,

It's twenty-five years since I came here for my interview in 1971; I took a taxi from New Street station – it cost 45p and I gave the driver a 50p piece and told him to keep the change, which I thought was pretty damn grown-up. I asked the porter where the Drama Department was, and he said, 'You go down the end of the corridor and follow the sound of screaming.' Then I sat outside the secretary's office and two tall, blonde girls[228] swept past me giving me this smile that said, 'We know all about Stanislavski and you're only from Lancashire.' I sat on this orange plastic chair and thought, Will I ever be sophisticated and knowledgeable and know about Lotte Lenya? Twenty-five years later I have to say, no probably not. Well, they gave me a place . . . They gave me a conditional place. The conditions were I had to get four S levels, clean the toilets and bring £10,000 in used fivers. And I turned up for freshers week and wandered around the campus not realising the number one rule of the Student's Survival Strategy – never make friends with the first girl you meet in the refectory because she will turn out to be either a) a nutcase, b) have a thing about Bamber Gascoigne[229] or c) be engaged to a mechanical engineer. But whatever it is, you'll loathe her after the first five minutes and spend the next three years trying to get rid of her . . . And she'll send you a Christmas card every year until you both die.

---

227 Comedian (1922–2012). Made twenty appearances at the Royal Variety Performance.
228 Jane Wymark and Jane Wynn Owen.
229 The presenter of *University Challenge* on ITV from 1962 to 1987.

My impression of the Drama Department was that it was full of girls whose fathers appeared regularly on television[230] and boys who had leading parts in productions in the National Youth Theatre.[231] My father was an insurance salesman and I had been in the school play, *The Winter's Tale*, the highlight of which for me was when the girl playing Leontes lost her voice and stood on the stage in costume doing the gestures while the dialogue was provided from the side of the stage by the Head of the English Department, Miss Morris, who was 103. This was an alienation technique I think Bertolt Brecht would have been rather keen on.

Of course, in the summer of 1971 I wasn't the glamorous, sophisticated figure that I never became. I had shoulder-length hair parted in the middle, clipped back by two little clips that looked like little polo mints – little white hair slides – and a scoop-neck green T-shirt with elbow patches in a contrasting lime green, loon pants with eighteen-inch flares, a pink acrylic cardigan – £1.99 from British Home Stores – and the *pièce de résistance* – a lavender canvas trenchcoat, which had cost something unbelievable like £13. And this was in the days of galloping inflation when it was not unusual to buy something in a shop, take it to the check-out and by the time you paid for it you couldn't afford it.[232]

I lived in a bedsitter in Lordswood Road which cost me £2.50 a week; for that I got a bed in the window and a lot of green and black wallpaper and the use of the Baby Belling on the landing that used

---

230 Jane Wymark's father Patrick Wymark, who died in 1970, had been in many films and TV dramas in the 1960s. Catherine Ashmore was the daughter of Rosalie Crutchley, who in the early 1970s played Catherine Parr in *The Six Wives of Henry VIII* and *Elizabeth R*.

231 George Irving and, arriving a year later, Robert Howie.

232 This was a favourite joke structure of VW's, often applied to waitresses. *W&W*: 'That girl is so slow. Honestly, you order cheesecake, you get penicillin.' Or the 1987 live show: 'I tipped her a quid. By the time she picked it up it was only worth seventy-five pence.' She also had it in for the Post Office. In a piece from the mid-1980s titled 'Wednesday, or a Month in the Country', VW stands in the queue for three days: 'By the time I reach the counter, the TV licence has gone up twice and my shoes are out of fashion.' And from her 1990 show: 'I had a letter from John Noakes saying my new design for a threepenny stamp had come third.'

to take thirty minutes to heat up a tin of soup. I could never wait that long so I used to drink it cold and hang my stomach over the gas fire.

I've been racking my brains this morning to think of the content of some of the lectures that I sat through and it has all gone – I can't think of anything. I can remember sitting in the small studio watching somebody push a knitting needle through somebody else's head, but whether that was part of the Theatre of Cruelty course or just somebody falling out over a borrowed leotard I'm not sure. You see, leotards loomed very large in the department . . . so did the bodies loom very large most of the time. People were always panicking about their weight. It was not unusual to come across a slumped figure sitting over a cup of Marmite going, 'I've got to lose 12lb by Thursday – Clive has just put a nude scene into *The Importance of Being Earnest*.'[233] But most people's way of losing weight was quite simple; it was to have sex all the time and spend all your grant cheque on an Afghan maxi coat. You may not remember these – they looked fabulous but they smelt terrible when they got wet. If you got four of them in a small room on a rainy day it was like the elephant house. But it was a very funny time in the early Seventies: we had inflation, we had power cuts – the telly went off at ten o'clock at night to save power, everybody just had sex all the time because it was easier than finding a clean cup and making somebody a cup of coffee. We were not political at all. We didn't sit in – we just lay down, really.

The second year I spent sharing a flat in Richmond Hill Road. It was a one-bedroom flat, so I had to go in the living room on a camp bed which used to collapse all the time and my friend[234] used to have to come in the middle of the night and unfold me. Then we lived on Rice Krispies, powdered tomato soup and white sliced bread. Every so often my friend would say, 'We really ought to eat more healthily,' and put honey on the sliced bread – there was a big Seventies myth that honey was good for you. This went along with the other Seventies

233 Clive Barker, drama department lecturer. VW was scathing about his wandering hands and exploitation of female students.
234 Jane Wynn Owen.

myths like smoking marijuana makes you an interesting conversationalist. And if you light enough joss-sticks nobody will realise your room is actually in a hall of residence.

I spent my third year in a flat in Priory Road, in a house which is now a private hospital. I can only say I hope they cleaned the bathroom when they took it over. You see hygiene was never very high on our list of priorities; we could take a pause in a Harold Pinter play with the best of them,[235] we could analyse the subtext in a Sean O'Casey but show us a can of Vim and a damp cloth and we were baffled.

But I am here anyway, forty-three, no hair slides, no trenchcoat, still no bloody idea what Stanislavski was all about, still friends with the two blonde girls that passed me that day I came for the interview. I'm glad I was here. I'm glad to be here today. Thank you to the University for the honour that they are granting me today. Thank you to the Government of 1971 who gave me a full grant – will they ever catch on again, I wonder? I'm off now to do what my education has qualified me to do, which is to get laughs from two thousand people at the Cliffs Pavilion, Southend, so if I can lay hands on a 50p piece, I'm getting in a taxi and going back to the station.

Thank you.

TO GEOFFREY

It makes me quite forlachan,
Some are dead like Delius,
Bach, and Williams (Vachan)
Hattie Jacques[236] and Dennis Brain[237]

---

235 'Giving Notes' (*ASOTV*): 'This is our marvellous bard, Barbara, you cannot paraphrase. It's not like Pinter where you can more or less say what you like as long as you leave enough gaps.'

236 Comic actress (1922–1980).

237 Pre-eminent French horn player (1921–1957) who died young in a car crash.

(That one who played the hachan),
Marshall (Arthur),[238] Austen (Jane)
And O'Casey (Sachan).

But one old fave who hasn't conked,
And so no cause to machan,
Is that old bloke from Methuen
Who's been there since the dachan
Of time; of whom it's often said
He is more brains than brachan.
But never were worn corduroys
More elegantly wachan.

Never was one's work received
With apathy or scachan,
Never was one pushed to publish
Cookery or pachan,
But now he plans to bugger off
And soon he will be gachan.
And I for one am sad to see
The back of Geoffrey Strawn.

---

238 One of the captains on *Call My Bluff*. VW was on his team several times between
1981 and 1984 and they corresponded regularly. She chose his collected works as her
book when she first appeared on *Desert Island Discs* in 1987.

13

ALL THE TRIMMINGS

'Don't panic, once I've done a bit more I will be able to see what we don't need and lose it. I think my idea of forty or so weeny items isn't going to happen, I think there will be bigger chunks, and that will probably be a more satisfactory programme to watch, more to get your teeth into.'[239]

Eager to return to sketch comedy for the first time in eight years, in 2000 Victoria planned an ambitious Christmas celebration. As ideas percolated, she kept her producer Jemma Rodgers in the picture. The same fax mentions, tantalisingly, a set of musical items: 'probably I'll lose Lesley Garrett, and just do Jayne Mcdonald [sic],[240] with the Sound of Music, Brassed Off, the Billy Cotton Band Show,[241] and the finale, that will be plenty of music for 45 minutes'. The Lesley Garrett item was no more than an idea for what she referred to as a 'big BBC1 type chummy opera show' but she dropped it to focus on other musical numbers. But the *Sound of Music* sketch was written, and it was only with great regret that Victoria agreed to discard it at the last minute in order to save money.

---

239 Fax to Jemma Rodgers, 14 August 2000.
240 VW never publicly acknowledged that Stacey Leanne Paige was based on Jane McDonald, the breakout star of the BBC One docusoap *The Cruise*.
241 This became 'Keyboard Collywobbles' featuring VW and Anne Reid duetting at the piano.

The recent experience of making *dinnerladies* had been salutary. Though it was a popular triumph, Victoria felt she'd been overtaken by innovative new comedies that did without a studio audience. Thus for her new show her first decision was to shoot everything on film. This meant the choice of what to cull had to be made before it went into production, as it would be wasteful to axe afterwards.[242] As an insurance policy she wrote more than ever. Among the casualties were 'A Bit of Spam', inspired by maverick detective dramas, and 'Where the North Is', which parodied the cockle-warming *Peak Practice*. 'The Herd' was a response to *Big Brother*, on Channel 4 for the first time just as she was starting to write. 'The House of Lolly Goggins', a mega-saga cramming into eight minutes an entire history of Britain in the twentieth century, would have proved far too costly to film. When it came to selection, Victoria's instinct was to favour the scripts which parodied film rather than television, and especially the ones that felt Christmassy. A seasonal parody of *Whistle Down the Wind* was nonetheless dropped, as was another film spoof set in the early 1960s.[243] There were slightly too many sketches set during the Second World War.

At the top of some scripts Victoria listed the names of actors alongside the roles they had been approached to play, and these are included here, although they were often only snapshots, as the casting changed on an almost daily basis. What to keep or cull was partly influenced by the availability of actors. Victoria wrote two sketches featuring James Bond and hooked Roger Moore to star in one of them, but Pierce Brosnan's Hollywood agent did not share his client's enthusiasm for taking the mickey out of the franchise.

---

242 The exception was the short skits for '1940s Newsreel' in which JW and VW play a mother and daughter from the East End who are cheerful in the face of the Luftwaffe. VW kept one of them back for Comic Relief.

243 When making *The Giddy Kipper* in 2010, VW would revisit the atmosphere of *Whistle Down the Wind*, which had also been shot in the Ribble Valley fifty years before.

There was even less room for all these scripts as Victoria expanded the idea of a framing device, of a show within a show. So Delia Smith was not required to share her method of heating baked beans. Nor was Bob Monkhouse called upon to choose his own coffin.

BOND

Int. Day. M's office. M behind desk looking at computers.[244] *Bond enters, brushing snow off his polar anorak.*

M: You managed to survive intact, I see.

Bond (*ironically*): Luckily, the nuclear winter was a little short this year.

M: You found someone to keep you warm, I gather.

Bond looks ironical.

I congratulate you, James. Not many men could consummate a relationship with a woman while they were bound back to back with steel rope, dangling from a rocket launcher.

Bond (*shrugs*): Don't forget, I was at public school.

M: Hang your coat up.

Bond: Thanks.

M: Use the loop, please, we don't hang by hoods here. Now – have you heard of toast?

Bond (*not sure*): The Telecommunications Observation and Surveillance Taskforce?

M: No, it's hot bread that's gone brown. People have it for breakfast.

Bond (*suggestively*): I'd like to try it.

M: The Russians have come up with a lethal device: once activated, it sends an infra-red micro laser beam to every toaster made after 1994.[245]

Bond: Will it kill?

M: Oh yes. If we don't stop them, James, in twelve hours everyone who eats toast will be dead. (*To intercom.*) Send in Q, please, Miss Moneypenny.

Bond: But people on diets would be safe.

---

244 Judi Dench was approached about appearing in other sketches, but not this one.
245 See also 'Email on Toast', p. 231.

M: Totally. But if you want to live in a world full of whingers with bad breath, I don't.[246]

Q in, with trolley of equipment.

Q: Now pay attention, 007. Hair mousse? Usual thing, body, shine, style that lasts all day ... rub some into the palm of your hand ... now put your palm on that slice of bread.

Bond does so, a screen starts beeping and flashing.

We'll pick up that signal from anywhere in the world. But be warned, it won't work on granary.

M (*reading screen*): We're losing time.

Q: Very well. X-ray contact lenses. Good for checking concealed weapons and looking at girls' underwear. Tube of wine gums, third one down is a self-inflating nuclear submarine. Gas-sensitive ballerina music box, any gas around, she'll start to spin and you'll hear 'Dance Ballerina Dance' as popularised by Nat King Cole.

M: You must go, Bond.

Q: Just this. It's a suppository.[247] Once inserted it will read computer files, in fact any video images will be projected directly onto the back of the eyeball.

M: Good luck, James.

He leaves, taking some of the things with him. M looks at Q and picks up the suppository.

M: He forgot this.

Q (*hurrying away*): It's only a sample, keep it. Whoops.

There is a slight collision as the tea lady[248] comes in with the trolley. She pushes it in a slow and challenging manner.

M: You're very late.

Tea Lady (*in similar ironic tones*): I know. It was unavoidable, the detention block had run out of Garibaldis. (*She looks around.*) This hasn't changed.

---

246 'Bond' is an odd place to find the most caustic joke VW ever made about dieting.
247 See also *ATT*'s Jane Austen spoof 'Plots and Proposals': 'Suppose? Suppose? I find you very suppository, miss!'
248 VW.

M: No. I boxed the pipes in the ladies' lav, but basically it's as you left it.

Tea Lady: Tea? (*She puts in sweeteners.*)

M: I don't take sweeteners.

Tea Lady: Don't worry, they're a new form of paralysis tablet, and unlike sweeteners, there's no bitter aftertaste. (*She gives M the tea.*)

M: I suppose it's no use my screaming for help.

Tea Lady: No use whatever. I believe it was your idea to staff the secretarial block entirely from women with hearing difficulties. It wasn't too taxing to block the frequencies of the hearing aids. Scream away, they won't hear a darn thing.

M: How long will I take to die?

Tea Lady (*looking in biscuit tin*): That depends how long it takes my little killer ants to chew through to your organs. The underwire of your bra might slow them up a bit.

M: So if I drink this tea, I'm dead.

Tea Lady: I'm so sorry, were you hoping to live?

M drinks the tea and starts to become paralysed. Tea lady looks around, sees the suppository and does something with it we can't see.

Tea Lady: Oh, Bridges of Madison County.

THE HERD

Ext. Day. Field of cows.

VO: Tonight on *The Herd*. Does Tania suspect the others are getting tired of her manipulative behaviour?

One cow looks over at group of cows.

        Is Emily still mad with Kaz?

CU of other cows.

        And will Alisha and Fran sort out that very special meal?

Two cows eating grass.

        The Herd. Live tonight and every night on the internet.

Huge close-up of cow's eye with security cameras reflected in them. Website
          address over.
www.theherd.co.uk[249]

A BIT OF SPAM[250]

Spam, middle-aged down-at-heel police detective: Michael Gambon
Lady Chief Constable: Penelope Wilton
Jan, in bakery: Victoria Wood
Pikelet, detective sergeant: Andrew Dunn
TV VO: Alan Titchmarsh
Ma: Clarissa Dickson Wright
Snout: Richard E Grant

VO: Last week on *A Bit of Spam*.
Int. Day. Chief Constable's office.
Lady Chief Constable: You were a brilliant detective, Spam, but look
          at you now – bitter, twisted and covered in crumbs – get out!
Spam bites into a baguette, stricken.

*Int. Day. Spam's hall. Wendy, his wife, is putting on coat, grabbing car
keys, etc.*
Wendy: I can't live like this, Derek, you leave the fridge door open,
          you roll in at three o'clock in the morning stinking of egg may-
          onnaise – I think I've got a loaf of bread – open the breadbin
          – it's gone! What happened to my needs, Derek? Do you never
          think I might like a slice of toast of a morning?
Spam (*eats*): I can change, Wendy.
Wendy: Do me a favour, Spam – skip the rest – I've heard it all before.

---

249 At the time of writing, the domain name remains available.
250 On television there had been a spate of grumpy or dysfunctional detectives often
equipped with some sort of quirk – among them *Inspector Morse*, *Prime Suspect*, *Dalziel
and Pascoe* – but at the top of the script VW wrote: 'Film/Contemporary Police Dra-
ma/ref Touch of Frost'.

She leaves. He calls after her despairingly.

Spam: Wendy! Whoops, tomato.

He pops a stray piece from his tie into his mouth.

Int. Day. Tiny café/bakery. Spam sits at tiny table, with coffee. Table is covered in debris, sandwich wrappers, etc.

Spam (*not looking up*): Another ham and pickle please, Jan.

Jan (*kindly*): Don't you think you've had enough?

He puts his head in his hands. Jan comes out from behind the counter.

>Look – I know this is none of my business – but have you ever thought of going to a—

Spam: A salad bar? Yeah, I've thought of it. Sometimes I've even got as far as choosing size of bowl, but—

Jan: I'll take you. It's not all lettuce leaves, you know – you can get quite big greasy lumps of potato.

Spam (*gently*): I know. You're a nice woman, Jan. But if I'm going to a salad bar, I'll go on my own.

Jan (*pointing to own face*): You've got brown sauce—

Spam (*it's no more than he expected*): I'll have it later. Take care of yourself, Jan.

Jan: And you, Spam.

She watches him leave.

Ext. Day. Spam's front door. He is in middle of heated argument with his detective sergeant, Pikelet, a fortyish man.

Pikelet: The force needs you, sir!

Spam: It's all over, Pikelet! Find another detective inspector! I've had it. Do you know what I do when I get up? I put both legs down one leg of my underpants and guess what – I stay like that all bloody day. Now go home, Pikelet – you're wasting your time.

Pikelet: I thought you were a copper's copper, sir – seems I was wrong.

He turns and leaves. Spam leans against the door frame.

Spam: You bloody fool, Spam.

Music.

Title caption: A BIT OF SPAM.

Int. Night. Spam's totally bare living room, just bare floorboards, walls, one box for him to sit on, and one with a small TV on it. The TV has sound working but just snow for a picture. Spam is eating a Ginsters pastry with the cellophane on.

TV VO (*Alan Titchmarsh*[251]): And of course the nice thing about concrete is, you'll never have to weed it.

Lady Chief Constable appears in doorway. Spam jumps up and turns off the TV.

Lady Chief Constable: I tried knocking on the door, but there wasn't one.

Spam: No my, er, wife took it.

Lady Chief Constable: I've just come from the station, Spam.

Spam: Which station, ma'am?

Lady Chief Constable: The police station. A big – what *is* that word? – 'crime' has been committed.

Spam: What, by villains?

Lady Chief Constable: There's villains, shooters, fences, grasses, my laddos having it away on their toes – it's bad.

Spam nods.

I need you to solve it for me.

Spam: I'm suspended, ma'am.

Pause. She looks around the room even though there's nothing to look at.

Lady Chief Constable: It seemed so simple at Police College, didn't it, Derek? Do you remember – when we were in the Brutality Squad?

They exchange a look.

Spam: I loved you, Chris.[252]

Lady Chief Constable: Look – I'll do a deal – I can get you back on the strength – no questions asked—

---

251 Alan Titchmarsh appeared as a gardener in 'Plots and Proposals'. In the Comic Relief sketch 'Wetty Hainthrop Investigates' (1999) he played his jealous twin Adam Titchmarsh.

252 The idea of pairing Michael Gambon and Penelope Wilton as old flames would have brought echoes of Pinter at his most romantic: in 1978 at the National Theatre they played the extramarital lovers Jerry and Emma in the original production of *Betrayal*.

Spam: But—

Lady Chief Constable: But – you have to have this place totally furnished and decorated – tastefully – by tea-time tomorrow – pelmets, scatter mats, dados—

Spam (*moved*): Thanks. Do you want to – stay? I could probably lay my hands on a tin of peas?

Lady Chief Constable (*fighting her softer side*): You can't open the same tin twice, Derek. Tea-time tomorrow.

VO: Next week on *A Bit of Spam*.

Int. Day. Small carpet shop. Spam shoves face into frightened face of Mr Crangle.

Spam: I'm losing patience with you, Mr Crangle. First you say an eighty twenty twist will do me all over the house, and now, apparently, I need something a little bit more heavy duty for the hall. And I think I'd like to hear quite a bit more about this so-called free underlay . . .

Mr Crangle nods, terrified.

Int. Night. Elaborately decorated feminine bedroom, all done cheaply. Spam interrogates sulky girl in kimono, Mandy, with black eye.

Spam: Nice place you've got here, Mandy.

Mandy: I'm a high-class call girl, Mr Spam, we're well paid.

Spam: Come off it, Mandy – you haven't worked in weeks – you've been off work with a cold – who paid for all this?

Mandy: I—

Spam: And how did you get that black eye?

Mandy: My pimp lost his rag.

Spam: Your pimp's been in Parkhurst since Christmas. (*Wheels round suddenly.*) It was a stencilling brush, wasn't it—

Mandy: No—

Spam: You were doing that top corner and it fell out of your hand—

Mandy: I—

Spam: You've decorated this whole place on a budget, haven't you, Mandy?

Mandy (*gives in*): Yeah, alright. I never meant to get involved – someone came round with a wallpaper border – I just thought I'd try it – well for a joke – I'd heard about people brightening up a north-facing wall.

Spam (*resigned*): And then, don't tell me – you had to do the other three walls—

Mandy: I had to, Mr Spam! Doing one made the other walls seem faded and lacklustre. You get sucked in – before you know where you are you're updating your curtains and giving a new lease of life to the bathroom with deckchair stripes in ice-cream pastels!

She bursts into tears. Spam pats her awkwardly. He gets his notebook.

Spam: OK, Mandy. Let's start at the beginning, shall we?

She nods.

You're stuck with an avocado bathroom suite – what choice of paint will best bring it into the twenty-first century?

Int. Day. Small egg and chips style café. Snout, a thin, shifty, dishevelled interior decorator turned informer is in one corner with a cup of tea. Spam is at the counter, paying for his teas.

Spam: What's the special, Ma?

Ma: Truffle-fed porcupine slow roasted with a giblet coulis.[253]

Spam: I'm a bit pushed for time.

Ma: Donkey?

Spam: Yeah, take away.

---

253 VW liked a pretentious recipe. Compare and contrast with the choice on offer at the Elbow Café in 'Just an Ordinary Man' (*ASOTV*): faggots in rum sauce, liver au poivre, sweet and sour haddock, or mixed grill. In 'Just an Ordinary School' the girls are served 'boring old' brochet aux champignons de rosée. In *Cakes on a Train*, the film script VW was working on at the end of her life, the main characters gather in a swanky restaurant:

Beautiful Waitress: Excuse me, I'm Tia and I'll be describing your bread for you today.

Gareth: Right.

Beautiful Waitress: We have a jewelled Persian flat bread, a mandelbrod—

Bertie: Sorry, what is that?

Beautiful Waitress: It's very like a mandelscorper. Perhaps a little more heavily textured. We have our East Meets West watercress naan, salted pretzel shards and our South African Yiddish kitkekaka.

He sits down opposite Snout.

Ma (*shouts to back*): Donkey in a bun, to go!

Snout: What is it, Mr Spam – I don't know nothing, honest.

Spam: I need some of these.

From a filthy old cloth he unwraps a small edging tile.

Snout (*panicking*): For God's sake, Mr Spam – do you want to get us both arrested? They haven't even got these at the Ideal Home Exhibition.

Spam (*out of corner of mouth*): Do you recognise it?

Snout (*reluctantly*): Well it's a hand-fired Tuscany rope twist edging tiles, isn't it?

Spam: What shade?

Snout (*whining*): I dunno, Mr Spam – they're bringing out new colour ranges all the time.

Spam: What shade?

Snout: Look – it's Azure Blue or Seascape – but—

Spam gets up to leave.

Spam: Ma! I'll skip the donkey!

End on puzzled face of Ma.

CHOOSE YOUR COFFIN

Bob stands by writing desk covered in family photos, hint of cosy middle-class study behind. He's looking at a brochure.

Caption: BOB MONKHOUSE.

Bob: Hi! I'm Bob Monkhouse and I'm ordering my coffin now, while I am still alive. Makes sense, doesn't it? That way I'm relieving loved ones of extra stress and worry, *and* I'm getting a coffin *I* want with the handles *I* like.

One phone call now, then when you die, the coffin you choose will be delivered anywhere in the UK free of charge in time for your funeral.

Caption: FOR EIRE AND I.O.M. ADD £3.95.

Order a brochure now, no salesman will call, and you won't need a medical, because you'll be dead. Ciao!

UP THE CANAL, SATURDAY[254]

Val, girl, twenties: Caroline Aherne? Maxine Peake?
Mum: Victoria Wood
Ronald, her boyfriend: Jim Broadbent
Prissy neighbour: Anne Reid
Mrs Barraclough, abortionist: Julie Walters
Mr Barraclough: Bob Monkhouse

Ext. Day. Urban stretch of canal, Manchester, 1962. Val, a blonde girl in her twenties, in jeans and reefer jacket, wanders along, swinging her bag. Vera, Val's mum, appears on the horizon, a tarty middle-aged woman in winkle pickers and laddered stockings. She's furious.

Vera: Come on, Val!

Val (*sulkily*): What?

Vera: Ronald's waiting, come on! Wandering about like, a – ooh never
 mind! Shift yourself, come on!

They set off.

Ext. Day. Their run-down street. Vera is hurrying Val along.

Vera: And you can put a smile on your face, Val – I can't believe
 Ronald's letting you come with us!

Val: Can I sit in the front?

Vera: Don't be a soft mollock. He can't rummage round my suspend-
 ers if I'm in the back, can he?

Val: I'll be sick.

Vera: You will not, and stop being so awkward.

Val: I feel sick now.

---

254 At the top of the script VW wrote: 'Feature film black and white 1961'. In *ASOTV* she had briefly been this way with a short parody of the new wave of early-Sixties black-and-white British films. Her sketch featuring northern lovers called Barry and Freda even had the same reveal, seeming to be about an unwanted pregnancy before swerving off in another direction: 'You'll just have to tell her t'truth. The whippet got wet, caught cold and died.'

Vera shoots her a significant look, then pushes her into the hall of their house. The house is big, old and neglected, lots of bells by the door.

Vera: Go and put a skirt on and don't show me up!

Int. Day. Vera's tiny cluttered living room. Ronald, a smooth car salesman type, is pouring a drink for himself and Vera.

Ronald: Cheers, my dear. Here's mud in your eye and hairs in your plughole.

Vera: Oh cheers, Ronald! (*Sips.*) Ooh, what have you put in this gin?

Ronald: Brake fluid.

Vera: It's lovely and tangy. (*Laughs, then smooches up to him.*) You do look nice in that car coat, Ronald.

Ronald: Do I? Tell you one thing, Vera, my dear – they're as good as a rug if you're after a spot of outdoor entertainment.

Vera: I don't know what you mean, you sauce box.

Ronald: Come on, Vera – I'm not wearing quick-release shower-resistant cavalry twills by chance, you know. I've heard you used to be pretty free with your favours.

Vera: That was in the war, just doing my bit for the lads. It was quicker than knitting a balaclava.

Ronald: I've heard you're still available.

Vera: It's not my fault they haven't abolished National Service. Anyway – I thought you were different. I thought you might take me out – I thought we could have half a grapefruit somewhere.

Ronald (*reaching for her chest*): They're four bob apiece in Didsbury – will I get back what I'm spending?

Vera (*slapping him*): Get out! You come in here lording it over us with your Ford Anglia and your drip-dry vest – what do you think I am?

Ronald: Let's just say you don't have to work in a pie shop to recognise an old tart.

He pushes her aside and leaves.

Vera: You could at least say, ta-ra!

She bursts into tears, Val appears in doorway, in different blouse, skirt half-zipped up.

Val: Mam—

Vera: You can put your donkey jacket back on – we're not going.

Val: Mam—

Vera (*blowing her nose, recovering*): What's up with you, stood there like a mop and bucket?

Val: It's my skirt – I can't zip it up.

Pause.

Vera: You silly, silly, silly little cow.

Ext. Day. Respectable street of terraced houses. Vera leads Val along, not sure of the way.

Val: Where are we going, Mam?

Vera: There's ways and means of putting these things right. At a price.

She approaches woman, who is scrubbing her path, tight-lipped in head-scarf, curlers and pinnie.

 Excuse me, love – does a Mrs Barraclough live along here?

Woman: Barraclough? Good name for her. Barraclough by name and – (*realises this isn't going to work*) – she's next door, if you can call it a door.

Vera: Thanks for your trouble.

Woman: I hear she does 'alterations'.

Vera: What's that to you?

Woman: Well it's nothing to me, because I'm a respectable woman. I keep my broom on my broom handle, it's a shame your lass here didn't do similar.

Vera: Come on, Val.

They go up adjoining path.

Woman (*going into her own house*): Some of us know how to keep a lid on our dustbins.

She slams the door.

Int. Day. Living room of Barracloughs' house. Neat, tiny, in style of twenty years before. Overdecorated with ornaments, photos etc. Val and Vera sit nervously on edge of chairs. Mr Barraclough, a strange elderly man with dyed black hair and fingerless gloves, comes into the room.

Mr Barraclough: Mrs Barraclough will not be one moment. May I enquire the nature of your business?

Vera: It's private. Ladies' business.

Mr Barraclough: Private ladies' business. We get a lot of that here.

Vera (*slapping Val's hand off her skirt*): Give over picking lint. Are you involved in the business side, Mr Barraclough?

Mr Barraclough: I'm not at the cutting edge, one might say, but someone has to pick up the pieces – is that not so? Ah – I hear my wife – excuse me.

He picks up an enamel bucket with lid and leaves.

Val: I don't want to have it done, Mam!

Vera: Shut up, you daft trollop.

Mrs Barraclough comes in, late-middle-aged, small, respectable, cosy but somehow sinister.

Mrs Barraclough: So sorry to keep you – I had an awkward client in another room.

Val and Vera exchange glances. Mrs Barraclough picks up a framed picture.

      Do you like Filey? Lovely sunsets. Let's talk business.

Vera: This girl's done something she shouldn't.

Mrs Barraclough: Let her talk for herself.

Val: I can't get my zip done up on my skirt.

Mrs Barraclough: Why come to me?

Val: I was given your name. My friend Deirdre.

Mrs Barraclough: Oh I know Deirdre. She's had lot of bother with zips, hasn't she? (*Pause – she sizes them up.*) Well, it's cash on the nail, half now and half in ten days when the job's complete. No talking, no paperwork and no comebacks if it doesn't work.

Vera: OK.

Mrs Barraclough (*brisk*): OK. Arnold! Get your skirt off.

Val takes her shoes and skirt off, stands nervously in blouse and under-skirt. Mr Barraclough comes in. Mrs B looks at the skirt.

Mr Barraclough: Need a hand, my dear?

Mrs Barraclough (*examining zip*): Nine-inch zip Arnold, please, it's a funny blue but we might get close.

Mr Barraclough (*leaving*): Nine-inch zip, it is.

Mrs Barraclough: We'll sort you out, don't you worry.

Val: Thanks, Mam.

Mrs Barraclough (*unpicking zip*): In a rush, you girls, you get the underskirt caught in the teeth – you tug away . . .

Vera: Oh I've told her.

DELIA'S BACK TO BASICS

Delia's kitchen.

Delia[255] *opens ring pull can of LATENIGHT brand beans, with a handy gadget.*

Delia: I'm using this because I know if you are very idle it can be difficult to pull up the ring by hand – then either put them in a pan—

Super caption: PUT THEM IN A PAN.

Or a very nice way to serve them is eat them straight out of the tin with the spoon you made the tea with.

Super caption: EAT THEM OUT OF THE TIN.

Delia takes used teabag off spoon and wipes it on her hip.

Another nice thing is, you don't have to sit down, just stand anywhere in the kitchen and cram them down your neck while gawping out of the window.

WHISTLE DOWN THE WIND[256]

John, a farmer: Pete Postlethwaite

Mary, his wife: Victoria Wood

Nicholas, a tramp: Michael Gambon

Policeman: Andrew Dunn

---

255 Also in *ATT*, Delia Smith plays a dull cook in 'Plots and Proposals' and 'A Christmas Carol'. For *MLX* she would play herself in 'Beyond the Marigolds: What Mrs Overall Did Next . . .'

256 VW described this as a 'feature film black and white 1961'. Aware that every precious second had to be accounted for, on the typescript she made a note of its duration as three minutes and fifty-four seconds.

Ext. Day. Lancashire moors. A bleak landscape. Amidst open farmland is an isolated stone barn. Silhouetted against the wintry skyline are three children in a line. They approach the barn. They are Susan (twelve), Pauline (nine) and Raymond (seven). They wear old coats, wellies and woolly hats.

Ext. Day. Dirty untidy farmyard. The farmer's wife, Mary, a grim worn woman in her forties, is hanging out huge underpants on the line. Her husband, John, an unshaven rough farmer, is tinkering with a bit of tractor. Mary shades her eyes to see the children better.

Mary: They're off up to that barn again, Susan, Pauline and Raymond. Our children.

John (*spitting*): Barn. They should be int yard with me on Christmas morning, fettling[257] gaskets, not boggering about wi' barns.

Mary: Christmas. Why did you tell our Raymond aged seven Father Christmas would bring him a pedal car?

John: I don't hecking know! Do you think I wanted to end up like this – scratting around to put custard on the table – can't give my own son a pedal car – can't even afford a collar for my damn shirt!

He breaks down, sobbing.

Mary (*going to the back door*): That tramp's still on the loose. Them at Home Farm's missing a red duffel coat and a pair of gum boots. Police reckon he's hiding out round about here somewhere.

Quick cutaway of barn.

John (*still sobbing*): Can't even give him a puppy to drown!

Mary (*in doorway, with plate*): John – someone's taken a mince pie – and some milk!

---

257 A favourite VW word. In 'Brontëburgers', her Haworth Parsonage guide lists wuthering as 'an old Yorkshire word; some other old Yorkshire words are parkin and fettle.' Fettling was on VW's mind as, elsewhere in *ATT*, 'Brassed Up' features the Associated Fettlers and Warp and Weft Adjusters Silver Band.

Ext. Day. The outside of the barn. The children climb the last gate and approach cautiously.

Susan: Have you got the mince pie, our Pauline?

Pauline: Yes, our Susan, and the milk.

Raymond: And then he'll give me a pedal car, won't he, our Susan, like my dad said?

Susan: Stop mithering, our Raymond. Come on.

Pauline: Be quiet though – he might be tired if he's been delivering toys all night.

They open the door.

Int. Day. Inside of barn. Nicholas the tramp lies on straw at the far end. It's very dark but, as the door opens, shafts of light reveal his white hair, and beard, his belted duffel coat, his black wellies with the tops turned over, a blood-stained bandage round his knee. Nearby are two abandoned split-soled boots. The children enter cautiously.

Pauline: Are you awake, Father Christmas?

Nicholas: What? Oh yeah, yeah.

Susan: Did you get all your presents delivered?

Nicholas: Eh? Yes I did.

Raymond: Where's your reindeer?

Susan: They'll be back at the North Pole, won't they? Are they back at the North Pole, Father Christmas?

Nicholas: Eh? Oh yeah – they like it better there, you know. Did you get the food?

Pauline passes over the bag containing a mince pie and a bottle of milk. He snatches it and gulps it down.

Susan: What have you done to your leg?

Nicholas: Fell off a roof.

Pauline: Getting down a chimney.

Nicholas: Chimney, that was it, yeah. Tricky things, chimneys.

Raymond: Father Christmas doesn't fall off chimneys – he's magic is Father Christmas.

Susan: Ssh, our Raymond.

Nicholas finishes the milk.

Pauline: Can we have our presents now?

Nicholas: Eh?

Pauline: That's what you do – we give you milk and a mince pie—

Susan: Only one thing each – it's in the note.

He picks up the note that has fallen out of the bag.

Nicholas: 'Dear Father Christmas – Please could we have some Rimmel Lily of the Valley talcum powder, *Fun for the Secret Seven* by Enid Blyton and a pedal car like you promised my dad for Raymond.'

Raymond: A red one.

Susan: Ssh, give over pestering.

Pauline: Where have you put them, Father Christmas?

Nicholas: Look – kids—

Raymond: He hasn't brung them! We were never getting them! He just wanted a mince pie! That's not Father Christmas! It's a feller!

He runs to the door, where John and Mary are coming in. He flings himself on John, crying.

Pauline: He's just showing off.

Policeman appears in the doorway. He calls outside.

Policeman: He's here alright!

Ext. Day. Outside barn. The children with Mary stand watching as Nicholas is helped by a policeman onto a flatbed trailer pulled by a tractor, driven by John. The trailer has various packets and boxes already on it. Nicholas pulls on a hat; the policeman hands him a sack. And as he sits down with the sack, he is silhouetted like Santa in his sleigh. Susan approaches him hesitantly.

Susan: Well I still believe in you.

Nicholas (*trying to let her down gently*): Ho ho ho.

Policeman (*gets in trailer*): Come on, let's move it.

John starts the engine.

Mary: Where's your cap, you? Go and get it.

Raymond runs into the barn. The others watch as the tractor slowly pulls the trailer away. They hear Raymond shouting from the barn.

Raymond: Mam! Mam!

They turn to see Raymond shoot out of the barn with a big brand new pedal car.

Raymond: It was him, Mam, it was him!

EMAIL ON TOAST

Video. Ad.

Lower-middle-class late-middle-aged couple at kitchen table. They sit happily eating breakfast.

Male VO: Want the convenience of the internet but don't have a computer?

CU. Toast pops up from toaster. They look at each other, delighted.

Now you can get email on your toaster!

Couple read a piece of toast, it's too hot, they drop it onto the table and continue to read while sucking their fingers.

Super caption: WON'T WORK WITH GRANARY

WHERE THE NORTH IS

Winnie, a community nurse: Victoria Wood
Alison, practice manager: Imelda Staunton
Janisha, community nurse: Shobna Gulati
Betty, old lady: Thelma Barlow
Jim, her husband: Michael Gambon
Mrs Pateley: Anne Reid
Boris, a depressive: Andrew Dunn
Keith, Winnie's husband: Bernard Wrigley

Ext. Early morning. Winnie's little car going along moorland road.

Ext. Early morning. Winnie's car pulls up outside modern Health Centre in little northern village. Local madman is waiting.

Madman: Nurse Winnie! Shall I watch your car?

Winnie: You watch it, Dilly, and that way you'll be doing me a favour, because I won't be worrying about it.

She winks chummily, he's thrilled.

Madman: I love you, Nurse Winnie.

Winnie: That's right, Dilly.

Int. Day. Health Centre office. Alison is at the filing cabinet, her back to the door. Winnie bustles in.

Winnie: Morning, Alison love, ooh the sun on the moors this morning – made you glad to be northern. Now, what have you got for me this morning? Alison – something wrong, love?

Alison turns round, face wracked with pain.

Alison: It's John. He's not coming back from Saudi. He's staying with that woman. I had the letter this morning.

Winnie (*embracing her*): Oh Alison love – well at least the post was on time.

Alison attempts a smile.

Alison: No, you're right. I should look on the bright side but at the moment I feel like no one will ever love me again.

Winnie (*sighs*): Well you better face it, love – they might not. (*Brightening.*) Now, come on – let's have that list.

Alison (*recovering herself*): Yeah. Now, where was I?

Janisha, Winnie's partner nurse, comes in.

Winnie (*putting kettle on*): Morning, Janisha love. Isn't it gorgeous this morning? Have you brought the sugar?

Janisha brims over.

Janisha: The solicitor called last night, Winnie – I'm not getting custody.

Winnie embraces her.

Winnie: Oh love.

Janisha: Was I not a good mother, Winnie?

Winnie: Well you can't have been, can you, my darling? Tuh. Anyway, *did* you bring the sugar?

Cut to:

Same, a little later. The three of them all blowing their noses and mopping up, Winnie and Janisha get coats on, ready to leave.

Winnie: Well, this won't do, three of us howling our eyes out when there's northern folks need looking after.

Alison: Are you alright, Winnie?

Winnie (*bravely*): Oh I'm alright – don't worry about me – it was just a bit of a shock finding it like that.

Alison: They can do loads of things with verrucas these days.

Winnie: I know. Ta. Come on, Janisha – let's go and sort out a few folks' lives for them.

Ext. Day. Moorland road. Winnie's car bowling along.

Ext. Day. Inside car. Winnie driving.

Janisha: You know I envy you, Winnie.

Winnie: Don't talk so daft – whatever for?

Janisha: Well – you're happily married, you've got lovely children, you're good at your job, you're dead popular—

Winnie (*pulling up*): I think you're forgetting something.

Janisha (*smiling*): What?

Winnie: I'm warm-hearted! Come on!

They get out of the car and approach the first in a row of lovely little terraced cottages (preferably a row standing alone). Two old faces, a man and a woman, appear at the window. They disappear and the lace curtain drops back into place.

Winnie rings the bell and consults her notes.

Janisha: What's this case, Winnie?

Winnie: Old couple. Betty and Jim. They can't cope on their own up here on the moors, you know, the moors up here – they're having trouble accepting it.

She knocks.

Betty! It's Nurse Winnie! They're stubborn and independent – and I respect that – they don't want folks like me telling them what to do.

Jim and Betty open an upstairs window.

Betty: We're not going in a home.

Winnie: You are!

Jim: We just want to be left alone.

Winnie: Right – I'm smashing the door down! (*Winks at Janisha.*)
     That'll do it!

Int. Day. Betty and Jim's tiny living room, a little later. They're finishing a cup of tea. Winnie picks up wartime wedding photo.

Winnie: Is that your wedding, Betty?

Betty: Yes. 1941. We've lived here all our married lives, haven't we, Jim?

Winnie (*putting down photo*): Terrible frock.

Jim: It's part of us, is this place, Winnie. I don't know how we'd cope in
     some new-fangled block – what's it called – accommodation?

Betty (*patting his hand*): Sheltered accommodation, love.

Jim: Sheltered! We don't want to be sheltered! We're old, but we're
     still people!

He goes out and slams the door.

Janisha: Can't we help Betty and Jim stay in their own home, Winnie?
     Can't we plug into the new patchwork system of homecare,
     on-line assistance and infra-red panic buttons?

Betty: Oh Nurse Winnie, we'd give anything.

Winnie: Oh alright then.

End on Betty's thankful face.

Ext. Winnie's car, parked as before. Winnie and Janisha are lashing Betty and Jim's table to the roofrack.

Janisha: Where now, Winnie?

Winnie: Just next door. (*Looks serious.*) Mrs Pateley's test results have
     come through – look, you nip and do old Mr Tomkinson's band-
     age down the far end – I think I best do this one on my own.

Ext. Day. Mrs Pateley's lovely little back garden.
Mrs Pateley is watering her geraniums. Winnie comes round the side of the house and watches her, sorrowfully.

Winnie: I thought I'd find you here.

Mrs Pateley: It's my own little world, Winnie – and I feel safe here.

Winnie: You have a real gift, my love.

Mrs Pateley: Each flower's a friend, Winnie, does that sound silly?

Winnie: Yeah.

Mrs Pateley: You haven't come here to talk gardens, have you, Winnie?

Winnie: No, love.

Mrs Pateley: I'm dying, aren't I?

Winnie pats her hand, welling up.

>Oh, don't cry. I knew all along really.

Winnie: No, I wasn't crying for that. It's just I found a lump on my foot this morning – I think it might be a verruca. (*Remembers.*) Ooh – now – these came free with *Bandage* magazine (*gets packet of seeds out of bag*). I thought of you – have them.

Mrs Pateley: Oh, I love these. (*Pause.*) Will I be here when they flower?

Winnie (*taking packet back*): Let's have a look – flowers June, July – no.

End on Mrs Pateley's face.

Ext. Day. Moorland near terrace. Janisha and Winnie sit by the car with sandwiches and a thermos of coffee admiring the view.

Janisha: Do you ever wish your life had taken a different turn, Winnie?

Winnie: That I'd ended up in the big city, do you mean?

Janisha: No, I didn't mean that – I meant—

Winnie: Yeah, Winnie's talking – thank you. No I don't, Janie love, I've got everything I could want here – ignorance, ulcerated legs – tuh – come on – getting philosophical when there's work to be done.

They start to pack up.

Janisha: Who's next? Is it Mr Morris?

Winnie: Boris. He and his wife Doris used to run the pub.

Janisha: Oh, Boris and Doris Morris?[258]

Winnie: Mm. She left him I'm afraid. Went off with that man from the flower shop, what's his name, Horace Norris.

Janisha: Oh yeah – I think I've seen their van.

Winnie: You will have done. Horace and Doris Norris, florists—

---

258 A favourite gag type of VW's at the time she was writing *ATT*. See also Valerie and Hillary Malory in 'Keyboard Collywobbles' and Phyllis and Dilys Willis in 'Plots and Proposals'.

Int. Day. Mr Morris's untidy neglected kitchen. He sits, untidy and neglected, at the table.

Winnie: Come on Boris, you've got to get over this, move on.

Boris: What's the point?

Winnie: Well, you've got children for a start.

Boris: No I haven't.

Winnie: Ooh no, sorry, wrong manic depressive.

Janisha: Look – shall I scour out your teapot – that always makes me feel life's worth living.

Boris: You can scour it all you like – it won't bring my wife back, will it?

He puts his head down on the table.

Janisha: Sorry, Winnie – I didn't mean to make a blunder with my emotional immaturity.

Winnie: No, Janice – it's Mr Misery here who needs to apologise. OK – we've tried the softly softly teapot-scouring approach and it didn't work. I'm known for my insightful warm-heartedness, Boris Norris, but it's gloves off time. So listen up, soppy – you look terrible, smell terrible – you were a laughing stock before your wife left you—

Boris (*stumbling out of the back door*): No!

Winnie: You've become a tragic waste of space, I'm afraid.

Janisha (*anxious*): Oh Winnie!

Winnie: Has to be done. It'll be make or break.

Sound of shot.

⬤ I'm gagging for a bap, are you?

Ext. Day. Moorland road. Inside Winnie's car as they drive along.

Janisha: Winnie, I just need to say something.

Winnie (*pulling up suddenly, angry hooting from behind*): Let's look at the view a minute, shall we?

The car behind them zooms past, driver gesturing angrily.

Ext. Day. Winnie and Janisha standing looking out over the valley, the wind whipping their hair.

Janisha: Winnie – I'm sorry I made all that fuss this morning about losing custody of my children.

Winnie: It's natural. Remember what a tizz I got into when I lost those cotton buds?

Janisha: Thanks, Winnie.

Winnie: Come here.

They embrace. Janisha spots something over Winnie's shoulder.

Janisha: Isn't that your Keith?

Winnie: Keith?

Janisha: Your husband.

Winnie: Oh, that Keith.

A lone figure stands some distance away. Winnie, suddenly worried, runs towards him.

Winnie: Keith! Keith love!

Keith: Winnie! (*They embrace.*)

Winnie: Why are you on the moors all alone, Keith?

Keith: I came up here to think. I phoned the Health Centre, they said you thought you might have a verruca – oh Winnie – I've been so worried!

Winnie: There's still hope, Keith. I thought I had athlete's foot once, do you remember, and I'd just stood on a croissant—

Keith (*fighting tears*): Yeah . . .

Winnie: We'll get through this.

Keith: Yeah.

Winnie: I love you, Keith Bago.

Keith: Oh, and I love you, Winnie Bago!

They embrace, cry etc.

WARTIME FOOD FLASH

Caption (on a card held up): A WARTIME CHRISTMAS PUDDING.
Nice middle-class lady in overall and turban behind table laid for cooking.

Lady: It's more important than ever that we have a jolly good Christmas, and that means plenty of Christmas pudding. Not so easy when squandering even an extra sultana could mean the hideous deaths of some of our brave boys at sea.

But never fear – here's an economical recipe that is tasty and nutritious. Pencils ready?

She indicates the ingredients ready in little bowls.

Simply mix together three ounces of grated carrots, two ounces diced turnip and a small minced onion. Add in yesterday's mashed potato, a nut cutlet, half a pint of cold tea, and for that authentic Christmas flavour, a raisin.

No more silver sixpences till peacetime, but a handful of nuts and bolts will keep the kiddies happy, and more importantly, combat anaemia and night fatigue.

Looks a bit thin? Don't worry – half a pound of shredded bloomer will give bite, body and lots of flavours.

We cut abruptly to the same set-up but closer. She holds the finished pudding and puts a spring of privet on top.

Who needs holly when privet is off the ration, and though we can't waste brandy in these dark days – a tuppenny tin of creosote will make Christmas go with a bang!

Caption of the list of ingredients. Muffled boom.

Lady (*OOV*): Oh golly . . .

THE HOUSE OF LOLLY GOGGINS[259]

Lady Goggins:[260] Judi Dench
Scrimmage, companion: Frances de la Tour
Siegfried Sassoon: Richard E Grant
Wilfred Owen: Famous Footballer
Laurel and Hardy: Alan Rickman
Geordie battleaxe: Kate Robbins
Young Tommy Steele: Lee Evans

---

259 At the top of the script VW described this as 'video/contemporary drama/ref. Barbara Taylor Bradford/Catherine Cookson mini-series'.

260 VW liked the name enough to hold onto it and give it to a character in 'Lark Pies to Cranchesterford' (*MLX*).

Young Margaret Thatcher[261]
De Gaulle: Duncan Preston
Edith Piaf: Imelda Staunton
Beverley Sisters: The League

VO: And now, a new fifty-two-part drama – Bella Taylor Cookson's
      – *The House of Lolly Goggins*.
Caption: LONDON, CHRISTMAS 1913.
*Ext. Night. The steps of a London town house, rain beating down. Lolly
knocks on the door and collapses.*
Caption: BELLA TAYLOR COOKSON'S – *THE HOUSE OF
      LOLLY GOGGINS*.

*Int. Night. Lady Goggins' gloomy drawing room. She sits in full widow's
weeds and veil over her face. Scrimmage fusses with the tea things nearby.
Butler enters.*
Butler: Your daughter Lolly Goggins is giving birth on the front step,
      my lady.
Lady Goggins: Move her on, it's hard enough keeping that step clean
      as it is. Scrimmage, kindly divvy up with my broth.
Butler (*leaving*): I'll get the Harpic, my lady.
Scrimmage: But my lady, to think of your own child in such a some-
      thing, would it not be, I knew this this morning, something
      something long sentence, daughter!
Lady: That will do, Scrimmage. I believe I asked for my broth.
Scrimmage (*brings bowl over to side table*): You'll have to suck it
      through your veil – she hasn't sieved it.

*Ext. Night. Steps as before. Rain. CU of door slowly closing. Lolly's
anguished face. We hear a baby cry. Lolly checks her clothing to find the
source of the noise.*

*Int. Night. Lady Goggins' drawing room, as before. Lady Goggins sits in
dusty widow's weeds.*

---

261 No name is attached to the role in the script.

Caption: LONDON, 1914.
Butler draws curtains. Noise of shelling.
Lady Goggins: What is that noise, Crupper?
Butler: It is the First World War, my lady . . .
Lady Goggins: Fair enough.

Int. Night. Drawing room as before. Sound of cheering.
Caption: LONDON, 1925.
Lady Goggins: What is that noise, Crupper?
Crupper (*drawing curtains*): It is the audience at the Criterion The-
        atre, my lady, cheering a play by Noël Coward, heralding the
        start of the Roaring Twenties.
Lady Goggins: Never! In this house we shall be forever oldeworlde![262]
Scrimmage (*OOV*): My lady?
Lady Goggins: Scrimmage? To you what has occurred?
*Scrimmage now has sharp black bob, short Chanel suit, red lips, cigarette
holder.*
Scrimmage: I'm emancipated, my lady. Vo de oh flipping doh.
She Charlestons out of the room with Crupper.

VO: Bella Taylor Cookson's – *The House of Lolly Goggins* – with Alan
        Rickman as Laurel and Hardy.
*Int. Day. Hollywood silent movie set. Laurel and Hardy face each other
angrily.*
Hardy: I'm tired of being the fat one, why don't you be the fat one
        for a change!
He storms off.
Laurel: Olly, come back!

VO: With Kate Robbins as Geordie battleaxe, Annie Murphy.
*Ext. Day. Slum street, Newcastle docks, 1930s. Bosomy battleaxe, all torn
blouse and stained pinnie, confronts Lolly II (played by Lolly I).*
Caption: THE DEPRESSION, 1934.

---

262 In her monologue 'Keeping Fit', VW surveyed the desolation of Morecambe in
winter: 'Even the giftie shoppie's shuttie.'

Battleaxe (*very strong Geordie accent*): Why aye young Lolly with your high-flown ways and fancy la-di-da strutting and pollocking about – you might think yourself a slice above the rest of us but I've heard your mother was no more wed decent than a beast of the field so that makes you more no and no less than a common – (*spits*) I won't soil my lips with the word – so what have you to say to that?

Lolly: Sorry, could you repeat the question, please?[263]

VO: From Blitz-torn London –

Ext. Night. Lady Goggins' town house as before, 1944. Sign over door says 'Government Brothel, Ten Shilling Limit'. Lolly II, in unconvincing grey wig and lines, lies on pavement, woman bending over her.

Lolly II: Where am I?

Woman: You're in war-torn London, dear, at the height of the London Blitz. 1939 to 1945.

Lolly II: Oh. Then I've had amnesia for twenty years. I'm Lolly Goggins.

Woman: Where do you live, dear?

Lolly looks at houses.

Lolly II: I live there.

Front door opens, young airman, drunk and dishevelled, staggers down the steps. His hat is thrown down after him by blowsy old Trout, henna'd hair, over made-up, silk kimono. There is a burst of raucous laughter and hot piano music.

Trout: And don't come back, Sonny! (*Looks closer.*) Don't I know you?

Lolly II: I'm Lolly Goggins.

Trout: Say hello to your mother, Lolly Goggins!

Peals of laughter from Trout, who we now see is Lady Goggins.

VO: With Duncan Preston as General de Gaulle.

Int. Day. Office of General de Gaulle, Paris, mid-60s (Eiffel Tower seen through window).

---

263 VW used the same punchline when being interviewed on stage by her future biographer in 2008. See *Let's Do It*, p. 9.

De Gaulle: Why are you here, Lolly Goggins?

Lolly Goggins III (*now in her fifties*): I have come on behalf of the British Government, to ask if we may join the Common Market.

De Gaulle: Why should I give you the yes, when for so many times the answer has been 'non'!

Lolly III: Because you are my father.

VO: With Imelda Staunton as Edith Piaf.[264]

Int. Night. Stage of Moulin Rouge.

Edith Piaf in panto version of her usual clothes, with possibly a glimpse of young Sacha[265] in background. They are doing the song sheet. Sound of children in audience.

Edith: That wasn't very loud, was it? So it's non – (*clap clap*) rien de rien, (*stamp stamp*) non, (*raspberry*) je ne regrette rien, quack quack. Êtes vous prêtes?

VO: With AN Other as Farrah Fawcett-Majors.[266]

Ext. Day. Set of Charlie's Angels, *early 70s. Farrah, Kate and Lolly III stand flicking their hair and preparing for the next take. A make-up girl quickly powders Lolly.*

Caption: LOS ANGELES, 1974.

Farrah Fawcett-Majors (*angrily*): Don't look at me like that, Lolly Goggins, I'm not just a blonde bimbo mouthing vapid words and worrying about my hair.

Lolly III (*American accent*): Who the hell are you then, Farrah?

Farrah Fawcett-Majors (*flick, flick*): Do you think I should turn these bits in?

VO: And in the concluding part of Bella Taylor Cookson's *The The House of Lolly Goggins.* (*To himself*) Did I say 'the' twice then?

---

264 Imelda Staunton played the title role in Pam Gems's play *Piaf* at Nottingham Playhouse in 1980.

265 Sacha Distel, French chansonnier (1933–2004).

266 VW sent out feelers to Daryl Hannah to play the role.

Int. Day. Head office of huge multi-national 'Goggins', the new present day. Lolly III, now aged sixty, all shoulder pads and big hair, looking stone-faced.

Caption: HEAD OF 'GOGGINS' MULTI-NATIONAL, 2001.

Lolly IV (*aged twenty, all lime green dreadlocks and body piercing*): Why should I listen to you, mother? You've never been there for me. You were always in meetings, flying round the world.

Lolly III: I did it for you!

Lolly IV: You didn't even give birth to me! You had me implanted in a host mother!

Lolly III: That was to get you used to boarding school. You don't understand! Being pregnant was difficult in the 1980s – the suits were fitted – we didn't have your elastic waistbands . . .

Lolly IV (*sighing wearily and turning away*): I'm going back to the other eco warriors. They're real people.

Lolly III: No, don't go, I'd like you to meet someone, someone very special . . .

She speaks into infra-red lapel intercom.

Call the nursing home, please, my daughter and I are making a family visit.

Int. Day. Bedroom, posh nursing home.

Nurse: She may not know you – she was born in the rain on the steps of a London town house in 1913.

Lolly III: We understand.

Lolly III and Lolly IV approach the bed, where Oldest Lolly, in worst wig, latex and lines so far, is lying.

Lolly III: Mother, I've brought Lolly to see you.

Oldest Lolly: Little Lolly. My my. It's all a very long way from 13 Oldeworlde Square, Belgravia.

Youngest Lolly: Whose house was that?

Oldest Lolly: It was the house of my mother.

Youngest Lolly: What was her name, Grandma?

Oldest Lolly: No idea. Sorry.

TRAILS FOR THE HOUSE OF LOLLY GOGGINS

1 Ext. Day. Dusty plain, India.

VO: With Duncan Preston as Gandhi, and Imelda Staunton as Elizabeth Taylor.

Elizabeth Taylor: You must eat, Mr Gandhi.

Gandhi: I won't, thanks very much.

2 Int. Café, 1930s.

VO: With Bob Monkhouse as Einstein.

Einstein: I think you've overcharged me.

Waitress: No – that's an eight not a three.

Einstein: Sorry – I don't usually have the cottage pie.

3 Ext. Day. Grantham street, late 40s.

VO: With AN Other as Margaret Thatcher.

Margaret bends over weeping Urchin.

Margaret Thatcher: What's the matter, urchin?

Urchin: I've dropped my milk, lady, will you give me threepence for some more?

Margaret Thatcher: I'll give you something worth more than threepence – the awareness that one must stand by the consequences of one's actions. In fact – one day – no child shall get milk for nothing![267]

Urchin (*defiantly*): Then I'll grow up and get a job, lady, and buy all the milk I want!

Margaret Thatcher: I wouldn't bank on it!

4 Studio floor, late 60s.

VO: With the League of Gentlemen as the Beverley Sisters.

The three stand in jaunty caps and trouser suits. We catch a mercifully brief snatch of 'Scarlet Ribbons'.

---

267 In 1971, when she was Secretary of State for Education in the Heath government, Margaret Thatcher was dubbed the milk snatcher for withdrawing free school milk for children over the age of seven.

SOUND OF MUSIC

The loo. VW by the washbasins with guidelines tome.[268]

VW: I don't want to do a flipping finale now, I tell you. It's got to celebrate the traditional family Christmas, but what is one? In my family we stayed in bed till four o'clock in the afternoon, watched *The Sound of Music*, cheering for the Germans, got Meltis new berry fruits stuck to the bottom of our new Pirelli slippers, got told off and went to bed.

Mo[269] *comes out of the loo and washes her hands.*

You are being filmed, Mo.

Mo: You don't surprise me.

She dries her hands on the roller towel. It comes away from the wall. She shrugs and leaves.

VW: I told you that would happen. You couldn't have *The Sound of Music* on the telly now, according to this. People crossing the Alps without proper safety equipment.

Backdrop of Austrian Alps.

Maria sits with the children who are all arguing about who lost a ball.

Maria: Children! Children! Stop arguing, it's only a ball.

They subside, sulkily.

Well, you are a lot of gloomies, what's wrong? Frederick?

Frederick: Toothache.

Maria: Too many sweets! Marthe?

Marthe: I was expecting a letter, it hasn't come.

Maria: Liesle?

Liesle: I'm in love with someone in the Hitler Youth, but I don't think he loves me.

---

268 VW wrote a lot of extra material for the *ATT* framing scenes, but this was the only section that overtly cued up a sketch.

269 It was VW's hope to cast the hugely popular Mo Mowlam, then Chancellor of the Duchy of Lancaster.

Maria: Never mind. Shall I tell you what I do when I feel gloomy?
They nod enthusiastically.
She sings.

> When I feel sad and blue
> As if I don't belong
> I don't pop out for glue
> I tra la la a song . . .

General hubbub from children.
Frederick: But we don't know any songs.
Marthe: Songs have complicated lyrics.
Maria: Not this one, listen!
Vamp till ready.
Kurt: Can't we try glue?
Maria laughs and sings.

> Even when the snow's about to fall
> Even when the postman doesn't call
> Even when your heart is breaking
> Even when your teeth are aching
> Even when you've lost your favourite ball
> And what a fuss you're making
> Just la la a song to change your mood
> Just la la to get your heart aglow
> I always take a few big la las
> Everywhere I go.

Liesle: Aren't we supposed to be in the curtains?
Maria: Oh, I forgot about the damn curtains. Can we just stop a
    minute?
Cut to:
Some, all now in curtains, one in a vertical blind.
Vamp till ready.
Maria: So what do we do when we're miserable?
Children: La la la!

Maria: That's it!

Even when the day seems grey and glum
Even when the needle pricks your thumb (*child mimes this*)
When the dentist keeps you waiting (*child mimes toothache*)
When your key falls down a grating (*child mimes upset*)
Even when your pants go up your bum
Now that is irritating
La la la to brighten up your day
Just try getting out your la las
See what happens then.

Cut to tea bar, where Chiara and Sandy are looking at The Sound of Music *on the TV.*
Sandy: We do have a child-free version, do we?
Chiara: Oh yes. It's been digitally remastered for political correct-ness.[270]
With the remote, she changes channel, we overlap the last few bars to see seven minorities capering about in the curtains.
Sandy: Very good. The one on the end?
Chiara: An asylum seeker.
Sandy: Excellent.
Back to the song as before.

When osteoporosis claims your hip
Your neighbour paints her front door kiwi
Both your slippers smell of wee wee
When you catch your scrotum in your zip
Everyone goes tee hee
La la la your gloomy cares away

---

[270] The following exchange is deleted at this point in the typescript:
Voice Off Camera: Er, we can't do this with children apparently.
Maria: What?
Voice: Child protection act. Can't put children in musicals any more.
Maria: What am I having then, seven adults?

Do it every time you're feeling blue
I won't be parted from my la las (*snort from camp man*)
That's enough from you . . .

Big musical finish. They all laugh, join hands, and prepare to cross the Alps.

14

PUTTING THE RECORD STRAIGHT

For most of the Noughties Victoria steered away from television comedy in favour of documentaries, drama and theatre. But in 2005 BAFTA honoured her with a lifetime achievement award in a televised celebration attended at the Theatre Royal Haymarket by many friends and colleagues. Although the evening was carefully scripted by Victoria, not everything went according to plan thanks to a malfunctioning autocue. One sequence in particular didn't quite land and a section of it went missing. It featured Jim Carter and Jim Broadbent as Malcolm and Willis, two killjoys through whom Victoria gave voice to her embarrassment at such a public fuss being made of her. Although the script doesn't specify, she may have seen them as a pair of snotty, sneering critics – of the type who would sit stony-faced through the press night of *Acorn Antiques: The Musical!* when it opened in the same theatre a few weeks later. This is the unexpurgated version which includes several disparaging references to Victoria's career.

UNTITLED

Willis and Malcolm at the podium – carefully combed hair, raincoats buttoned to the neck. They speak in considered plonking tones.

Willis: I'll speak, shall I – you paid for the Scotch egg – er, no, what we'd like to do if we may – Malcolm and I have been looking at Miss Wood's career over the years, and granted this is a ballyhoo and whoop di doo occasion, and we don't want to put a dampener on things.

Malcolm: We'd like to put a bit of a dampener . . .

Willis: I should say we're looking at reducing the fun element here by around 27 per cent.

Malcolm: Push on, Willis, people are waving.

Willis: Well, what we feel, Malcolm and I, is that Miss Wood has been over-praised.

Malcolm: Way over.

Willis: Her reputation is founded on very rocky foundations.

Malcolm: Sandy!

Willis: Eh?

Malcolm: Sandy foundations.

Willis: Oh, I thought you'd spotted Miss Toksvig.[271]

Malcolm: I was making the point, sand is a notoriously inadequate foundation.

Willis: You're not wrong.

Malcolm: As is jelly.

---

271 As ever with her allusions to other comedians, there was a context to this name-check. When turning up for the first week's rehearsal of *DL* in the BBC's rehearsal rooms in North Acton, the cast found Sandi Toksvig and several actors devising a sitcom. 'This is not the most welcome news,' VW tutted in the *Radio Times*, 'to someone who has spent the past six months in an office swearing over a 200-page refill pad trying to write one.' The sitcom was not commissioned.

Willis: That's right.

Malcolm: As are sponge fingers.

Willis: Steady, ladies present. Er – where was I?[272]

Malcolm: Miss Wood's reputation – unfounded.

Willis: *Start the Week* – it didn't![273] We start our week on a Thursday.

Malcolm: *That's Life!*

Willis: It wasn't!

Malcolm: *Pat and Margaret?*

Willis: She didn't look like a Margaret.

Malcolm: And as for *dinnerladies*—

Willis: They were not ladies, and they never made dinner!

Malcolm: Someone's gesticulating with their fingers.

Willis: Ignore it – it's the sign of a poor vocabulary.

Malcolm: Should we not say one complimentary thing before we go?

Willis (*thinks*): No.

---

272 Accidentally or not, this is where the presentation was cut, and the following eight lines were never heard.

273 VW made thirteen appearances on the Radio 4 programme between May 1977 and September 1979. In all of these she performed songs. There was another booking in December 1986 but she got stuck in traffic on the way to Broadcasting House and didn't make it in time. Although mortified, she did at least dodge an encounter with Roland Rat, who had also been booked. Only a couple of weeks earlier on *ASOTV*, VW had warned against sharing a studio with *TV-am*'s puppet rodent in her lusty spoof of *The Good Old Days*, sung by JW:

So please take this as your slogan,

Go on *Aspel*, go on *Wogan*

But for Gawd's sake never work with Roland Raaat!

15

MID LIFE CHRISTMAS

In 2009 it had been a long time since Victoria had written a sketch comedy. As with her two previous Christmas specials, she now conceived a festive entertainment that would have an underlying theme. *Victoria Wood's Mid Life Christmas* was packed with gags about failing bodies. At the heart of it was an extravaganza inspired by the Beijing Olympics. The idea of creating her own Olympiad seized Victoria's imagination and it was a big production effort to create and capture the action in a borrowed football stadium. As usual she had written more than could fit into the available space and so, without any trace of sentiment, she wielded the knife. 'Have been to the edit today armed with huge cuts,' she told her producer John Rushton. 'We have wiped out a lot of the Olympics – it's the easiest one to lose, but have kept a few of the studio gags and all the archive footage and the driving.'[274]

'SWATCH Team' was the last of her parodies of detective drama. As with 'Clancy – Interior Decorator' and 'A Bit of Spam', she found comedy in the idea of a gnarled copper policing the public's decorative failings. But once more she had to let it go, in this case along with an ad for ugly sofas.

The last time Victoria acted with Julie Walters was in 'Beyond the Marigolds: What Mrs Overall Did Next . . .' While a fitting conclusion to their thirty-year screen partnership, in fact Victoria had

274 Email to John Rushton, 8 October 2009.

written another sketch for them to do together. 'I would love to be able to shoot one extra sketch with Julie the week we are filming with her in September,' she told John Rushton. 'This will be a simple set up of a news studio, so basically a desk and a backing flat. We would need a wig each but nothing elaborate, and a contemporary costume each – a suit or a blouse and skirt, nothing fancy.'[275] 'Middle Aged News' was never made.

275 Email to John Rushton, 29 June 2009.

MIDDLE AGED NEWS

Two middle-aged ladies sit behind the news desk.[276] *They have laptops set into the counter, but also a box of tissues, cough sweets, several pairs of reading glasses, a half-full bottle of vanilla smoothie etc. They are peering uncertainly at the autocue. There is a burst of very loud theme music, with much percussion.*

First Lady: Hello – ooh that was loud, wasn't it? – do you think it's always going to be that loud? We need to find that boy . . .

Second Lady: It wasn't as loud this afternoon I don't think.

First Lady: No I don't think it was.

Second Lady: Any road up. Yes, hello – ooh sorry, I'm taking your hello off you.

First Lady: No, you're alright. I need to clear my throat.

Second Lady: Yes, so, hello – this is the nine o'clock news, for people who want to be in bed by ten.[277]

First Lady: And it's not so hard-hitting.

She clears her throat.

First Lady: Too much cheddar.

Second Lady: I can't read that.

First Lady: Ask her to make it bigger – she can make it bigger. The trouble is if it's too big you never get the whole word.

Second Lady: No it's alright, I'll put my readers on. (*She puts on glasses.*) That's worse, if anything. Are these yours?

First Lady: They might be – have they got a bit of emulsion paint on the . . .

Second lady pounces on another pair.

---

276 Although the typescript doesn't say, it seems likely that VW would have played First Lady and JW Second Lady.
277 The BBC's *Nine O'Clock News* moved to 10 p.m. in 2000.

Second Lady: These are mine! That's better. What are yours – one
    point five?

First Lady: Mm. What are yours – two?

Second Lady: I'm not sure. They were in a bin at the services. Right.
    This is the – no no I said that, didn't I? Nine o'clock thingy.
    Right – the Prime Minister – shall we start with that?

First Lady: Sounds good, Jose!

Second Lady: I thought he looked tired today, the Prime Minister.
    Oh, what else – there was an altercation at *Gardeners' Question
    Time—*

First Lady: You don't mean *Gardeners' Question Time—*

Second Lady: Prime Minister's question time – I've got *Gardeners'
    Question Time* on the brain – get it right, Gillian! And the
    other one – I want to say Doctor Cameron—

First Lady: Out of *Doctor Finlay's Casebook*[278] – the original!

Second Lady (*adopting Scottish accent*): Doctor Cameron! And Doctor
    Snoddie! He said that, didn't he – Dorctor Snordie . . .

First Lady: Coming up – the cod liver oil thing.

Second Lady: Oh yes – where's she gone? Is no one winding it on?
    Anyway, from memory – it now turns out it might not be as
    effective as they thought. I get so annoyed about this! We had
    all this with the Atkins, didn't we? It's good then it's bad, they
    want to buck their ideas up.

First Lady: I've given up with nutrition – I say to my husband, just
    put it on the table – monkey's I cannot give.

INSURANCE AD

Three matching mid shots of couples on sofas.
First sofa.
A middle-aged couple. Their sofa is garishly floral.

---

278 Based on a 1935 novella by AJ Cronin, the drama was shown on the BBC from 1962
until 1971.

First Man: They couldn't have been more helpful, one phone call and
      we were insured.

Cut to:
Second sofa.
This sofa has scalloped back. A slightly prim-looking woman.
Woman: I called and got my quote straight away – it was so simple.
Cut to:
Third sofa.
A younger couple. This is a bright-coloured leather sofa.
Man: We wanted to insure our sofa – but some sofa insurance firms
      make it so complicated!
Girl: But with uglysofas dot com we got insurance straight away. And
      we saved twenty-five pounds.
They smile.
Male voiceover: Uglysofas dot com – because people are a bit weird.[279]

COFFEE PALAVER[280]

A small coffee shop.
*Running along the front of the counter are baskets of coffee beans all with
a rustic-looking wooden label bearing a description. There are packets on
the counter as well in smaller baskets, also with labels. Two anxious-look-
ing middle-aged ladies approach the counter.*
First Lady: You sit down, Jean. Now. What to have . . . this sounds
      nice – fine-bodied with earthy overtones and subtle hints of
      vanilla. Jean – yep? Sorry – can I just check, is that organic?
Barista: No.
First Lady: Oh. It's not organic, Jean – (*to barista*) – can I just see
      what else . . .

---

279 The domain name remains available (although uglysofa.com is taken).
280 In an email to John Rushton VW asked for 'Coffee Palaver to be dressed for winter
– so heavy coats for both ladies'. It was filmed with VW as First Lady and Harriet
Thorpe as Second Lady. They performed it twice the following year – once at a charity
event in Hendon, then at Theatre Royal Haymarket as part of *The Angina Monologues*.

Barista: It is Fairtrade though.

First Lady: OK. Well I might come back to that one. Jean, how do you feel about this one – bursting with citrus and floral aromas it packs a nutty kick? And is that Fairtrade?

Barista: Yes.

First Lady: And is it organic? Oh yes, I can see it is organic. It says here – organic. So Jean – that's Fairtrade, organic and packing a nutty kick?

Second lady thinks.

Second Lady: Air miles.

First Lady: Yes, sorry – was it flown here?

Barista: Yes.

First Lady: It was flown here, Jean! Sorry, that's not sitting with us quite so . . . (*she looks around*). Ooh, little aeroplane with a cross through – Jean – this has a superb interplay of musky flavours delivering a full-bodied tastebud temptation. Yes? And that's come by ship.

Barista: Yes.

First Lady: And it's organic.

Barista: Yes.

First Lady: Shall we go for that, Jean? Organic, no air miles and delivering a musky interplay?

Second Lady: Lovely. Just ask them if it's Fairtrade?

First Lady: Sorry – this one – the tastebud temptation interplay musky doings – is that one Fairtrade?

Barista: No.

First Lady: It's not Fairtrade. How strongly are we feeling about that, Jean?

Second Lady: Well . . .

First Lady: How unfair would the trading be, do we think? Are they badly exploited, these particular workers? Or are they perhaps just not happy with their canteen? If they're being paid a pittance and working all hours then obviously we're not going to drink it, but if it's just girls grumbling about their uniforms I think we could stretch a point. Jean?

Second Lady: Are there any others?

First Lady: Ooh hang on. Hang on a minute. Ooh yes – ready for this, Jean – reaching you by sea and guaranteed organic this Fairtrade breakfast coffee has a spiky – said spiky then – spicy backtaste and all the smoky bouquet you would expect from a Blue Mountain single estate bean. Ticks all the boxes, Jean – Blue Mountain? Spicy backtaste? Smoky bouquet?

Second Lady: What was the first one again?

First Lady: Jean – they close in ten minutes – I've described every blessed bean in the place – could you please make your mind up?

Second Lady: About what?

First Lady: About what flipping coffee you would like to drink!

Second Lady: Oh I thought *you* wanted a coffee – I'm happy with a Horlicks.

DENTURES

Int. Kitchen. Day.
Man looks at apple in fruit bowl, picks it up and ruefully puts it down.
Male voiceover: There is an alternative to dentures!
Man looks interested.
Male voiceover: It's this!
Black and white still of old bloke with collapsed gummy face.
Man: Thanks. I'll just have a banana then.

SWATCH TEAM

Pulsing music. Very short title sequence – very heavily messed about with – slowed down, colour changed, details burnt out etc. A heavy-set woman in boxy skirt suit and low court shoes running down a street with a male detective sergeant behind her. She bangs on a door and when it's opened she holds up her warrant card which drops down concertina-style to reveal a long strip of colour swatches.

Dilys: Detective Dilys Willis.[281] SWATCH team.

The title comes up.

S.W.A.T.C.H. TEAM

Int. Day. Small modern living room.

Dilys and her sergeant Maurice are interviewing a tearful young woman.

Dilys is holding a green jumper.

Dilys: Come on, love – he's been here, hasn't he – this is his jumper.

Girl: No – (*desperately.*) It's my jumper, honest!

Dilys: Really. Had your colours done lately?

Girl: Maybe.

Dilys: What were you? A cool spring? Warm spring?

Girl: Warm spring.

Dilys: Oh. Funny – I didn't know springs could wear sage – did you, Maurice?

Maurice: No, ma'am.

Dilys: No. We know you can wear apple. We know you can wear leaf. You might even be able to carry off a pale mint – but sage?[282]

She grabs the girl and drapes the jumper round her neck.

Dilys: Is that flattering her complexion, Maurice? Brightening her eyes?

Maurice: No, ma'am.

Dilys (*shouting suddenly*): No it isn't! Because you know and I know you can only wear sage if you're a red-headed autumn! Kyle Ellis – get out here now!

A red-headed boy comes out slowly from behind an armchair.

Dilys: Cuff him, Maurice. Use the dark green.

She shakes her head wearily as Maurice chooses a pair of handcuffs from the pairs of every colour he has attached to his belt.

---

281 See note 258.

282 When VW, aged eight, saw Joyce Grenfell at Buxton Opera House, she was much struck by the way Grenfell said to the audience, 'I'm going to give you a minute to decide whether my dress is leaf green or lettuce green.'

Int. Café. Day.
Maurice bringing two mugs of tea over to Dilys.
Dilys: Thanks, Maurice.
He nods and sits down, sighing.
Dilys: Cheers. Welcome to SWATCH team – you did well.
Maurice: Thanks, boss.
He looks away.
Dilys: Everything OK? Settled in alright?
Maurice: Everyone's been great – it's just – oh it doesn't matter.
Dilys: Go on. Call it off the record. Just because I've got a big bust
       and court shoes doesn't mean I'm not approachable.
Maurice: I can't wear navy, I have to be really careful with yellow.
Dilys: Tell me about it. When you're young you want to do everything,
       wear everything – I thought I could have it all, job, mar-
       riage, diagonal stripes – here I am – divorced and lucky if I
       can carry off a two-tone trim. Be careful what you wish for,
       eh . . .
Maurice: You're a bloody good copper, boss.
She sighs and stands up.
Dilys: Come on – let's get a bit of fresh air – you can sit too long in
       mixed fibres.
They get up and leave.

Ext. Park. Day.
*They are crossing through a small park. Across the road is an ice-cream
van and a man selling something from a suitcase. A crowd of teenage
schoolkids are milling around.*
Dilys: What the – come on, Maurice!
She breaks into a slow run.

Ext. Street. Day.
*As they run across the road the man with the suitcase hastily packs it up
and legs it. The crowd of girls stand back in shock.*
Dilys: Don't move, girls! Call for back-up, Maurice!
*They run after the man into an alley, Maurice calling into his phone for
back-up.*

Ext. Back alley. Day.

The man has run into a dead end. He stands cornered, panting as Dilys and Maurice run up to him.

Dilys: Stay where you are – SWATCH team.

She lets her swatch book drop. The man groans.

Maurice: Shall I look in the case, ma'am?

She nods. He bends down to open it. We are looking at his back and can't see into the case. He turns to her.

Maurice: Ma'am?

Cut to close-up of Dilys touching up her lipstick.

Dilys: Hang on.

She puts her lipstick away.

Dilys: OK.

She looks down at the case.

Dilys: You scum.

The case is full of cheap pashminas.

Dilys: Seen this stuff before, Maurice?

Maurice: Is it scarves, boss?

Dilys: Worse. Pashminas. Those girls were – what – fourteen, fifteen?

Man: They knew what they were doing.

Dilys: You think it's OK, do you, for a fifteen-year-old girl to wear a pashmina?

She snatches a blue one out of the case.

Dilys: Sell a lot of these, do you?

He nods.

Dilys: Do you know who's supposed to wear hyacinth blue?

He nods.

Dilys: Middle-aged women. Women with fading complexions. Women with no self-esteem. Women who are learning languages of countries they will never ever go to! You don't sell hyacinth blue to a girl!

A policeman comes running up the alley.

Dilys: Take him away. Is restyling here?

Policeman: Yes, ma'am.

Sad music. The policeman hustles the man away and Maurice closes the case. Dilys walks slowly back down the alley.

Ext. Street. Day.
A small crowd is gathered. A sobbing girl is clutching a blue pashmi-
na and a uniformed woman in a hi-vis style vest, lettered on the back
'RESTYLING', is trying to take it off her. Dilys walks slowly past. Her
work is done.

Int. Police station. Day.
The next day. Hustle and bustle. Dilys going cheerfully up the stairs carrying
an evidence bag which contains a clutch bag and some evening shoes. Her
boss, a silver-haired Police Superintendent, stops her as she reaches the top.
Superintendent: Can you come in here a minute?
Dilys: Of course, sir.
He leads her into his office, presses a button on his laptop and turns the
screen towards her. It is CCTV footage of a woman crossing the road at
night.
Superintendent: Well?
Dilys: It's me, sir.
Superintendent: Yeah. (*He sighs and opens a folder.*) You had everything
            going for you, Dilys – you could wear any blue you wanted,
            all the pinks, cream that wasn't too yellowy, splashes of topaz –
            but it wasn't enough for you, was it? – you had to go and wear
            black. And you are stupid enough to get caught doing it.
He slams down the lid of the laptop.
Superintendent: What the hell were you thinking? Black?
Dilys: It's slimming! I've got a bulky outline!
Superintendent: Jesus, Dilys – charcoal you could have got away with,
            deep kingfisher – but not this—
He presses a button on his desk intercom.
Superintendent: Get Maurice Norris in here – Dilys Willis is off the
            SWATCH team.
Thudding music.
Caption: NEXT WEEK ON *S.W.A.T.C.H. TEAM*.

Ext. South Bank, London. Day.
Maurice, strolling along in civvies, stops and stares at someone on the
bench.

Maurice: Boss?

We see it is Dilys, in clashing patterns and wild colours.

Maurice: Boss? What's going on? What's happened to you?

Dilys: This is what happens when you're taken off the SWATCH team – you get – uncoordinated.

She looks at him defiantly.

WRINKLES

Int. White-walled art gallery. Day.

A woman in her late thirties peers at a piece of modern sculpture.

Male voiceover: Time brings wisdom. But it can also bring tiny lines and wrinkles.

The woman frowns into a hand mirror.

Male voiceover: New DermaRevive plumping serum contains active cellular peptides that penetrate deep into the skin.

Diagram of arrows penetrating sub dermis.

Caption: It doesn't really.

The woman smoothes cream on her skin.

MIDLIFE OLYMPICS 2009

OLYMPICS ONE

Studio. Commentary box.

Two presenters. One is a youngish man, a typical sports commentator, the other a middle-aged lady, with nicely done hair and a smart blazer. Behind them we can see down into the arena, which is sparsely attended and has a few officials walking around checking equipment etc.

Steve: Welcome back to Bedford[283] – to the Midlife Olympics 2009 and a cracking start as you saw earlier – Robert Carmichael

---

283 Bedford in the original script, changed to Brentford after the production was given permission to film at the ground of Brentford FC.

and his team bringing home the Gold for Great Britain in the 4 x 400 Hedge Trimming. Finland as we just heard disqualified when third man Essa Hakonen snipped through his own cable. The Finns aren't going to be happy with that. But now it's very much the turn of the ladies – as you can see, we're back in the Women's Arena and plenty of action coming up, Carol.

Carol: Well later on we'll be going live to the Ladies' Outdoor Reversing – British girl Carol Dacres hoping to come good this year after Rome 2005 where of course she knocked down a low wall and a Punch and Judy booth.

Steve: We haven't done great on Ladies' Driving Events generally.

Carol: No, we haven't. We've had injury problems – you remember Pam Jessop was stretchered off in Tokyo with a loose moccasin, and then of course Marnie Sutherland was disqualified in the Multi Storey Parking event, when she got – flustered.

Steve: So – just to be clear – because many of you have texted in – this is the Middle-Aged Ladies' Pentathlon – not the Menopause Pentathlon – which is part of the separate Menopause Olympics – the Menopolympics.

Carol: Teams just coming into the arena now here but I can just tell you that the British Menopause Sudoku champion Sally Ryan, who looked to be out of the running when she couldn't find her glasses – they were on her head.

Steve: And we can go over to Deirdre Gumbarton down in the Women's Arena – Deirdre, how are spirits in the British camp?

Cut to:

Arena.

Deirdre is standing in front of the coffee shop set-up. She is in a pastel tracksuit, she's about thirty, athletic and cheerful. Piano music comes from the loudspeakers. Behind her march in the competing teams, four women in each, all in team tracksuits.

Deirdre: Spirits are high, Steve. I visited the athletes in the Olympic village last night and they seemed pretty confident that they can deliver at least a silver in the stadium today.

Steve: Not an event you've competed in as yet, Deirdre – the Middle-Aged Ladies' Pentathlon.

Deirdre: No, indeed. All that to come!

Steve: Could come sooner than you think!

Deirdre: Absolutely!

The camera stays on her a moment too long and catches her scowling and talking to the cameraman.

Deirdre: What did he mean by that? Idiot!

Cut to:

Commentary box.

Down in the arena the teams are warming up, practising little movements etc.

Steve: Just talk us through the five events, Carol. Is it very different from the Men's Pentathlon?

Carol: It's similar – in the shopping event the women have a smaller trolley, or they have the option of a wheeled basket – but instead of the Men's Skimped Hoovering, the Women have the Dead Mouse on a Shovel 100 Metre Dash.

Steve: Sounds easy but you have to remember they will have their eyes shut.

We see down in the arena the teams lining up in the coffee shop section. Janey, a thin tough-looking woman, is warming up aggressively.

Steve: Teams lining up there for Ladies' Individual Coffee Shop. Tyne and Wear's Janey Johnson[284] warming up – did so well in Helsinki in the Decaffeinated Sugar-Free Pairs.

Carol: She may struggle in the individual—

We intersperse the relevant shots of the course. Or a computer simulation of the event with a stick figure.

If we can just see the course – it's all about level of difficulty – athletes have to choose their coffee – complicated coffee is more points, but obviously a simple latte or Americano will get them away from the counter quicker – they've got to order, queue, collect their drinks – make their way to an empty table—

---

284 Changed to Kerry Perry in the shooting script. She was played by Dorothy Atkinson. Having had a small role in *H49*, she would go on to have a much larger one in *That Day We Sang*.

Steve: They can take a spare seat at somebody else's table—

Carol: They can – but it's risky. The person may have just got up for a paper napkin – someone may have saved that place for a friend – it can backfire!

Steve: And they have to clear away.

Carol: They have to clear away. Which is where the Kenyans fell down last year, if you remember – got two soya cappuccinos all the way to a high counter, moved a newspaper, wiped the table – didn't clear away – instant disqualification. Which was tragic. In fact I'm not sure we'll see Nandi Mbuso come back from that and carry on competing at this level.

Steve: And we're off.

Cut to:

Arena.

This event is set up with four identical coffee counters, collection points, bin, tables, with uniformed 'customers' at them, bits of carefully placed litter.

Everything is in the Olympic colours. The four competitors are bouncing up and down on their toes, warming up. They have to start by pushing a swing door to reach the counter. We have a British, a Japanese, a Kenyan and a Canadian. The whistle blows. They push the door and run to the counter. There are four tracksuited girls to take their order and another four making the drinks. Some competitors grab just one drink and go to find a table, some take a few drinks on a tray. They weave their way through the tables, buzzers go off if they bump into anyone or knock something off a table as they go past.

Carol (*VO*): That was a very good start for the British girl – she's put in a lot of door work over the winter, it's really paid off.

Steve (*VO*): And the Kenyan's gone for tea!

Carol (*VO*): That can work – it's a quicker delivery – but she will have to remember to dispose of her teabag or she'll be looking at that automatic three-second penalty we were talking about earlier. No, she's done it!

They are all taking their drinks and finding a seat, weaving their way through the tables, avoiding the planted customers.

Steve (*VO*): Look at the Canadian go – that was a heck of a body swerve—

Carol (*VO*): Yes, she's been trained by Paulo Moretti – he really builds his girls up – ah! – you see – she's taken too many paper napkins – she'll be penalised for that – and two wet rings on the table – that could lose her the Gold.

Steve: Oh, and the little Japanese girl has finished—

Carol: Kim Kurasawa – knocked out in the semis last year with a damaged tray – she's come back fighting.

Steve: And Deirdre's there with Janey – just waiting for the judges' marks there.

Cut to:

Arena.

Deirdre with a panting Janey, putting on her track jacket.

Deirdre: How was that?

Janey: Yeah – it went pretty well – I knocked a newspaper off a table, also I didn't get all my lids completely closed – but – yeah – pretty pleased—

Deirdre: And a very high level of difficulty.

Janey: I said to my family I would go for the hardest level – three frappuccinos extra cold and no tray!

Deirdre: I think we've got a message from them!

Cut to:

Janey's family at home.

A family group in the garden, banners and balloons everywhere with Good Luck Janey on them, Janey for Gold etc. Her elderly parents beam into the camera.

Parents: All the luck in the world! Janey for Gold!

Cut to:

Arena.

Janey wipes away a tear.

Deirdre: Judges' marks!

They stare up at the scoreboard.

Ninety-three – risk paid off! (*Groan from the crowd.*) Oh – and the Canadian's been disqualified. Wow!

Canadian team staring up at the scoreboard in disbelief.
Cut to:
Commentary box.
Steve: And we'll have to wait to hear the reason for that
    disqualification—
Carol: I think it was the wet rings—
Steve: And the Canadian coach going off to the judges' table there –
    Paulo Moretti – not happy.
They get the wind-up.
Carol (*gabbling a little to end in time*): Well – she was sailing close to
    the wind with her extra napkins – serviettes, sorry – they've
    changed the official wording – she took a risk – and at this
    level, Steve – doesn't always pay off.
Steve: More from us, after this.

OLYMPICS TWO

Commentary box.
Steve: And you join us back in the Women's Arena – the Middle-Aged
    Ladies' Pentathlon – halfway through the phone event – the
    Long Hold – just run us through the event, Carol.
*Down in the arena we can see the competitors seated at identical chairs,
with pads of paper, pencils and identical phones, sitting silently. Above
each of their heads is a lighted switchboard giving the status of their call
– on hold/just being put through/all operatives busy etc.*
Carol: This is the final part of the phone section – the athletes have to
    dial a given number – could be directory enquiries, could be
    customer services—
Steve: And can they use reading glasses to help them dial?
Carol: No – no glasses – no holding the piece of paper at arm's length
    and squinting at it and no calling out to a younger family
    member – I can't see a bloody thing in this light, you do it.
Steve: So they're calling a number – they may have a complaint, or a
    query—
Carol: That's right, and of course at some point they will be put on

hold – and then it's a waiting game – it's all about holding your nerve, and not getting rattled when the athlete in the next lane seems to be getting through her menus quicker – and actually getting through to a living person—

Steve: Let's just see—

Cut to:

Arena.

Japanese girl is sitting calmly.

Steve (*VO*): Japanese girl looks to be doing very well – she's been sent back to the main menu three times and she's not even drumming her fingers – that is classy.

The Kenyan woman stands up in frustration.

Carol (*VO*): Oh – the Kenyan's stood up – she's out! Automatic disqualification of course for standing up—

The umpire indicates the Kenyan girl should leave the phone area and she walks away shaking her head and miming earache.

Carol: She stuck twelve minutes of Celine Dion and 'My Heart Will Go On', so she did pretty well, Steve.

Steve (*VO*): Britain's Janey Johnson there – been training hard she tells me by calling British Gas every day and trying to report a billing error and a change of address.

Carol (*VO*): Oh – and the Canadian's given up – she's disconnected! She's out!

The Canadian ends her call.

Steve (*VO*): She's shaking her head – I think she's saying, I coped with the voice recognition – I managed to enunciate the name of the cinema, I chose the film – and then I got put straight back to pensioners' opening times – I'm out of here!

Cut to:

Commentary box.

Carol: Janey looking pretty good there, Steve.

Steve: She did very well in the semis, that's given her confidence.

Carol: Yes, because that was a tricky one – getting the Norwich bus times from a Bangalore switchboard.

Steve (*getting the wind-up*): Absolutely. Long Hold living up to its name there – we'll be back later with the rest of the Ladies'

Pentathlon and all the latest from the Men's Posturing Arena with the Synchronised Boasting and the Individual Non-Stop Whinge – after this.

OLYMPICS THREE[285]

Commentary box.
Carol and Steve are chatting, he gets the nod that he's on air, smiles, and then holds his earpiece.
Steve: Oh and we're just hearing that one of the British team may have failed a drugs test – what's happening, Deirdre?
Cut to:
Arena.
Deirdre is looking anxiously at Janey, who is in back of shot being led away by Olympic officials, followed by her coach. The other British team members are shocked and puzzled.
Deirdre: All I can tell you, Steve, is that a couple of minutes ago, Olympic officials entered the Women's Arena where as you know we're awaiting that result on the shopping relay – and asked Janey Johnson to accompany them for interview. That's all I can tell you at the moment. Hopefully it's some sort of mistake and she'll be back competing shortly.
She shrugs at the camera hopefully.
Cut to:
Commentary box.
Steve: Well if that is indeed the case that will be a sad, sad day for British sports and for middle-aged people everywhere. Back after this.

---

285 VW spared a section that falls here in the script, involving the Supermarket Check-out Relay and a brief history of previous Midlife Olympiads.

OLYMPICS FOUR

Commentary box.

Steve: We're live from Bedford at the Midlife Olympics – here at the Women's Arena where as you heard on the news, Ladies' pentathlete Janey Johnson has allegedly failed a random drugs test – the event has been suspended while we await that result. Carol?

Carol: Well, I'm wearing my lucky blazer – let's hope it's a silly mistake – because if Janey has tested positive for the drug in question it's a sad, sad, sad day for British sport.

Steve: And let's not beat about the bush, Carol – these are not just relatively harmless steroids or amphetamines – this is serious mood-altering stuff for middle-aged people – we should call it by its name. Carbs.

Carol: Yes, it's carbs, to use its street name. Carbs and sugar. We've been trying to root this out of British sport for many years – the whole Pedalo team at Helsinki in '92, you'll recall, caught not just with jam but with jam-spreading equipment – and of course Maurice Colley – you remember that stupendous world-beating Wheelie Bin Trundle.

Steve: Indeed. And what shock waves there were when Colley was stripped of his Trundle title after tests revealed he was using a cocktail of banned substances including carrot cake and Grecian 2000.

Carol: Tragic.

Steve: Let's turn to something a bit more cheerful – Andy Cafferty down in the Olympic Car Parking Stadium . . .[286]

---

286 The next section made the final cut. It concluded with a short exchange which was culled:

Arena.

They have cut by mistake. Everyone is just hanging about. Deirdre is chatting to someone behind the camera.

Deirdre: Yeah, great – they're in the Olympic village and we're what, like in some – well, it's not even a Holiday Inn, is it? I haven't even got an ironing board.

OLYMPICS FIVE[287]

Commentary box.

Steve: And I think we now join Deirdre Gumbarton in the Women's Arena – let's catch up with event four – the Dead Mouse on a Shovel 100 Metre Scuttle And Fling.

Cut to:

Arena.

A track is marked out as if for the long jump. In another corner is the balance team, with teams warming up nearby. A Kenyan is warming up, running on spot etc. She picks up her shovel and swings it around a bit. A whistle blows.

Carol (*VO*): Kenya's Doris Nkruma making her third attempt.

Odd bits of crackly music and scattered applause come from other bits of the stadium. Doris holds out her shovel and a dead mouse is placed on it. She closes her eyes. Starting pistol. With screwed-up face she runs down the track and at a marked point stops and flings the mouse off the shovel. She opens her eyes to see where it has landed and two officials in blazers mark it with a flag.

Carol: A good throw. And now Britain's Sue Codlington – replacing Janey Johnson of course – she's unlikely to top the Kenyan.

Sue takes off her warm-up jacket and does similar warm-up with shovel etc.

Steve (*VO*): And of course this is where the British team pay the price for that very costly Viennetta.

Carol (*VO*): Well, Viennetta and victory start with the same letter, Steve – but they couldn't mean two more different things.

Steve: Same two letters, Carol.

Carol: Indeed.

The whistle blows. The mouse is put on the shovel. Starting pistol. She runs. She steps over the line as she throws. A red flag goes up. Groans all round.

---

287 The opening exchange, confirming that Janey Johnson had tested positive for Viennetta, made the final cut.

Steve: It's a no throw.

Sue walks back to her coach disconsolately and puts her jacket back on.

Cut to:

Commentary box.

Carol: From the get go I wasn't convinced—

Steve: Let's look at that again.

Cut to:

Footage of mouse fling. We see the sequence again in slow mo.

Carol (*VO*): She never really gets the shovel up—

Steve (*VO*): She half commits, and then – there you are! Foot over the line – it was never going to happen. Ooh – we're going over to Deirdre?

Cut to:

Arena.

Deirdre: Yes, we've just been told Janey Johnson, disqualified after she tested positive for carbs and sugar, is going to make a statement.

Cut to:

Another part of the arena.

A flurry of camera flashes and shouted questions as the press gather round Janey, who is with her coach. She reads from a prepared statement in a flat voice.

Janey: Today I tested positive for a banned substance. I deeply regret my actions and am sorry for the embarrassment and pain I have caused to the British team, to my coach and to my family. There is a lot of pressure competing at this level – and when I was given access to a slice of Viennetta, in a moment of weakness I did make use of it, by eating it. This unfortunately led to me having some malt loaf. And a handful of All-Bran. And the last of the glacé cherries. Thank you.

She turns away and is led away by her coach. The press shout out questions.

Press Person One: What sort of malt loaf, Janey?

Press Person Two: Who gave you the Viennetta? Who else had it?

Cut to:

Arena.

Deirdre (*who has been watching this on a monitor*): And I think we can
     go over to Janey's family – obviously a very disappointing day
     for them.

Cut to:

Janey's family at home.

*The old dad is pouring water to put out the barbecue. People are stabbing
the good luck balloons, carrying the party food inside and taking down
the bunting. Nobody takes any notice of the camera.*[288]

FRAGILE TISSUE[289]

Ext. Beach. Day.

*A sixtyish woman in elegant casual clothes walking barefoot on the beach.
She turns to the camera. She's American.*

Woman: After menopause a woman's intimate tissue can lose its
     elasticity – become drier and more fragile—

Cut to:

Int. Living room. Night.

Two teenage boys dumbstruck with horror as they watch this on TV.

---

288 'Olympics Six' was used in the final programme. In a montage of British successes,
one section was not included:

   Ladies' Arena.

   The British competitor from the Long Hold holding up her phone in triumph.

   Steve (*VO*): She's through! Held in a queue for twenty minutes but she's through!

289 This has a lot in common with the opening monologue of the second episode of
Victoria Wood's Big Fat Documentary (2004) in which VW, walking along a beach in
Santa Monica, plays a Californian version of herself hawking a weight-loss product
called ColonToGO! The dumbstruck boys were played by VW's son Henry and his
friend Gabriel. Although the sketch was cut, their cameo was used at the very end of
Victoria Wood: What Larks!, the documentary about the making of *MLX*.

16

LAST WORDS

Victoria's last official performance as a comedian to be filmed and broadcast was in December 2010 when she emceed *The Angina Monologues*. But she couldn't resist the lure of an audience and continued to accept occasional bookings. She pretended to feel ambivalence about thrusting herself back on stage. In her speech notes for one of these appearances she wrote, 'Just introducing the show – I can't do much – I've had the comedy equivalent of a gastric band fitted – if I do more than a tiny bit of comedy I throw up . . .'[290]

In 2011 she hosted a memorial to the trumpeter James Watson and compèred a London Jazz Festival night at the Barbican Centre, enjoying the latter enough to front the same event in 2013. During the busy first half of that year, while she was adapting *That Day We Sang* for television, Victoria hosted a gala celebrating slapstick comedies of the silent age, made a presentation in tribute to Delia Smith, gave a speech to the Grand Order of Lady Ratlings and handed out the prizes at University College School.

---

290 One joke VW wrote in this period suggests that she found it impossible to stay off the subject of bad television: 'Sky are doing a new programme – it's a cross between *Through the Keyhole* and *Celebrity Detox* – the celebrities have to swallow a miniature camera and you have to guess which celeb is which by looking at their colon. It's called *Through the Arsehole*.'

This last invitation came from Kenneth Durham, her former brother-in-law who had been headmaster at the independent school in Hampstead since 1996.[291] Victoria would go on to address other audiences, some of them very grand. Sundry royals and celebrities heard her pay tribute to Sir Marcus Setchell, her gynaecologist and theirs, at his retirement lunch in 2014. In 2015 the Chancellor of the Exchequer George Osborne hosted an event at 11 Downing Street, where Victoria banged the drum for the Manchester International Festival. In all these bookings she would discreetly recycle an interchangeable portfolio of tried and tested gags, as she did in the last third of her prizegiving speech. But like all her best speeches stretching back over three decades to the launch of *The Lucky Bag Songbook*, her routine for a roomful of teenagers was original, and personal, and suggested that her inner comedian would not be silenced. That said, the pay-off was clearly addressed to the teenagers' parents.

Victoria stood up and entertained an audience with an original piece of writing for the final time at the wedding of her friends Beth Willis and Jonny Campbell.[292] The venue was Wilton's Music Hall in Wapping, east London, the date 7 December 2013. She had not composed or performed verse since the mid-1980s but, for 'Whitney's Wedding', she took as her inspiration 'The Lion and Albert' (1931),[293] the most famous of the verse monologues recorded by Stanley Holloway that were often played in the Wood household when Victoria was a child. With the newlyweds standing either side of her, she brought the house down.

---

291 This was his final term. Kenneth Durham died in August 2016, four months after VW, also aged sixty-two.

292 Respectively, the executive producer and director of *Eric & Ernie*. In 2016 they were expecting their second child and, in their friend's memory, named her Ida Victoria.

293 By Marriot Edgar, a comic poet who was born, VW fans may be delighted to learn, in Kirkcudbright.

PRIZEGIVING SPEECH AT
UNIVERSITY COLLEGE SCHOOL

This is quite an unusual situation for me – to be in a school and not be in trouble. I spent most of my school career being sent out of the room – and I'm only here today because Ken, or Mr Durham as I call him, did a big emotional blackmail number on me. I'm sure you know he can be very persuasive – though I'm not sure I should have let him tarmac my driveway.

I said to Mr Durham, 'This is quite a young audience for me. I don't usually find myself standing in front of so many people who have their own hips.' I said I don't think you're going to get it. He said, 'Don't worry, they won't be listening. You're old – it's just white noise to them.'

It makes a change from my last guest appearance which was at a big show-business lunch with some quite famous people. They're nerve-wracking, those big show-business dos. You're always slightly wondering, is the Operation Yewtree van going to be backing up to the kitchen entrance?[294]

I've been trying to think back to my own school prizegivings – what would I want to hear if I was sitting where you are? I would want to hear the words, 'I'm not going to talk, just do shadow puppets.' I would want to hear the words, 'There is an ice-cream van out the back and everyone who's not getting a prize can have a free 99.'

How can I explain what life was like in the Sixties? We had old money – which was enormous. With a threepenny bus fare it was like handing over three pan lids. And if your bus journey was going to be sixpence, you just didn't go, you stayed at home. You watched

---

294 The police investigation into sexual abuse allegations was set up in October 2012. At the time of VW's speech several celebrities had been arrested, including Gary Glitter, Rolf Harris, Stuart Hall and Max Clifford, who would all later be imprisoned.

Jackanory, which was just someone reading out of a book. And sometimes they would show you one of the illustrations. We were happy with that.[295]

We didn't have internet. We didn't have phones. If you arranged to meet someone and they didn't turn up you had to stand there for a week looking round hopefully, and if something had happened to them you might only read it in the paper a year later when it was wrapped around some chips.

We didn't have teachers we liked – they were all tweed-suited freaks of nature whose main qualification for teaching seemed to be that they could hit a moving child with a board rubber at about twenty-five yards.

We had a terrible school orchestra – I've had two children in school orchestras, so I've heard some eye-wateringly terrible things of an evening, but mine was the worst. We had one trumpet, that was me – and about thirty-seven clarinets – that was all the girls who came in on the train and wanted something easy to carry – and one cello, played by a girl called Joy. And the unfortunate thing about Joy was she had enormous hips so really she was shaped like a cello. You'd come in and go, 'Have we got two cellos? Oh no, it's Joy.'[296]

And French. Now even in 1964 they had language labs. Not in my school. We had a projector – it's hard to describe this. Imagine the old film with the sprocket holes. Imagine seeing that one frame at the time – so a slide would come up. It was a drawing – not even a photograph – of a woman. While we were gawping at that, a voice from a tape recorder would go, 'Le train est départ.' While we were reeling

---

295 VW read for *Jackanory* five times between 1984 and 1991: *Little Mabel Wins* by Jilly Cooper, *The Tiger Who Lost His Stripes* by Anthony Paul, *Ten in a Bed* by Allan Ahlberg (with Martin Jarvis and Rosalind Ayres), *Matilda* by Roald Dahl and finally a story by a winner of a *Jackanory* competition.

296 This section was a filleted version of the longer account of orchestral life VW gave in speeches to support Jessie's Fund, the charity of which she was patron. It was founded by her schoolfriend Lesley Schatzberger, who was one of those thirty-seven clarinettists in the Bury Grammar School orchestra and went on to become principal clarinet of the London Classical Players, English Baroque Soloists and Orchestre Révolutionnaire et Romantique.

from that onslaught of foreignness another voice would say, 'The train has departed.' And then in the final step to our multicultural future we would all mumble, 'Le train est départ.' Then the tape would go 'Beep' and that meant wind on to the next picture. So we could all say some things in French but we would never move onto the next topic unless someone said 'Beep'.

I've only got four O levels – I know they don't call it an O level now – what do they call it? A degree. So I only got four when you were supposed to have five to apply to university – but I managed to make up the shortfall with a life-saving certificate and some green shield stamps.

While I was at university this part of my career you might be able to identify with – I was on a TV talent show. This was in 1973. I auditioned for the big hit *X Factor* of its day which was called *New Faces*. They held auditions all over the country and I was at university in Birmingham and the auditions were at the Dolce Vita nightclub. I hadn't realised how many people would turn up and when I got there the queue was round the block – luckily in those days the queue wasn't part of the programme – and I wouldn't have been seen but a friend of mine was a make-up girl at ATV. She was quite important – she did Noele Gordon's eyebrows for *Crossroads* – and she put my form to the top of the pile and I got seen. I auditioned for a man called Les Cox. A lot of people thought that was a three-man drag act but actually he was the producer.

Some of the *New Faces* winners were given their own show called *The Summer Show* – there was me and a comedian called Marti Caine and a very young Lenny Henry. They didn't really know what to do with me in this sketch show because I was fat – so there was always a problem about my costumes. In those days no one was fat – there was Hattie Jacques and Fred Emney[297] and that was about it. And I wasn't huge – I was too fat for most of the costumes – and I wore denim dungarees which they didn't like.

---

297 Character actor (1900–1980) who often wore a monocle. Weighed twenty-two stone.

So they would take me to Angels or Bermans and the costume woman would go to a rail of clothes and sweep along the hangers and say, 'If you would only lose two stone you could wear all these of Felicity Kendal's.'[298] I was mortified. Now I'd just say, 'Yeah and if she put on two stone she could wear all my dungarees, get over it.'

I wasn't fat like people are fat now. Nobody would bat an eyelid. You're not really considered fat now unless the fire brigade have to knock a hole in the wall to take you shopping on a low loader.

So we're all doing this sketch show – and we're all staying at the Spider's Web Motel in Borehamwood – and we were on a hundred and twenty quid a week. I'd been on the dole, which was thirteen quid a week – I was living the dream – and one day we all get taken up to London for a photo session for the cover of the *TV Times*. And the day that the *TV Times* came out I came down to breakfast. A copy was lying on the table – and it was just a picture of Marti – none of the rest of us – and someone had burnt her eyes out with a cigarette. I don't think that would happen now. Because you can't smoke in hotel restaurants.

After *New Faces* I eventually ended up at Granada Television, where I got my first series *Wood and Walters* – which didn't go that well. Granada were brilliant for *Coronation Street* and drama and current affairs – but sketch shows weren't their thing. We recorded in front of a live audience – let me rephrase that: in front of an audience. I don't know how they got that audience – I think maybe they sent a bus around Manchester saying, 'If you're over eighty and you don't like fun – get on!'

And Julie and I would come out and say hello and say, 'This is a sketch set in a boutique.' You'd hear them say, 'What's a boutique?' I remember one night, one sketch was received in total silence and the woman said, 'We're missing *Brideshead* for this.'

Every job is a new challenge. I've just been filming a documentary – it's about depression. We flew a group of people who suffer from depression – we flew them out to swim with dolphins – and it's very

---

298 For many years the thin actress in this story was Anna Massey, but her name would have meant nothing to this audience.

therapeutic and it does lift the spirits. The dolphins absolutely hate it. They come home at night. 'How was your day?' 'Don't even talk to me.'

No, I've been making a documentary about tea.[299] I've been to China and India – I went to Kolkata, which was great because I've got a friend there – not a close friend – just someone I got chatting to in Directory Enquiries.

I've been flying all over the place. I've got all the travel gadgets – the ioniser and the neck cushion. I was coming back from Shanghai, and the man next to me had this very posh seat cushion – I recognised it from the website. It was the calming aromatherapy lumber support cushion with the flatulence-absorbing charcoal layer. And he was sitting next to me – and it was very annoying, because you knew he was farting but you didn't know when. It was all fine till we hit some turbulence. His cushion went into reverse – he got three shots of water lily and ginseng up his bum and we were all begging for the oxygen masks.

But I nearly had to cancel this. I was all geared up to come here and then yesterday I got this problem with my eye. I got a lump on my eye. I do have problems with my eyes – I wear hard contact lenses and sometimes they get bits of dirt behind them – it's very painful – it's worse on the Tube in London because the Tube is so dirty – all dust and bits of grit and mice – and sometimes I get mice in my eyes.[300]

And someone said I could get my eyes lasered, then I wouldn't need to wear lenses. There's a place up the road in Swiss Cottage that does eye lasering. Except I've been past it on the bus and I know that in the same building they do body hair lasering. That's asking for trouble, isn't it? Hairy people too embarrassed to look where they're going and short-sighted people blundering about – all in the same waiting room. You could go in for a bikini wax – couldn't you? – going through the

---

299 In fact, *Victoria Wood's Nice Cup of Tea* had been broadcast on BBC One a couple of months earlier.

300 Mice often popped up in VW's imagination. See 'Pardon?' and 'Hi Chaps 3' in this collection but also 'Service Wash': 'For years we had to make our own rugs. We used to stitch mice on to pieces of sacking.'

wrong door – they've got their backs to you. You say, 'Things are getting a bit fuzzy.' 'Can you read the top line?' 'Not with my pants, no.'

So I had this lump on my eye and I phoned the NHS helpline – it's automated – it said, 'Please state your symptoms slowly and clearly.' I said, 'I have a lump on my eye.' 'We think you are saying the Odeon Muswell Hill.' Anyway, I went to the eye hospital in Marylebone Road – lovely – got seen straight away – they had a look – they said, 'We think you are suffering from a combination of fat and tears.' I said, 'You don't even know me.'

And then I got into an argument in the supermarket where they were trying to sell me a bag for life. I said, 'I've already got a bag for life.' She said, 'Do you want another one?' I said, 'How many lives are you expecting me to have?' Luckily there was a diversion – there was a boy trainee at the next till – someone had a packet of maxi pads and he beeped them through as white Hovis.[301]

Anyway, thank you for inviting me here. I'm trying to get home in time for *Midsomer Murders* on ITV4. Everyone's been so lovely. They said, 'How shall we introduce you?' I said, 'Just don't call me a national treasure – it's very overused – I don't claim to be one. There's only a few at a time.' Madonna would like to be a national treasure but she's never going to be because she's not English[302] – and wearing a flat cap and looking miserable doesn't make you English – and anyway she can't be a national treasure because she's a cougar – you can't do both. You've got to choose. Demi Moore – cougar. Delia Smith – national treasure. Carol Vorderman – she could go either way.[303] Obviously our main national treasure was Thora Hird and then when she died, I thought it's going to go to Judi Dench, but then Joanna Lumley came up on the rails . . . Judi Dench is a bit bitter about that – apparently she's sat at home with a fag and a can of lager going, 'I wish I'd thought

<hr />

301 This joke was borrowed from 'Midlife Olympics'.

302 This cultural reference was a bit past its sell-by date in 2013. Madonna had filed for divorce from Guy Ritchie, her British husband, five years earlier.

303 VW had several variations of this national treasure riff. In a previous version she used Lynda Bellingham here but her name would have meant less to teenagers.

of saving the bloody Gurkhas.'

Thanks again for inviting me and I will leave you with my wishes for the future but you can choose which of these will happen first.

That there will be world peace.

That all disease will be eradicated

That one night our teenage children will say, 'I won't go on the internet tonight – I feel like folding some laundry.'

WHITNEY'S WEDDING

There's a famous seaside place called Blackpool.
You'll have the next line on your lips –
It's noted for fresh air, and also for fun
And mugging, and drag acts and chips.[304]

And Blackpool's the scene for my story,
A wedding, one morning in May.
When Mr and Mrs Ramsbottom
Gave their only child Whitney away.

They'd worried she'd never get married,
That the way to her heart would stay barred.
Cos she only liked sitting ont sofa,
And *Strictly*, and *Bake Off*, and lard.

But Cupid we know is capricious,
We can't choose the target he picks.
And love came to Whitney Ramsbottom
And she'd only popped out for a Twix.

---

304 The first verse of 'The Lion and Albert' goes like this:
    There's a famous seaside place called Blackpool
    That's noted for fresh air and fun
    And Mr and Mrs Ramsbottom
    Went there with young Albert, their son.

She was having a quick flick through *Closer* –
Will Jen find the love she deserves?
Madonna will only eat kiwis,
And Kerry's embracing her curves.

It was then that she looked up and saw him.
He leaned in and he gave her a shove.
He said, Hutch up I can't reach the Pringles.
And bang that was Whitney – in love.

They met for a drink the next evening.
He ordered, as he was the man,
A two-litre bottle of Tango.
They swigged it in turns in his van.

He proposed in their favourite bistro,
They'd just ordered a pair of Scotch eggs.
It wasn't exactly a bistro.
To tell you the truth it was Greggs.

The wedding was planned to the second,
Each detail was honed to the hilt.
And because of the whole Scotch egg moment,
She thought he'd look nice in a kilt.

She hadn't lost weight by the fitting,
They couldn't zip it up in the shop.
In the end they just stitched in elastic
And chucked a pashmina on top.

The hen night it started off sober –
Nice little place that played jazz.
Then they started inventing new cocktails,
With Baileys, Red Bull and Shiraz.

The groom ended up on a bollard,
Stark naked and, let's be frank, pissed.
And a short silent film of his scrotum
Was sent to his Christmas card list.

The wedding day dawned bright and sunny,
The groom in his kilt looked a treat.
But all was not well at the bride's house,
For Whitney was getting cold feet.

The groom was just stood at the altar,
Not knowing if things were on track,
Fiddling about with his sporran –
That didn't look great from the back.

Mum said, This is up to you, Whitney,
You must follow your heart and your mood.
I'll support you in any decision,
But remember we've paid for the food.

The car drove around as she dithered.
Was she really in love, or mistook?
Dad said, Ne'er mind suited and booted,
He's kilted and jilted by't look.

Then the music struck up on the organ,
The groom turned around with a smile.
As Whitney grabbed hold of her father,
And plodded her way down the aisle.

The vicar said, Whitney Ramsbottom,
Do you take him for good or for ill?
She thought for a good thirty seconds
And then she said, Sod it – I will!

ACKNOWLEDGEMENTS

I am grateful to Lucy Ansbro for permission to dive back into the Victoria Wood archive, and to Adele Fowler for enabling me to gain access to it. My thanks too go to Libby Gregory and Cathy Edis for sorting and cataloguing Victoria's archive. Not everything in this book came from that vast collection of folders, files and boxes: I would like to thank Alison Lloyd, Chrissie Poulter and Robert Howie for retrieving the pieces Victoria wrote for them to perform at Birmingham University, and Beth Willis and Jonny Campbell for sharing 'Whitney's Wedding'. I am grateful to Geoffrey Strachan for giving his blessing to the inclusion of 'To Geoffrey', and for much else. I am also indebted to those who allowed their memories to be tapped in relation to work done a long time ago – or sometimes, in the end, not done: Jim Broadbent, Geoffrey Durham, David Firman, Dusty Hughes, Celia Imrie, Rosalind March, Marcus Mortimer, Geoff Posner, Duncan Preston, Jemma Rodgers and Julie Walters. I would also like to thank VW scholar-fans Steven Flavell and Claire Mortlock for generously sharing their store of knowledge.

My thanks to all at Orion and beyond who helped bring this book to fruition: Jamie Coleman, Pippa Wright, Lucinda McNeile, Paul Murphy, Victoria Hunt, Clarissa Sutherland, Folayemi Adebayo, Natalie Dawkins, Emily Taylor, Helen Ewing and Virginia Woolsten-croft. My debt to James Gill of United Agents is, as ever, outstanding.

IMAGE CREDITS

All images courtesy of the Victoria Wood Archive except for the following:

Section one
p. 2 (above) Courtesy of Robert Howie and Chrissie Poulter.
p. 2 (below) John Sturrock/Report IFL Archive/reportdigital.co.uk.
p. 5 Arena Pal.
p. 6 Daily Star.
p. 7 (below) Shutterstock/Rex Features/ITV.
p. 8 (below) Don Smith/Radio Times/Getty Images.

Section two
p. 1 (below) Don Smith/RadioTimes/Getty Images.
p. 4 (above) PA Archive/PA Images/Alamy.
p. 5 (above) Chris Chistodoulou.
p. 5 (below) Emma Cattell/Mirrorpix/Getty Images.

CREDITS

Trapeze would like to thank everyone at Orion who worked on the publication of *Victoria Wood Unseen on TV*.

Agent
James Gill

Editor
Jamie Coleman
Pippa Wright

Copy-editor
Paul Murphy

Design
Nick Shah
Rabab Adams
Steve Marking
Charlotte Abrams Simpson
Debbie Holmes
Joanna Ridley
Nick May
Helen Ewing
Clare Sivell
Natalie Dawkins

Audio
Paul Stark
Jake Alderson

Proofreader
Victoria Hunt

Editorial Management
Clarissa Sutherland
Jane Hughes
Charlie Panayiotou
Tamara Morriss
Claire Boyle

Production
Nicole Abel
Fiona McIntosh

Operations
Jo Jacobs
Sharon Willis

Sales

Jen Wilson
Victoria Laws
Esther Waters
Frances Doyle
Ben Goddard
Georgina Cutler
Jack Hallam
Anna Egelstaff
Inês Figueira
Barbara Ronan
Andrew Hally
Dominic Smith
Deborah Deyong
Lauren Buck
Maggy Park
Linda McGregor
Sinead White
Jemimah James
Rachael Jones
Jack Dennison
Nigel Andrews
Ian Williamson
Julia Benson
Declan Kyle
Robert Mackenzie
Megan Smith
Charlotte Clay
Rebecca Cobbold

Marketing

Folayemi Adebayo

Publicity

Virginia Woolstencroft

Contracts

Anne Goddard

Rights

Susan Howe
Krystyna Kujawinska
Jessica Purdue
Ashley Kinley
Louise Henderson

Finance

Nick Gibson
Jasdip Nandra
Rabale Mustafa
Elizabeth Beaumont
Ibukun Ademefun
Afeera Ahmed
Levancia Clarendon
Tom Costello